MANITOBA BIRDS

Palmer
Mutcheson

Phone   number
(425) 308-4496

Andy Bezener
Ken De Smet

LONE
PINE

The Publisher: Lone Pine Publishing
10145–81 Ave.
Edmonton, AB   T6E 1W9
Canada

Website: http://www.lonepinepublishing.com

Canadian Cataloguing in Publication Data

Bezener, Andy, (date)
   Manitoba birds

   Includes bibliographical references and index.
   ISBN 1-55105-255-5

   1. Birds—Manitoba—Identification. I. De Smet, Ken D. II. Title.
QL685.5.M35B49 2000   598'.097127   C00-910996-X

Editorial Director: Nancy Foulds
Project Editor: Eloise Pulos
Editorial: Eloise Pulos, Eli MacLaren
Production Manager: Jody Reekie
Layout & Production: Monica Triska
Book Design: Rob Weidemann
Cover Design: Rob Weidemann
Cover Illustration: Western Grebes, by Gary Ross
Illustrations: Gary Ross, Ted Nordhagen, Ewa Pluciennik
Cartography: Lana Anderson-Hale, Elliot Engley, Monica Triska
Separations & Film: Elite Lithographers Co., Edmonton, Alberta

We acknowledge the financial support of the Government of Canada through the
Book Publishing Industry Development Program (BPIDP) for our publishing
activities.

PC: P7

CONTENTS

ACKNOWLEDGEMENTS

Many thanks go to Gary Ross and Ted Nordhagen, whose skilled illustrations have brought each page to life. The book owes its final form to discussions with Shane Kennedy, Nancy Foulds, Eloise Pulos, Roland Lines and Jody Reekie at Lone Pine Publishing. John Acorn and Chris Fisher provided much of the initial text for this book by way of their book, *Birds of Alberta*, which was also published by Lone Pine. Rudolf Koes and Peter Taylor are owed thanks for their great help in reviewing the checklist and range maps. Special thanks go to our families and friends, especially Kindrie Grove and Bev, Shannon and Melissa De Smet for their unwavering support and encouragement. Final thanks are extended to the growing family of ornithologists and dedicated birders who have offered their inspiration and expertise to help build Lone Pine's expanding library of field guides.

Common Loon
size 80 cm • p. 20

Pied-billed Grebe
size 34 cm • p. 21

Horned Grebe
size 35 cm • p. 22

Red-necked Grebe
size 50 cm • p. 23

Western Grebe
size 65 cm • p. 24

American White Pelican
size 160 cm • p. 25

Double-crested Cormorant
size 80 cm • p. 26

American Bittern
size 72 cm • p. 27

Great Blue Heron
size 115 cm • p. 28

Black-crowned
Night-Heron
size 62 cm • p. 29

Turkey Vulture
size 74 cm • p. 30

Snow Goose
size 70 cm • p. 31

Canada Goose
size 89 cm • p. 32

Tundra Swan
size 135 cm • p. 33

Wood Duck
size 47 cm • p. 34

American Wigeon
size 52 cm • p. 35

Mallard
size 60 cm • p. 36

Blue-winged Teal
size 38 cm • p. 37

Northern Shoveler
size 49 cm • p. 38

Northern Pintail
size 62 cm • p. 39

Green-winged Teal
size 36 cm • p. 40

Canvasback
size 54 cm • p. 41

Lesser Scaup
size 42 cm • p. 42

Bufflehead
size 37 cm • p. 43

Common Goldeneye
size 46 cm • p. 44

Hooded Merganser
size 45 cm • p. 45

Common Merganser
size 63 cm • p. 46

Ruddy Duck
size 40 cm • p. 47

Osprey
size 60 cm • p. 48

Bald Eagle
size 98 cm • p. 49

Northern Harrier
size 51 cm • p. 50

Sharp-shinned Hawk
size 31 cm • p. 51

Northern Goshawk
size 58 cm • p. 52

Swainson's Hawk
size 50 cm • p. 53

Red-tailed Hawk
size 55 cm • p. 54

American Kestrel
size 27 cm • p. 55

Merlin
size 28 cm • p. 56

Gray Partridge
size 32 cm • p. 57

Ruffed Grouse
size 43 cm • p. 58

Spruce Grouse
size 41 cm • p. 59

Sharp-tailed Grouse
size 45 cm • p. 60

Sora
size 23 cm • p. 61

American Coot
size 37 cm • p. 62

Sandhill Crane
size 103 cm • p. 63

Killdeer
size 25 cm • p. 64

American Avocet
size 45 cm • p. 65

Spotted Sandpiper
size 19 cm • p. 66

Marbled Godwit
size 46 cm • p. 67

Least Sandpiper
size 15 cm • p. 68

Common Snipe
size 28 cm • p. 69

Wilson's Phalarope
size 23 cm • p. 70

Franklin's Gull
size 36 cm • p. 71

Ring-billed Gull
size 48 cm • p. 72

Herring Gull
size 61 cm • p. 73

Common Tern
size 37 cm • p. 74

Black Tern
size 24 cm • p. 75

Rock Dove
size 35 cm • p. 76

Mourning Dove
size 31 cm • p. 77

Eastern Screech-Owl
size 22 cm • p. 78

Great Horned Owl
size 55 cm • p. 79

Snowy Owl
size 60 cm • p. 80

Burrowing Owl
size 26 cm • p. 81

Great Gray Owl
size 72 cm • p. 82

Short-eared Owl
size 38 cm • p. 83

Common Nighthawk
size 24 cm • p. 84

Chimney Swift
size 13 cm • p. 85

Ruby-throated Hummingbird
size 9 cm • p. 86

Belted Kingfisher
size 32 cm • p. 87

Red-headed Woodpecker
size 23 cm • p. 88

Yellow-bellied Sapsucker
size 22 cm • p. 89

Downy Woodpecker
size 17 cm • p. 90

Black-backed Woodpecker
size 24 cm • p. 91

Northern Flicker
size 33 cm • p. 92

Pileated Woodpecker
size 45 cm • p. 93

Olive-sided Flycatcher
size 19 cm • p. 94

Least Flycatcher
size 14 cm • p. 95

Eastern Phoebe
size 18 cm • p. 96

Western Kingbird
size 22 cm • p. 97

Eastern Kingbird
size 22 cm • p. 98

Northern Shrike
size 25 cm • p. 99

Warbling Vireo
size 14 cm • p. 100

Red-eyed Vireo
size 15 cm • p. 101

Gray Jay
size 29 cm • p. 102

Blue Jay
size 30 cm • p. 103

Black-billed Magpie
size 51 cm • p. 104

American Crow
size 48 cm • p. 105

Common Raven
size 61 cm • p. 106

Horned Lark
size 18 cm • p. 107

Purple Martin
size 19 cm • p. 108

Tree Swallow
size 14 cm • p. 109

Cliff Swallow
size 14 cm • p. 110

Barn Swallow
size 18 cm • p. 111

Black-capped Chickadee
size 14 cm • p. 112

Red-breasted Nuthatch
size 11 cm • p. 113

White-breasted Nuthatch
size 15 cm • p. 114

Brown Creeper
size 13 cm • p. 115

House Wren
size 12 cm • p. 116

Marsh Wren
size 13 cm • p. 117

Golden-crowned Kinglet
size 10 cm • p. 118

Ruby-crowned Kinglet
size 10 cm • p. 119

Eastern Bluebird
size 18 cm • p. 120

Swainson's Thrush
size 18 cm • p. 121

American Robin
size 25 cm • p. 122

Gray Catbird
size 22 cm • p. 123

Brown Thrasher
size 29 cm • p. 124

European Starling
size 22 cm • p. 125

Cedar Waxwing
size 18 cm • p. 126

Tennessee Warbler
size 12 cm • p. 127

Yellow Warbler
size 13 cm • p. 128

Magnolia Warbler
size 13 cm • p. 129

Yellow-rumped Warbler
size 14 cm • p. 130

Palm Warbler
size 13 cm • p. 131

Black-and-white Warbler
size 13 cm • p. 132

American Redstart
size 13 cm • p. 133

Ovenbird
size 15 cm • p. 134

Mourning Warbler
size 14 cm • p. 135

Common Yellowthroat
size 13 cm • p. 136

Scarlet Tanager
size 18 cm • p. 137

Eastern Townhee
size 20 cm • p. 138

Chipping Sparrow
size 14 cm • p. 139

Clay-colored Sparrow
size 14 cm • p. 140

Vesper Sparrow
size 16 cm • p. 141

Savannah Sparrow
size 14 cm • p. 142

Song Sparrow
size 16 cm • p. 143

White-throated Sparrow
size 18 cm • p. 144

Dark-eyed Junco
size 16 cm • p. 145

Lapland Longspur
size 16 cm • p. 146

Snow Bunting
size 17 cm • p. 147

Rose-breasted Grosbeak
size 20 cm • p. 148

Bobolink
size 18 cm • p. 149

Red-winged Blackbird
size 21 cm • p. 150

Western Meadowlark
size 24 cm • p. 151

Yellow-headed Blackbird
size 24 cm • p. 152

Brewer's Blackbird
size 23 cm • p. 153

Common Grackle
size 31 cm • p. 154

Brown-headed Cowbird
size 17 cm • p. 155

Baltimore Oriole
size 19 cm • p. 156

Pine Grosbeak
size 23 cm • p. 157

Purple Finch
size 14 cm • p. 158

White-winged Crossbill
size 16 cm • p. 159

Common Redpoll
size 13 cm • p. 160

Pine Siskin
size 12 cm • p. 161

American Goldfinch
size 13 cm • p. 162

Evening Grosbeak
size 20 cm • p. 163

House Sparrow
size 16 cm • p. 164

INTRODUCTION

In recent decades, birdwatching has evolved from an eccentric pursuit practised by a few dedicated individuals to a continent-wide phenomenon that boasts millions of professional and amateur participants. There are many good reasons why birdwatching has become such a popular activity. Many people find it simple and relaxing, while others enjoy the outdoor exercise it affords. Some see it as a rewarding learning experience, an opportunity to socialize with like-minded people and a way to monitor the health of the local environment. Still others watch birds to reconnect with nature or to nurture personal spiritual growth.

Whether you are just beginning to take an interest in birds or have already learned to identify many, this field guide has something for you. To get you started, we've selected 145 of the province's most common and noteworthy birds. Some live in specialized habitats, but most are common species that you have a good chance of encountering.

BIRDWATCHING IN MANITOBA

Birdwatching is an age-old practice that continues to evolve in our province. First Nations people, who have lived in Manitoba for thousands of years, first observed birds as symbols of seasonal change, indicators of impending weather and spiritual guides. They also valued birds as a source of food, especially when huge migrating flocks descended upon Manitoba's marshes and plains. The eggs of ducks, gulls, shorebirds and even songbirds supplemented their summer diets, and Bald Eagles and Sharp-tailed Grouse were celebrated as spiritual symbols.

When European explorers and fur-traders first visited what is now Manitoba, birds provided them with a reliable source of food, especially when their provisions ran low. When ornithology became a popular science, a number of Manitoba birds were 'discovered' and collected as specimens for prominent Old World naturalists and taxonomists. At that time, birds were doubtlessly valued for esthetic reasons, but they were also viewed by many as scientific specimens of which the shooting, classification and trading represented the advance of knowledge, and perhaps, a living wage.

Bald Eagle

Attitudes have changed in modern times. Today, we find that understanding and awareness, spawned through the melding of these interests, has enabled thousands of people to more readily, and more thoroughly, enjoy the miracle of birds.

Manitoba has a long tradition of friendly birdwatching. In general, Manitoba birders are willing to help beginners, share their knowledge and involve novices in their projects. Christmas bird counts, breeding bird surveys, nest box programs, migration monitoring studies, feeder watch programs and birdwatching lectures and workshops all provide a chance for birdwatchers of all levels to interact and share the splendour of birds. So, whatever your level of knowledge, there is ample opportunity for you to learn more and get involved.

MANITOBA'S TOP BIRDING SITES

We are truly blessed by the geographical and biological diversity of our province. Indeed, Manitoba is quickly acquiring a reputation as one of North America's bird-watching 'hotspots.' Because we are situated near the geographic centre of the continent, our province is home to a combination of northern and southern species as well as birds from the East and from the West. From the rugged Canadian Shield, the

Golden-crowned Kinglet

lush grasslands and rolling parklands, the Hudson Bay coast and the agricultural plains of southern parts, Manitoba offers some of the most diverse and accessible birding sites on the continent.

There are hundreds of good birding areas throughout the province. The following areas have been selected to represent a broad range of bird communities and habitats, with an emphasis on diversity and accessibility.

Prairie
1. Upper Assiniboine WMA
2. Poverty Plains, Mixed-grass Prairie Preserve and Broomhill WMA
3. Oak/Plum lakes
4. Lauder Sandhills
5. Alexander–Griswold Marsh
6. Minnedosa pothole region
7. Assiniboine River Trail (Brandon)
8. Brandon Hills
9. Souris River Bend WMA
10. Whitewater Lake
11. Turtle Mountain PP
12. Pembina Valley
13. Pelican Lake
14. Tiger Hills
15. Glenboro Marsh
16. Spruce Woods PP
17. Pinkerton Lakes
18. Portage Sandhills WMA
19. Crescent Lake (Portage la Prairie)
20. Lake Manitoba Narrows
21. Delta Marsh and St. Ambroise PP
22. Lake Francis
23. Shoal Lakes
24. Oak Hammock Marsh
25. Beaudry PP
26. Assiniboine Park and Fort Whyte (Winnipeg)

Boreal Plains
27. Tall Grass Prairie Preserve
28. Rat River WMA and St. Malo WMA
29. Birds Hill PP
30. Netley–Libau Marsh
31. Hecla/Grindstone PP
32. Interlake area and Mantagao Lake WMA
33. Dog Lake
34. Crane River
35. Waterhen River
36. Riding Mountain NP
37. Duck Mountain PP
38. Porcupine Provincial Forest
39. Clearwater Lake PP

Boreal Shield
40. Spur Woods WMA
41. Moose Lake PP and Birch Point PP
42. Mars Hill WMA
43. Grand Beach PP
44. Whiteshell PP and Pinawa area
45. Nopiming PP
46. Grass River PP
47. Paint Lake/Pisew Falls PP

Taiga Shield
48. Sand Lakes PP

Hudson Plains and Southern Arctic
49. Churchill
50. Wapusk NP

PP = Provincial Park
NP = National Park
WMA = Wildlife Management Area

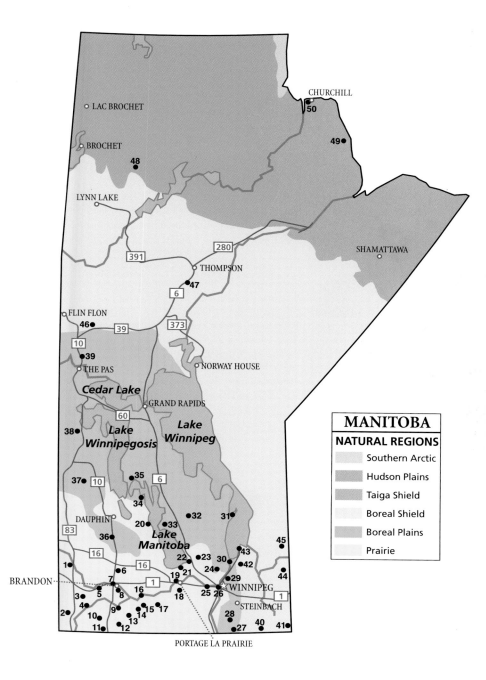

LAC BROCHET

CHURCHILL
50

BROCHET

49

48

LYNN LAKE

SHAMATTAWA

391   280

THOMPSON

47

6

FLIN FLON
46
39

10

39

THE PAS

Cedar Lake

GRAND RAPIDS

60

Lake
Winnipegosis

Lake
Winnipeg

38

37   10

35

6

34

DAUPHIN

32   31

83

20   33

36

Lake
Manitoba

45

16

22   23   30

43

6

21   24

42

BRANDON

19

29

44

1

7

16   1

WINNIPEG

3   5   8

16

25 26

STEINBACH

2

4

9

18

1

10   15 17

14

28

27   40   41

11   13

12

PORTAGE LA PRAIRIE

MANITOBA

NATURAL REGIONS

Southern Arctic

Hudson Plains

Taiga Shield

Boreal Shield

Boreal Plains

Prairie

NORWAY HOUSE

13

Poverty Plains, Broomhill Wildlife Management Area & Mixed-Grass Prairie Preserve

Manitoba's mixed-grass prairie is found in the extreme southwest of the province in the Poverty Plains area that stretches from Broomhill to Lyleton. While much of the area is privately owned, there is public access to the Mixed-grass Prairie Preserve in the heart of the Poverty Plains and to several local wildlife management areas, including Broomhill, Berniece and Pierson. Open pasturelands, haylands and mixed-grass prairie support impressive concentrations of nesting Sharp-tailed Grouse, Gray Partridges, Ring-necked Pheasants, Ferruginous Hawks, Say's Phoebes, Willow Flycatchers, Upland Sandpipers, Loggerhead Shrikes, Sprague's Pipits, Chestnut-collared Longspurs, Baird's Sparrows and Grasshopper Sparrows. Burrowing Owls have been found here, and in years of low rainfall, Lark Buntings can be plentiful. Field shelterbelts in the Lyleton area support, among other species, Gray Partridge, Orchard Oriole and Brown Thrasher.

Loggerhead Shrike

Oak Lake–Plum Lakes

The Oak Lake–Plum Lakes complex, located 60 kilometres west of Brandon, is what remains of Lake Souris in the wake of glaciers that retreated here some 12,000 years ago. A wooded ridge at the east edge of Oak Lake is home to a small cottage development, but there is still a rich variety of birdlife to observe, including Ruby-throated Hummingbirds, White-breasted Nuthatches, Eastern Phoebes, Eastern Kingbirds, Western Kingbirds, Brown Thrashers, Baltimore Orioles and Orchard Orioles. Further south along the narrow beach ridge are numerous marshland birds, including the Canada Goose, Western Grebe, Black-crowned Night-Heron, American Bittern, Sora, Black Tern, Franklin's Gull and Song Sparrow. The grasslands surrounding these marshy lakes support healthy populations of nesting Swainson's Hawks, Sharp-tailed Grouse, Gray Partridges, Wilson's Phalaropes, Marbled Godwits, Upland Sandpipers, Sprague's Pipits, Mountain Bluebirds and Chestnut-collared Longspurs.

Turtle Mountain Provincial Park

Amidst the beautiful, rolling landscape of Turtle Mountain Provincial Park (which includes over 200 lakes and over 1000 smaller wetlands), visitors can engage in cross-country skiing, mountain biking, canoeing, hiking, camping, and, of course, birdwatching. Noteworthy avian residents here include the Common Loon, Red-necked

American Redstart

Grebe, Pied-billed Grebe, Black-crowned Night-Heron, American Wigeon, Green-winged Teal, Wood Duck, Bufflehead, Canvasback, Lesser Scaup, Ring-necked Duck and Spotted Sandpiper. Birds you are likely to see in forested areas of the park include the Sharp-shinned Hawk, Ruffed Grouse, Ruby-throated Hummingbird, Yellow-bellied Sapsucker, Blue Jay, White-breasted Nuthatch, Gray Catbird, American Redstart, Mourning Warbler, Ovenbird, Rose-breasted Grosbeak and White-throated Sparrow.

Spruce Woods Provincial Park

Mountain Bluebird

Located southeast of Brandon along both sides of the Assiniboine River, this large park is blessed with a unique and intriguing mix of rolling sand dunes, native prairie, mixed forests, creeks, ponds and mature riparian woodlands. These diverse habitats, made accessible by the park's extensive system of trails, support quite a diverse collection birds. Specialties here include the Wood Duck, Hooded Merganser, Turkey Vulture, Broad-winged Hawk, American Kestrel, Ruffed Grouse, Common Nighthawk, Belted Kingfisher, Pileated Woodpecker, Mountain Bluebird, Golden-crowned Kinglet, Orange-crowned, Chestnut-sided, Yellow-rumped and Black-and-white warblers, Ovenbird, Scarlet Tanager, Eastern Towhee and Pine Siskin.

Oak Hammock Marsh

This restored marsh is only a remnant of an extensive marshland that once existed. It is still one of the best migratory bird viewing areas in North America, however, and some 285 birds, including over 90 nesting species, have been recorded in this marsh. Common summer residents include the Pied-billed Grebe, Great Blue Heron, American Bittern, Northern Pintail, Northern Shoveler and Ruddy Duck, Northern Harrier, Sora, Common Snipe, Marbled Godwit, Wilson's Phalarope, Franklin's Gull, Black Tern, Short-eared Owl, Marsh Wren and Common Yellowthroat. Grassland birds include the Western Meadowlark and Clay-colored, Savannah and Vesper sparrows. Huge flocks of waterfowl, Sandhill Cranes, numerous shorebirds and a variety of raptors pass through on migration, and tens of thousands of Snow Geese and Canada Geese arrive between April and early May, reappearing again in late September and October.

Marsh Wren

Assiniboine Park & Forest

This large park borders the Assiniboine River to the west of downtown Winnipeg, and it is one of the city's most productive and popular birding spots. Its open, wooded lawns, lush forest, gardens and ponds attract a wide variety of birds—5 vireo, 16 sparrow and 27 warbler species have been seen here. It is one of the best places to visit during spring and fall (typically from mid-April to late May and from late August to early October), and if you visit in winter, there is a good chance you will see waxwings, grosbeaks, crossbills and other winter finches. Species that nest here include the Wood Duck, Spotted Sandpiper, Common Nighthawk, Chimney Swift, Ruby-throated Hummingbird, Eastern Kingbird, Blue Jay, White-breasted Nuthatch, Gray Catbird, Cedar Waxwing, American Redstart, Ovenbird, Tennessee Warbler, Rose-breasted Grosbeak and Baltimore Oriole.

Rose-breasted Grosbeak

Hecla Provincial Park & Grindstone Provincial Park

Yellow-bellied Sapsucker

The waters that embrace the peninsulas and islands of these parks are home to a variety of birds, including the Common Loon, Western Grebe, Common Merganser, American White Pelican, Double-crested Cormorant, Common Tern, Bald Eagle and Osprey. Boardwalks, viewing towers and viewing blinds at Grassy Narrows Marsh provide access for observing marshland species up close. Early morning strolls along the forest trails should bring encounters with birds, such as the Red-tailed Hawk, American Kestrel, Yellow-bellied Sapsucker, Least Flycatcher, Eastern Phoebe, Gray Jay, Ruby-crowned Kinglet, Red-eyed Vireo, Mourning Warbler, Ovenbird and White-throated Sparrow.

Riding Mountain National Park

Riding Mountain, Manitoba's first national park, is situated about an hour north of Brandon. Two-hundred and sixty species of birds have been seen here, including specialties, such as the Black-backed Woodpecker, Brown Creeper, Winter Wren, Golden-crowned Kinglet, Great Gray Owl, Northern Goshawk, Spruce Grouse, Olive-sided Flycatcher, Connecticut Warbler and White-winged Crossbill. Other enticing species that are common in the park include the Common Loon, Black-crowned Night-Heron, American Wigeon, Green-winged Teal, Bufflehead, Common Goldeneye, Common Merganser, Ruddy Duck, Broad-winged Hawk, Merlin, Ruffed Grouse, Forster's Tern, Northern Saw-whet Owl, Belted Kingfisher, Gray Jay, Boreal Chickadee, Red-breasted Nuthatch, Mountain Bluebird, Swainson's Thrush, Dark-eyed Junco and Purple Finch.

Northern Goshawk

Clearwater Lake Provincial Park & Grass River Provincial Park

These two readily accessible northern parks, located between The Pas and Flin Flon, abound with birdlife. Excursions by canoe will reveal Common Loons, a variety of waterfowl, American White Pelicans, Double-crested Cormorants, Bald Eagles, Ospreys and Belted Kingfishers, and if travelling on land, portage trails offer good opportunities to meet Spruce Grouse, Gray Jays, Pileated Woodpeckers, Olive-sided Flycatchers, Boreal Chickadees, Red-breasted Nuthatches, Golden-crowned Kinglets, Swainson's Thrushes, White-winged Crossbills, Pine Siskins and Evening Grosbeaks. Over 20 colourful warblers and vireos—including the Blue-headed Vireo, Magnolia Warbler, Tennessee Warbler, Ovenbird, Connecticut Warbler and American Redstart—are common nesting birds you might come across if you visit these parks.

Boreal Chickadee

Whiteshell Provincial Park & Nopiming Provincial Park

These popular parks are part of a rolling landscape of granite outcroppings topped by mixed boreal forest and interlaced by a network of streams, lakes, bogs and ponds. Common nesting species here include the Common Loon, American White Pelican, Double-crested Cormorant, Great Blue Heron, Wood Duck, Common Goldeneye, Common Merganser, Turkey Vulture, Northern Harrier, Bald Eagle, Osprey, Sandhill Crane, Common Snipe, Spotted Sandpiper, Ring-billed Gull, Common Tern, Common Nighthawk and Whip-poor-will. In spring and summer, these parks are busy with the movements of Ruffed Grouse, Pileated Woodpeckers, Yellow-bellied Sapsuckers, Olive-sided Flycatchers, Eastern Phoebes, Blue Jays, Gray Jays, Common Ravens, Ruby-crowned Kinglets, Swainson's Thrushes, Rose-breasted Grosbeaks and Pine Siskins. Several species of owls are found here year-round, and the area also supports an impressive array of nesting warblers.

Turkey Vulture

Paint Lake Provincial Park & Pisew Falls Provincial Park

Northern Hawk-Owl

Pisew Falls and nearby Paint Lake, located 65 kilometres south of Thompson, offer birdwatchers a chance to meet the Northern Hawk-Owl, Boreal Owl, Spruce Grouse, Boreal Chickadee, Golden-crowned Kinglet and various woodpeckers, vireos, warblers and sparrows. Birding in these parks might even lead to glimpses of black bear, moose, mink, otter and marten.

Churchill

In recent years, the Churchill area has become a mecca for tourists, not for its polar bears, beluga whales, bearded, ringed and harbor seals, wildflowers or northern lights displays, but for its birdlife. Situated on the southern shore of Hudson Bay, where marine, tundra and coniferous forest habitats converge, the Churchill area offers innumerable birding opportunities. In June, when the ice breaks on Hudson Bay, rafts of sea ducks, including eiders, Long-tailed Ducks, scoters, Arctic, Pacific and Red-throated loons ply the open waters. Further inland, migrants and arctic-nesting species abound, so watch for Lapland Longspurs, Snow Buntings, Bald Eagles, Ospreys, Rough-legged Hawks, Peregrine Falcons, Gyrfalcons, Merlins, Snowy Owls and Short-eared Owls. Gull enthusiasts have the chance to see various species, including the Bonaparte's, Thayer's, Sabine's, Ross' and Little gulls and Arctic Terns and Long-tailed, Parasitic and Pomarine jaegers. Nearby Akudlik Marsh is a favoured site to get up-close observations of numerous shorebird species (15 of these shorebird species nest on the surrounding tundra).

Surf Scoter

ABOUT THE SPECIES ACCOUNTS

This book gives detailed accounts of 145 of the most common and noteworthy bird species found in Manitoba. As well as discussing the identifying features of the birds, each species account also attempts to bring the birds to life by describing their various character traits. Personifying a bird helps us relate to it, but the characterizations presented should not be mistaken for scientific propositions. Our limited understanding of non-human creatures, our interpretations and our assumptions most likely fall short of truly defining birds. Nevertheless, we hope that a lively, engaging text will communicate our scientific knowledge as smoothly and effectively as possible.

One of the challenges of birdwatching is that many species look different in spring and summer than they do in fall and winter. Many birds have what are generally called nesting and non-nesting plumages, and immature birds often look different from their parents. This book does not try to describe or illustrate all the different plumages of a species; instead, it focuses on the forms that are most likely to be seen in our area. Most of the illustrations are of adult birds. The order of the birds and their common and scientific names follow the American Ornithologists' Union's Check-list of North American Birds (7th edition, July 1998, and its supplements).

ID: It is difficult to describe the features of a bird without being able to visualize it, so this section is best used in combination with the illustrations. Where appropriate, the description is subdivided to highlight the differences between male and female birds, nesting and non-nesting birds and immature and adult birds. The descriptions use as few technical terms as possible, and favour easily understood language. Birds may not have 'jaw lines,' 'moustaches' or 'chins,' but these and other terms are easily understood by all readers, in spite of their scientific inaccuracy. Some of the most common features of birds are pointed out in the glossary illustration.

Size: The size measurement, an average length of the bird's body from bill to tail, is an approximate measurement of the bird as it is seen in nature. The size of larger birds is often given as a range, because there is variation between individuals. In addition, wingspans are given for some of the larger birds that are often seen in flight. Please note that birds with long tails often have large measurements that do not necessarily reflect 'body' size.

Status: A general comment, such as 'common,' 'uncommon' or 'rare,' is usually sufficient to describe the relative abundance of a species. Situations are bound to differ somewhat since migratory pulses, seasonal changes and centres of activity tend to concentrate or disperse birds. Some birds are more abundant in some parts of the province than in others. Therefore, some of the status comments include a reference to specific regions of the province, followed by the time of year in which they are usually present.

Habitat: The habitats we have listed describe where each species is most commonly found. In most cases, it is a generalized description, but if a bird is restricted to a specific habitat, the habitat is described precisely. Because of the freedom flight gives them, birds can turn up in almost any type of habitat, but usually they will be found in environments that provide the specific food, water, cover and, in some cases, nesting habitat that they need to survive.

Nesting: The reproductive strategies used by different bird species vary: in each species account, nest location and structure, clutch size, incubation period and parental duties are discussed. Remember that birdwatching ethics discourage the disturbance of active bird nests. If you disturb a nest, you may drive off the parents during a critical period or expose defenseless young to predators. All of the 145 focal bird species nest in Manitoba.

Feeding: Birds spend a great deal of time foraging for food. If you know what a bird eats and where the food is found, you will have a good chance of meeting the bird you are looking for. Birds are frequently encountered while they are foraging; we hope that our description of their feeding styles and diets provides valuable identifying characteristics, as well as interesting dietary facts.

Voice: You will hear many birds, particularly songbirds, which may remain hidden from view. With practice you will be able to identify most birds without having to see them. Memorable paraphrases of distinctive sounds will aid you in identifying species by ear. The paraphrases we have provided often only loosely resemble the call, song or sound produced by each bird. Should one of our paraphrases not work for you, feel free to make up your own—this creative exercise will reinforce your memory of the bird's sound.

Similar Species: Easily confused species are discussed briefly. Subtle differences in colour, shape or behaviour are often all that separates the appearance of one bird from another. As you are learning, you might find it useful to consult this section before finalizing your identification. By concentrating on the most relevant field marks, it is usually fairly easy to distinguish similar-looking species. Keep in mind that even experienced birders can make errors in identification, and eliminating similar species lessens your chances of mistaking a bird's identity.

Best Sites: If you are looking for a particular bird in Manitoba, you will have more luck in some places than in others, even within the range shown on the range map. We have listed places that, besides providing a good chance of seeing a species, are easily accessible. As a result, many conservation areas and provincial and national parks are mentioned.

Range Maps: The range map for each species represents the overall range of the species in Manitoba in an average year. Most birds will confine their annual movements to this range, although each year some birds wander beyond their traditional boundaries. These maps do not show differences in abundance within the range—areas of a range with good habitat will support a denser population than areas with poorer habitat. These maps also cannot show small pockets within the range where the species may actually be absent, or how the range may change over time. Some rare or occasional species may be indicated as such under 'status,' but because of the irregular or scattered nature of their distribution, the range map may not represent these occurrences. Unlike most other field guides, we have attempted to show migratory pathways—areas of the province where birds may appear while en route to nesting or winter habitat. Many of these migratory routes are 'best guesses,' which will no doubt be refined as new discoveries are made. The representations of the pathways do not distinguish high-use migration corridors from areas that are seldom used. Although large water bodies within each bird's range have been coloured over, only waterbirds will be found on these water bodies.

Range Map Symbols

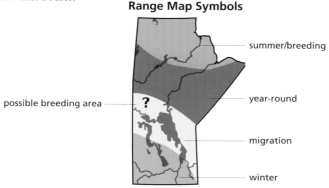

possible breeding area

summer/breeding

year-round

migration

winter

COMMON LOON

Gavia immer

These large, goose-sized waterbirds are most common in our province on remote shield-country lakes. Common Loons are a classic symbol of northern wilderness, and indigenous people in Manitoba once believed that these birds possessed supernatural powers. At one time, it was thought that the loon's haunting call was the voice of the Great Spirit, Manitou. • Loons are well adapted to their aquatic lifestyle: the reduced buoyancy effect of their nearly solid bones (most birds have hollow bones) facilitates deep dives, and their feet are placed well back on their bodies to enhance underwater propulsion and steering. On land, however, their rear-placed legs make walking awkward, and because of their heavy bodies and small wing size they require a lengthy sprint before taking off. Because they are vulnerable on land, Common Loons always build their nests close to water. • Common Loons were more common in the late 1800s, when they were referred to as 'Big Helldivers' or 'Great Northern Divers.' Since that time, some nesting populations have experienced serious declines owing to a combination of habitat loss, recreational activity near nest sites, mercury pollution and acid rain.

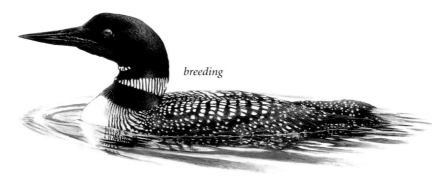

breeding

ID: iridescent green-black head; stout, black bill; striped 'necklace'; white breast and underparts; black and white checkered back; red eyes. *In flight:* long wings beat constantly; hunchbacked appearance; large, webbed feet trail beyond the tail.
Size: *L* 70–90 cm; *W* 1.2–1.5 m.
Status: rare to uncommon in the north and south; fairly common in central parts; mid-April to mid-November.
Habitat: large wetlands, lakes and rivers, especially in the boreal forest.
Nesting: on a muskrat lodge, floating mound of vegetation or on the ground; always near the water's edge, usually along small islands or secluded shorelines; may nest on an artificial nest platform; nest mound is built from aquatic vegetation; pair incubates 2 olive brown eggs, sparsely marked with black or brown, for 29 or 30 days; young hatch asynchronously.
Feeding: pursues small fish underwater; may also take large aquatic invertebrates and some amphibians.
Voice: alarm call is a quavering tremolo; contact calls include a lengthy wail and soft, short hoots. *Male:* territorial call is a complex yodel.
Similar Species: *Red-throated Loon:* smaller; slender bill; red throat and grey head and neck in breeding plumage. *Pacific Loon:* smaller; dusty grey head often has a silvery look; purple throat. *Yellow-billed Loon:* yellow, slightly upward-curving bill.
Best Sites: Whiteshell PP; Nopiming PP; Interlake area; Turtle Mountain PP; Duck Mountain PP; Grass River PP.

PIED-BILLED GREBE

Podilymbus podiceps

The Pied-billed Grebe is the smallest and wariest of Manitoba's grebes, but it is also the most defiant. When frightened, this grebe will compress its feathers to alter its specific gravity, enabling it to sink slowly until only its eyes and nostrils remain above water. If competing ducks, grebes or even loons enter a Pied-bill's territory, this bird will not hesitate to attack. Its tactics include hunching itself in a threat posture or launching an underwater diving assault. Perhaps this grebe's aggressiveness is what earned it the nickname 'Helldiver.' • Pied-billed Grebes are elusive birds, and they are far more common than encounters might lead one to believe. They are usually revealed by their loud, whooping calls, which often emanate from dense emergent vegetation in wetland habitats. Like most other grebes, male and female Pied-bills call in duets. • The scientific name *podiceps* means 'rump foot,' in reference to the way this bird's feet are located toward the back of its body.

breeding

ID: small, stubby, light-coloured bill with a black ring; tail is more noticeable than on other grebes; greyish-brown body; black throat patch; white undertail coverts; pale belly; pale eye ring; black eyes. *Non-breeding:* browner overall; yellow bill lacks the black ring; white 'chin.' *Juvenile:* striped head and neck.
Size: *L* 30–38 cm; *W* 58 cm.
Status: rare in the north; uncommon in central parts; common in the south; mid-April to mid-October.
Habitat: ponds, marshes and shallow lakes with thick emergent vegetation.
Nesting: in thick vegetation near lake edges; floating platform nest of wet and decaying plants is anchored to thick emergent vegetation; mostly the female incubates 3–10 bluish-white eggs for about 23 days.

Feeding: makes shallow dives or gleans the surface for aquatic invertebrates, small fish, adult and larval amphibians and some aquatic plants.
Voice: loud, whooping call that begins quickly, then slows down: *kuk-kuk-kuk cow cow cow cowp cowp cowp;* also 'whinnies.'
Similar Species: *Horned Grebe* (p. 22): red eyes; thin bill; gold 'horns' and red neck in breeding plumage; white cheek and foreneck in non-breeding plumage. *Eared Grebe:* red eyes; thin bill; golden ear tufts, black neck and chestnut sides in breeding plumage; white cheek and foreneck in non-breeding plumage. *American Coot* (p. 62): all-black body; white bill extends onto the forehead.
Best Sites: Oak Hammock Marsh; Netley-Libau Marsh; Delta Marsh; Turtle Mountain PP; Minnedosa pothole region.

HORNED GREBE
Podiceps auritus

Cold, mucky wetlands might not seem very inviting, but nothing is more appealing to nesting Horned Grebes. Their propensity for these habitats starts early in life—Horned Grebe eggs are incubated on soggy, floating platforms among dense emergent vegetation. Once they hatch, the young are often brooded on the wet nest before they are ready to follow their parents into open water. • In Ernest Thompson Seton's 1891 publication, *Birds of Manitoba*, he noted that Horned Grebes were 'abundant summer residents of general distribution.' They were listed as common to abundant in the Red River valley near Winnipeg, the Turtle Mountains, Portage la Prairie and Pembina, and they were the most common grebes on most prairie ponds. Today, Horned Grebes are not nearly as common, and according to recent breeding bird surveys, their numbers are declining in the prairie provinces and throughout North America.

breeding

ID: red eyes. *Breeding:* rufous neck and flanks; black head with golden 'horn' tufts; black back; white underparts; flat, uncrested crown. *Female:* slightly duller. *Non-breeding:* lacks the 'horn' tufts; black upperparts; white cheek, foreneck, flanks and underparts.
Size: *L* 30–40 cm; *W* 60 cm.
Status: rare in the north; uncommon to fairly common in central parts; common in the south; mid-April to October.
Habitat: *Nesting:* smaller, often weedy wetlands; also small dams, dugouts and semi-permanent ponds. *In migration:* larger lakes and rivers.
Nesting: usually singly; floating platform nest of aquatic plants and rotting vegetation is anchored to thick emergent vegetation; pair incubates 3–7 bluish-white eggs for about 24 days.

Feeding: makes shallow dives and gleans the surface for aquatic insects, crustaceans, mollusks, small fish and adult and larval amphibians.
Voice: series of croaks and shrieking notes similar to, but much softer than, the Red-necked Grebe's calls; a sharp *keark keark* during courtship.
Similar Species: *Eared Grebe:* head is more crested; black neck; splayed, golden ear tufts extend below the eyes in breeding plumage; darker neck in fall. *Pied-billed Grebe* (p. 21): thicker, stubbier bill; mostly brown body; dark eyes. *Red-necked Grebe* (p. 23): much larger; dark eyes; lacks the ear tufts; white cheek in breeding plumage; long, heavy bill.
Best Sites: Delta Marsh; Minnedosa pothole region; Riding Mountain NP; Churchill; Wapusk NP.

RED-NECKED GREBE

Podiceps grisegena

Like many fish-eating birds, grebes eat feathers. The feathers protect the stomach lining from sharp bones, and they might slow the passage of food to allow more time for the absorption of nutrients. • Unlike most other waterbirds, grebes lack webbing between their toes. Instead, each toe is wide and flat, or 'lobed,' to assist them while swimming. • Young Red-necked Grebes ride on their parents' backs for much of the first week after hatching. Although the striped young can stay aboard when the adults submerge underwater, they often free themselves and float to the surface during extended dives. • Nesting Red-necked Grebes are easily recognized by their unusual braying calls, which end in a horse-like 'whinny.' • Studies on Red-necked Grebes in Manitoba's Turtle Mountain Provincial Park during the 1980s revealed that the birds had low nesting success. Predation by raccoons and eggshell thinning caused by high levels of PCBs in the grebes' wintering areas were identified as the major contributing factors. • Many old-timers still refer to this grebe by its former name, 'Holboell's Grebe.'

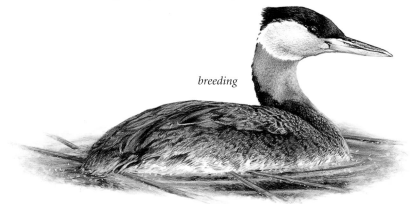

breeding

ID: reddish neck; grey-white cheek patch; black crown; straight, heavy bill is dark with a yellowish base; black upperparts; grey sides; light underparts; dark eyes. *In flight:* hunchbacked appearance; feet trail behind the body; white patches at the front and the back of the wing.
Size: *L* 43–56 cm.
Status: uncommon to fairly common; mid-April to mid-September.
Habitat: shoreline vegetation in medium-sized lakes and ponds, secluded bays of larger lakes and in offshore reed beds; occasionally along quiet rivers. *In migration:* open, deeper lakes.
Nesting: usually singly, but sometimes in loose colonies; floating platform nest of decaying aquatic vegetation is anchored in shallow water to emergent reeds, underwater plants or sticks; pair

incubates 2–6 eggs for 22 or 23 days; eggs are initially blue-white, but often become stained by vegetation in the water; young hatch asynchronously.
Feeding: dives and gleans the surface for small fish, aquatic invertebrates, crayfish, leeches and amphibians.
Voice: often repeated, excited braying: *ooh-ah ooh-ah ooh-ah* or a shorter *ah-ah-ah-ah-ah.*
Similar Species: *Horned Grebe* (p. 22): dark cheek; golden 'horns'; red eyes. *Eared Grebe:* black neck; fanned-out, golden ear feathers. *Pied-billed Grebe* (p. 21): much smaller, stubby bill with a black ring; mostly brown body. *Western Grebe* (p. 24) and *Clark's Grebe:* blackish upperparts; white foreneck and underparts; red eyes.
Best Sites: Turtle Mountain PP; Riding Mountain NP; Crane River; Waterhen River; Duck Mountain PP.

WESTERN GREBE

Aechmophorus occidentalis

The courtship displays of the Western Grebe are among the most elaborate and beautiful rituals in the bird world. During the 'weed dance,' the male and female swim with their torsos and heads held high, caressing each other with aquatic vegetation held in their bills. The 'rushing' display, which Western Grebes are most famous for, involves two or more individuals exploding into a paddling sprint side by side across the water's surface. The grebes stand high, feet paddling furiously, with their wings stretched back and heads and necks held rigid, until the race ends with the pair breaking the water's surface in a graceful, headfirst dive. • Western Grebe eggs hatch at regular intervals. Parental duties are often divided, with each parent feeding half the fledged young. • Western Grebes nest in colonies on large freshwater lakes. They are sensitive nesters, and, unlike their Red-necked relatives, seem unable to adjust to the disturbances created by cottagers and recreationalists on their summer range.

ID: long, slender neck; black upperparts from the base of the bill to the tail; white underparts from the 'chin' to the belly; long, thin, yellow bill; white cheek; black on the face extends below the red eyes.
Size: *L* 56–74 cm; *W* 76–102 cm.
Status: rare to uncommon in central parts; fairly common in the south; early May to late October.
Habitat: large, deep lakes with emergent vegetation for nesting.
Nesting: usually colonial; floating nest of fresh and decaying vegetation is anchored or placed among emergent vegetation; pair incubates 2–7 bluish-green to buffy eggs for about 23 days.
Feeding: gleans the water's surface and dives for small fish, amphibians and aquatic invertebrates.
Voice: high-pitched, double-note *crreeet-crreeet*; call sounds like a squeaky wheel when repeated in series.
Similar Species: *Clark's Grebe:* white of the face extends above the eyes; orange-yellow bill; single-note call. *Double-crested Cormorant* (p. 26): immature has a thicker, crooked neck, a longer tail and a yellow-orange throat patch. *Red-necked Grebe* (p. 23): shorter, stockier neck; dark eyes; darker sides and neck in non-breeding plumage.
Best Sites: Netley-Libau Marsh; Hecla/Grindstone PP; Dog Lake; Lake Francis; Delta Marsh; Pelican Lake/Ninette.

AMERICAN WHITE PELICAN

Pelecanus erythrorhynchos

A significant proportion of North America's American White Pelican population nests on islands in Manitoba's 'great lakes' (Winnipeg, Manitoba and Winnipegosis). Although these birds often lay two or three eggs, only a single chick usually survives—the other chicks are usually harassed and outcompeted for food by the eldest sibling. During the nesting season, adult pelicans disperse from their colonies, occasionally travelling hundreds of kilometres in search of productive fishing grounds. Most sightings in southern Manitoba are of non-breeding adults or birds foraging at great distances from their nest colony. • Groups of foraging pelicans swim in formation, deliberately herding schools of fish into shallow water, from which the birds dip and scoop the prey with their bills. In a single scoop, a pelican can hold up to 12 *l* of water, which must be drained from the sides of its mouth before swallowing its meal.

non-breeding

ID: very large, white bird; long, orange bill and throat pouch; black primary and secondary wing feathers. *Breeding:* small, keeled plate develops on the upper mandible; often has a dark crown and nape. *Non-breeding* and *Immature:* white plumage is tinged with brown.
Size: *L* 1.3–1.8 m; *W* 2.8 m.
Status: uncommon to fairly common; April to late September.
Habitat: large lakes and rivers.
Nesting: colonial; often associated with cormorants, gulls, terns and other waterbirds; on bare, low-lying islands; nest scrape or mound may be lined with pebbles, plant stems and debris; 1–3 large, white eggs are incubated for 29–36 days; young hatch at 1 or 2 day intervals.
Feeding: surface dips for small fish; may take crayfish or salamanders; often feeds in groups; young are initially fed by regurgitation.
Voice: generally quiet; adults rarely issue pig-like grunts.
Similar Species: *Snow Goose* (p. 31) and *Whooping Crane:* do not fold their neck back when in flight. *Tundra Swan* (p. 33): white wing tips; much smaller bill.
Best Sites: Red River near Lockport; Hecla/Grindstone PP; Shoal Lakes; Delta Marsh; Pelican Lake; Turtle Mountain PP.

DOUBLE-CRESTED CORMORANT
Phalacrocorax auritus

Manitoba's large lakes provide ideal habitat for the Double-crested Cormorant. Whether they are lined up along a gravel bar, perched high on a naked branch or swimming with only their heads breaking the surface, their beauty can take longer to appreciate than that of other species. These slick-feathered birds often appear dishevelled, and they typically smell of fish oil, but their mastery of aquatic environments is virtually complete. Double-crested Cormorants lack the ability to waterproof their feathers, which helps them during underwater dives by decreasing their buoyancy. Often, a waterlogged cormorant can be seen struggling to reach a patch of land or an elevated tree perch, where it will sit with its wings partially spread in an attempt to dry its flight feathers. Also aiding this bird's aquatic lifestyle are its long, rudder-like tail, excellent underwater vision and sealed nostrils. • Cormorants are often persecuted by commercial fishermen. However, recent studies in Manitoba have revealed that most of the cormorants' prey consists of undesirable, non-commercial fish species.

breeding

ID: all-black body; long, crooked neck; fairly long, straight bill with a hooked tip. *Breeding:* bright orange-yellow throat pouch; black plumes trail from the eyebrows. *Immature:* brown upperparts; whitish or buff throat and breast; yellowish throat patch. *In flight:* rapid wingbeats; kinked neck.
Size: *L* 80 cm; *W* 1.4 m.
Status: common to locally abundant; mid-April to mid-October.
Habitat: deeper lakes and large rivers.
Nesting: colonial; often nests near pelicans, terns and gulls; on the ground on low-lying islands or in treetops along lakes or rivers;

platform nest, made of sticks, aquatic plants and drift materials, is lined with fine materials; incubates 2–7 bluish-white eggs for 25–29 days.
Feeding: dives underwater (up to 9 m deep) for small schooling fish and rarely invertebrates; occasionally surface-dips for amphibians.
Voice: generally quiet; may issue pig-like grunts or croaks at nest colonies.
Similar Species: *Canada Goose* (p. 32): white 'chin' strap; lacks the all-black body. *Common Loon* (p. 20): shorter neck; black and white checkered back.
Best Sites: Whiteshell PP; Hecla/Grindstone PP; Delta Marsh; islands in Lake Manitoba, Lake Winnipeg and Lake Winnipegosis; Turtle Mountain PP.

AMERICAN BITTERN

Botaurus lentiginosus

This skilled hunter of Manitoba's marshlands is renowned for its cryptic camouflage and secretive lifestyle. American Bitterns are common inhabitants of marshes throughout the province, but their tendency to stay hidden within dense vegetation means that most nature enthusiasts have never seen one. When threatened, a bittern's first reaction is to freeze—its bill points skyward, and its streaked brown plumage blends perfectly with the cattails, bulrushes and tall shoreline grass of its marshland habitat. When possible, the bittern will face an intruder, moving ever so slowly to keep its camouflaged underside toward the source of danger. The bittern will even rock gently side-to-side like a reed swaying in the breeze, and most prowlers pass by without detecting it.
• At night, and occasionally during the day, American Bitterns advertise their presence by issuing deep, resonant calls.

ID: brown upperparts; brown streaking from the 'chin' through the breast; straight, stout bill; yellow-green legs and feet; short tail; black streaks from the bill down the neck to the shoulder. *In flight:* primaries are darker than the rest of the wing; head and neck are drawn back over the shoulders.
Size: *L* 60–85 cm; *W* 1.2 m.
Status: rare to uncommon in the north; fairly common elsewhere; mid-April to late September.
Habitat: among tall, dense grass, sedges, bulrushes and cattails in marshes, wetlands and lake edges.
Nesting: singly; on dry ground or above water in dense vegetation; nest mound or platform is made of grass, sedges, twigs and dead reeds; nest has separate entrance and exit paths; incubates 2–6 buff-brown eggs for 24–29 days.

Feeding: patient stand-and-wait predator; strikes at small fish, amphibians, reptiles, small mammals and large insects; young are fed by regurgitation.
Voice: deep, resonant, repetitive *pomp-er-lunk* or *onk-a-BLONK*, is most often heard at night.
Similar Species: *Black-crowned Night-Heron* (p. 29), *Least Bittern* and *Green Heron:* immature lacks the dark streak from the bill to the shoulder; immature night-herons are more greyish with white-flecked upperparts.
Best Sites: Netley-Libau Marsh; Dog Lake; Delta Marsh; Minnedosa pothole region; Riding Mountain NP; Churchill.

GREAT BLUE HERON

Ardea herodias

The sight of a Great Blue Heron is always memorable for Manitobans with a passion for the outdoors. Whether you are observing its stealthy, often motionless hunting strategy, or tracking its lazy wingbeats as it returns to a nesting colony, it's hard not to notice this bird's graceful beauty. • While in their treetop rookeries, Great Blue Herons are extremely sensitive to human disturbance. If you are fortunate enough to discover a nesting colony, it's best to observe the birds' behaviour from a distance. Because herons do not nest every year, and because nesting birds can forage far from their rookery, the presence of herons in an area does not necessarily mean that a nesting colony is nearby. • Great Blue Herons are fairly common in central and southern parts of our province, appearing along shallow river edges and lakeshore fringes. • This heron is often mistaken for a crane, but cranes hold their necks outstretched in flight.

breeding

ID: large, blue-grey bird; long, curving neck; long, dark legs; straight, yellow bill. *Breeding:* plumes streak back from the crown and throat. *In flight:* crooked neck; legs trail behind the body; deep, lazy wingbeats.
Size: *L* 1.0–1.3 m; *W* up to 1.8 m.
Status: fairly common; April through October.
Habitat: along the edges of rivers, shallow lakes and marshes; also seen in fields and wet meadows; nests on islands in Manitoba's larger lakes.
Nesting: colonial; in a tree or shrub or on the ground; flimsy to elaborate stick and twig platform is lined with leaves, is augmented, often over years, and can be up to 1.2 m in diameter; pair incubates 3–7 light bluish-green eggs for about 28 days.
Feeding: patient stand-and-wait predator; takes small fish and mammals, amphibians, nestlings, aquatic invertebrates and reptiles; rarely scavenges.
Voice: usually quiet away from the nest; may give a deep, harsh *frahnk* (usually during take-off).

Similar Species: *Black-crowned Night-Heron* (p. 29) and *Green Heron:* much smaller; shorter legs. *Egrets:* all are predominately white. *Sandhill Crane* (p. 63): red cap; flies with its neck outstretched. *Whooping Crane:* white overall; black wing tips.
Best Sites: Whiteshell PP; Birds Hill PP; Oak Hammock Marsh; Grand Beach PP; Hecla/Grindstone PP; Turtle Mountain PP.

BLACK-CROWNED NIGHT-HERON

Nycticorax nycticorax

When the setting sun has driven most wetland waders to their nightly roosts, Black-crowned Night-Herons arrive to hunt the marshy waters and to voice their hoarse squawks. Under the evening sky, these small herons patrol the shallows for frogs and small fish, which they can see in the dim light with their large, light-sensitive eyes. A popular hunting strategy for Black-crowned Night-Herons is to sit motionless atop a few bent-over cattails. In this scenario, anything passing below the perch becomes fair game—even ducklings, small shorebirds and young muskrats. • This heron's white 'ponytail' is present for most of the year, but it is most noticeable during the nesting season. • Immature night-herons are occasionally seen around large cattail marshes in fall. Because of their brown-streaked underside, they are easily mistaken for American Bitterns. • *Nycticorax*, meaning 'night raven,' refers to this bird's distinctive night-time calls.

breeding

ID: black cap and back; white cheek, foreneck and underparts; grey neck and wings; dull yellow legs; stout, black bill; large, red eyes. *Breeding:* 2 white plumes trail down from the crown. *Immature:* lightly streaked underparts; brown upperparts with white flecking.
Size: *L* 58–66 cm; *W* 1.1 m.
Status: rare in central parts; fairly common to uncommon in the south; mid-April to early October.
Habitat: shallow cattail and bulrush marshes, small lakes and slow rivers.
Nesting: colonial; in cattails and shrubs; loose platform nest is made of twigs and reeds and lined with finer materials; male gathers the nest material; female builds the nest; nests are used year after year; pair

incubates 3–5 pale green eggs for 21–26 days.
Feeding: often at dusk; stands motionless and waits for prey; stabs for small fish, amphibians, aquatic invertebrates, reptiles, small mammals and birds.
Voice: deep, guttural *quark* or *wok*, often heard as the bird takes flight.
Similar Species: *Great Blue Heron* (p. 28): much larger; lacks the black back. *Green Heron:* adult has a red face and neck; lacks the black back; immature has heavily streaked underparts. *American Bittern* (p. 27): similar to an immature Black-crowned Night-Heron, but the bittern has a black streak from the bill to the shoulder.
Best Sites: Oak Hammock Marsh; Glenboro Marsh; Turtle Mountain PP; Oak/Plum lakes; Riding Mountain NP.

TURKEY VULTURE

Cathartes aura

The Turkey Vulture may appear grotesque with its red, featherless head, but this adaptation, while unsightly, is beneficial because it allows the bird to remain relatively clean while digging through messy carcasses. Vultures eat carrion almost exclusively, and their bills and feet are not nearly as powerful as those of other raptors, which kill live prey. • Turkey Vultures soar at spectacular heights over the Manitoba landscape. With a wingspan of up to 1.8 m, these birds make use of the slightest wind updrafts or rising columns of warm air ('thermals'), becoming airborne when other soaring birds are grounded. Although most birds lack a good sense of smell, Turkey Vultures rely heavily on this sense to locate decomposing food. • Turkey Vultures seem to have mastered the art of regurgitation. The ability to regurgitate meals allows parents to transport food over long distances and also enables engorged birds to repulse an attacker, or to 'lighten up' for an emergency take-off. • Recent studies have shown that Turkey Vultures are most closely related to storks, not hawks as previously thought.

ID: very large, eagle-sized, all-black bird; bare, red head; yellow-tipped, red bill. *Immature:* bare, black-grey head; grey bill. *In flight:* rocks or tilts side-to-side while soaring; silver-grey flight feathers contrast with the black wing linings; wings are held in a shallow V; head is barely visible.
Size: *L* 66–82 cm; *W* 1.7–1.8 m.
Status: uncommon; early April to late September.
Habitat: usually seen flying over open country, forest edges, river valleys or along roads.
Nesting: on a cliff ledge, cave crevice or among boulders on islands; rarely in abandoned buildings; minimal or no nest material is used; pair incubates 2 creamy white eggs for up to 41 days.
Feeding: entirely on carrion (mostly mammalian); young are fed by regurgitation.
Voice: generally silent; may produce a hiss or grunt if threatened.
Similar Species: *Bald Eagle* (p. 49) and *Golden Eagle:* wings are held flat in flight; often show white on the underside of the wings and tail; do not rock from side to side when soaring; head is larger and feathered.
Best Sites: Whiteshell PP; Assiniboine River valley; Spruce Woods PP; Riding Mountain NP; Duck Mountain PP.

SNOW GOOSE

Chen caerulescens

There is hardly a more memorable sight than thousands of Snow Geese settling over the Manitoba prairie at sunset. Each spring and fall, Snow Geese pass through our province along the Mississippi flyway, a migration route that takes them back and forth from the Arctic and their wintering grounds in the Gulf of Mexico. October in particular brings flocks numbering over 100,000 birds. The event is spectacular, even though the birds stop only briefly to rest and refuel before continuing their migration. • In recent decades, an abundance of food along Snow Goose migratory routes and on their winter range has allowed populations to increase several times over. Unfortunately, this burgeoning population is destroying its own tundra nesting grounds through overgrazing. • Snow Geese come in two colour morphs: blue (less common) and white. In fall, Snow Goose plumage is often stained rusty red from the iron-rich aquatic substrates of their summer feeding grounds. • Unlike Canada Geese, which fly in well-formed Vs, migrating Snow Geese fly in unorganized, oscillating, wavy lines.

ID: white overall; black wing tips; dark pink feet and bill; dark 'grinning patch' on the bill; plumage may be stained rusty red. *Blue morph:* white head and upper neck; dark blue-grey body. *Immature:* grey plumage; dark bill and feet.
Size: *L* 60–80 cm; *W* 1.3–1.5 m.
Status: common to abundant in the north; rare, non-nesting summer resident and abundant migrant elsewhere; early April to mid-November.
Habitat: *Nesting:* on tundra along a pond, lake or island shoreline. *In migration:* shallow wetlands, lakes and fields.
Nesting: colonial; on a ridge or hummock of tundra; female fills a shallow depression with plant material and down; female incubates 4–7 whitish eggs for 22–25 days; pairs may mate for life.
Feeding: grazes on waste grain and new sprouts; also eats aquatic vegetation, grass, sedges, insects and roots.
Voice: loud, nasal, constant *houk-houk* in flight.
Similar Species: *Ross's Goose:* smaller; shorter neck; lacks the black 'grin.' *Tundra Swan* (p. 33): larger; white wing tips. *American White Pelican* (p. 25): much larger bill and body. *Whooping Crane:* larger overall; much longer legs and neck.
Best Sites: Churchill; Wapusk NP; Oak Hammock Marsh; Delta Marsh.

CANADA GOOSE

Branta canadensis

Canada Geese are some of the first birds to return to our province in spring, so when their V-formation flocks fly overhead, Manitobans are reminded that winter is nearly over. • In recent decades, these bold geese have inundated golf courses, city parks and picnic sites, and today many people consider them pests. Few people realize, however, that at one time these birds were hunted almost to extinction. If not for the work of dedicated conservationists, such as Jack Miner and Manitoba's Alfred A. Hole, we may have missed the experience of living with these wild geese. • Canada Geese often maintain life-long pair bonds, and they generally return to the same nesting site year after year. The fuzzy goslings are irresistible, especially to children, but Canada Goose parents can cause harm to unwelcome strangers. Low, outstretched necks and hissing sounds are signs that you should give these birds some space. • There are several subspecies of Canada Goose in Manitoba, ranging from the duck-sized 'Richardson's Canada Goose' to the 'Giant Canada Goose,' which can weigh over 11 kg.

ID: long, black neck; white 'chin' strap; white undertail coverts; light brown underparts; dark brown upperparts.
Size: *L* 55–122 cm; *W* to 1.8 m.
Status: common to abundant; late March to mid-November; a few are present in winter.
Habitat: lakeshores, riverbanks, ponds, farmlands and city parks.
Nesting: on islands and shorelines; usually on the ground; sometimes in a shrub, on a muskrat or beaver house or on any platform raised above the water; nest of plant materials is lined with down; female incubates 4–7 white eggs for 25–30 days while the male stands guard.

Feeding: grazes on new sprouts, aquatic vegetation, grass and roots; tips up for aquatic roots and tubers; also takes seeds, grain, insects and invertebrates.
Voice: loud, familiar *ah-honk*.
Similar Species: *Greater White-fronted Goose:* brown neck and head; lacks the white 'chin' strap; orange legs; white around the base of the bill; dark speckling on the belly. *Brant:* lacks the white 'chin' strap; white 'necklace'; black upper breast. *Blue morph Snow Goose* (p. 31): white head and upper neck.
Best Sites: Whiteshell PP; Oak Hammock Marsh; Interlake area; Whitewater Lake; Oak/Plum lakes; Churchill.

TUNDRA SWAN

Cygnus columbianus

Before the last of winter's snows have melted, Tundra Swans can be found foraging in flooded fields and pastures throughout southern Manitoba. The snow and ice they encounter there will not be the last on their journey, because they generally reach their tundra nesting grounds well before the spring thaw. In southern and central regions, migration typically occurs from early April to mid-May and from September to mid-November. • Churchill is a great place to see Tundra Swans and other arctic species on their nesting grounds. Incubating swans tend to be conspicuous on their high nest mounds, but predators such as gulls, Arctic Foxes and weasels keep their distance—an adult swan is powerful and can inflict serious wounds with its bill and wings. • Swans were hunted legally in North America until the early 1900s, and most species suffered serious declines. Unlike the Trumpeter Swan, which still remains extirpated in many provinces, the Tundra Swan was able to recover with the passage of the Migratory Birds Act in 1918.

ID: white plumage; large, black bill often shows yellow lores; black feet; neck and head tend to show a rounded, slightly curving profile. *Immature:* grey-brown plumage; grey bill.
Size: *L* 1.2–1.5 m; *W* 1.8–2 m.
Status: fairly common in the north; uncommon in central parts; common in the south; early April to mid-November.
Habitat: *Nesting:* coastal arctic tundra. *In migration:* shallow areas of lakes and wetlands, agricultural fields and flooded pastures.
Nesting: on tundra, often on islands or along shorelines; pair builds a large mound of vegetation; mostly the female incubates

4 or 5 creamy white eggs for 31 or 32 days; both adults tend the young.
Feeding: tips up, dabbles and surface gleans for aquatic vegetation and invertebrates; grazes for tubers, roots and waste grain.
Voice: high-pitched, quivering *oo-oo-whoo* is constantly repeated by migrating flocks.
Similar Species: *Trumpeter Swan:* loud, bugle-like voice; lacks the yellow lores; neck tends to be straighter and the head tends to be more angular in profile; extremely rare in Manitoba. *Snow Goose* (p. 31) and *Ross's Goose:* shorter neck; black wing tips.
Best Sites: *Nesting:* Churchill; Wapusk NP. *In migration:* flooded fields and large marshes; Oak Hammock Marsh.

WOOD DUCK

Aix sponsa

The male Wood Duck is one of Manitoba's most colourful birds: its iridescent plumage glows with almost all the colours of the rainbow, including the green, red and gold of Manitoba's tartan. • Wetlands and slow-flowing rivers bordered by stands of old, cavity-filled cottonwood trees are blessed each summer by the presence of the spectacular Wood Duck. Despite their splendid attire, Wood Ducks are usually heard before they are seen—from high in a tree, they often mutter squeaky, conspicuous, high-pitched calls. • Few birds are routinely forced into the adventures of life as early as Wood Ducks. Shortly after they hatch, young ducklings must jump to the ground from their nest cavity, which is often 15 m high in a tree, to follow their mother to the nearest source of water. • Female Wood Ducks and their offspring may return to the same nest site year after year. Sometimes clutches of 15 to 50 eggs can be found in a single Wood Duck nest—this is usually the result of several females 'dumping' eggs in a particular female's nest. • The scientific name *sponsa* is Latin for 'promised bride,' suggesting that the male appears formally dressed for a wedding.

ID: *Male:* very colourful; glossy green head with a few white streaks; crest is slicked back from the crown; white 'chin' and throat; white-spotted, purple-chestnut breast; black and white shoulder slash; golden sides; dark back and hindquarters. *Female:* white, tear-shaped eye patch; mottled brown breast is streaked with white; brown-grey upperparts; white belly.
Size: *L* 43–50 cm; *W* 70–75 cm.
Status: fairly common; April to mid-October.
Habitat: rivers, ponds, marshes and lakeshores with wooded edges.
Nesting: in a tree cavity, hollow or artificial nest box; usually near water; nest cavity is lined with wood chips and down; female incubates 8–15 white to buff eggs for 28–32 days.
Feeding: surface gleans and tips for aquatic vegetation, especially duckweed and aquatic sedges and grass; eats more fruits and nuts than other ducks.
Voice: *Male:* ascending *ter-wee-wee*. *Female:* squeaky *woo-e-e-k*.
Similar Species: *Hooded Merganser* (p. 45): male has a black head with a white crest patch; slim, black bill; black and white breast.
Best Sites: Whiteshell PP; Hecla/Grindstone PP; Spruce Woods PP; Souris River; Turtle Mountain PP.

AMERICAN WIGEON

Anas americana

The American Wigeon is generally a vegetarian. Although it frequently dabbles for food, nothing pleases a wigeon more than stems and leaves of pond-bottom plants—in shallow water, this wigeon is commonly seen tipping its hind end into the air. These plants grow far too deep for most dabbling ducks, however, so wigeons often pirate food from by accomplished divers, such as American Coots, Canvasbacks, scaups and Redheads. These birds are commonly observed grazing on shore, and they are good walkers compared to other ducks. Lightly grazed fields, city parks and golf courses with nearby sources of water usually support at least a few American Wigeons. • Male wigeons have distinctive whistled calls that stand out among the wetland symphony of buzzes, quacks and ticks. Upon hearing these birds, you'll probably realize where toy makers got the sound for rubber duckies! • The male's bright white crown and forehead have led some people, especially hunters, to call it 'Bald Pate.'

ID: large, white wing patch; cinnamon breast and sides; white belly; black-tipped, grey-blue bill; green speculum. *Male:* white forehead; green swipe running back from each eye. *Female:* greyish head; brown underparts.
Size: *L* 46–58 cm.
Status: uncommon in the north; fairly common in central parts; common in the south; early April to early November.
Habitat: pothole, sloughs, marshes and lake edges.
Nesting: nest is well concealed in tall vegetation and is built with grass and leaves and lined with

down; female incubates 8–11 white eggs for 23–25 days.
Feeding: dabbles and tips up for aquatic leaves and the stems of pondweeds; also grazes and uproots young shoots in fields; may eat invertebrates.
Voice: *Male:* nasal, frequently repeated whistle: *whew WHEW wheew. Female:* soft, seldom heard *quack.*
Similar Species: *Gadwall:* lacks the large, white forewing patch; male has all-black hindquarters and lacks the green eye swipe.
Best Sites: Pinawa area; Mantagao Lake WMA; Minnedosa pothole region; Duck Mountain PP; Churchill.

MALLARD

Anas platyrhynchos

The Mallard is by far the most abundant duck in Manitoba during the nesting season, and it is probably safe to say that most of us have seen this bird at one time or another. Some Mallards will overwinter in our province where open water is available, but most of these birds winter in the U.S. • Like most male ducks, male Mallards do not participate in the incubation duties or the raising of young. After mating, they retreat to larger lakes, usually in the company of other males (in 'bachelor' flocks), where they undergo a moult that leaves them flightless for a short period of time. This is when males adopt their dull 'eclipse' plumage, which looks similar to that of the female. As is true for many other ducks, this eclipse plumage lasts only for a few months until the birds regrow their brighter feathers, sometime before the end of fall.

ID: dark blue speculum bordered by white; orange feet. *Male:* glossy green head; yellow bill; chestnut breast; white 'necklace'; black tail feathers curl upward. *Female:* mottled brown overall; orange bill splattered with black.

Size: *L* 50–70 cm; *W* 75–100 cm.

Status: uncommon to common in the north and in central parts; uncommon to abundant in the south; March to late December; rare in winter.

Habitat: widespread; in beaver ponds, lakes, rivers, city parks, agricultural areas and sewage lagoons.

Nesting: in tall vegetation or under a bush; usually near water; often in an artificial structure or in an abandoned stick nest; nest is made of grass and other plant material and is lined with down; female incubates 8–12 light green to white eggs for 26–30 days.

Feeding: tips up and dabbles in shallows for the seeds of sedges, willows and pondweeds; also eats aquatic invertebrates, larval amphibians and fish eggs.

Voice: *Female:* loud quacks; very vocal. *Male:* deeper *quack*.

Similar Species: *Northern Shoveler* (p. 38): much larger bill; male has a white breast. *American Black Duck:* darker than a female Mallard; purple speculum lacks the white borders. *Common Merganser* (p. 46): male lacks the chestnut breast; blood red bill.

Best Sites: Whiteshell PP; Assiniboine Park; Delta Marsh; Turtle Mountain PP; Oak/Plum lakes.

BLUE-WINGED TEAL

Anas discors

The small, speedy Blue-winged Teal is renowned for its aviation skills. Small groups of teals can be identified in flight by their small size, colourful upperwing patches and the sharp twists and turns that they execute with precision. • Blue-winged Teals are found throughout Manitoba, but they are most common in southwest parts of the province among the marshes and sloughs of the 'prairie pothole' region. Over the past 60 years, many of our wetlands have been drained for agriculture, and in some areas of the province, these birds have been forced to adapt to life in less than ideal habitats, including roadside ditches, canals and rural dugouts. • The Blue-winged Teal is closely related to the Northern Shoveler and the Cinnamon Teal, which is accidental in Manitoba. These birds have broad, flat bills, pale blue forewing patches and green speculums. The female Cinnamon Teal and the female Blue-winged Teal are so similar in appearance that even expert birders and ornithologists have difficulty distinguishing them in the field.

ID: *Male:* blue-grey head; white crescent on the face; black-spotted breast and sides. *Female:* mottled brown overall. *In flight:* blue forewing patch; green speculum.
Size: *L* 35–40 cm; *W* 60–80 cm.
Status: rare in the north; fairly common in central parts; abundant in the south; mid-April to mid-October.
Habitat: wetland edges, shallow lakes, flooded fields and ditches.
Nesting: in grass along shorelines and in wet meadows; usually near water; nest is usually concealed by vegetation and is built of grass and considerable amounts of down; female incubates 9–12 white eggs

(may be tinged with olive) for 23 or 24 days.
Feeding: gleans the water's surface for sedge and grass seeds, pondweeds, duckweeds and aquatic invertebrates.
Voice: *Male:* soft *keck-keck-keck*. *Female:* soft quacks.
Similar Species: *Green-winged Teal* (p. 40): female has a black and green speculum and lacks the blue forewing patch. *Northern Shoveler* (p. 38): much larger bill; male has a green head and lacks the white crescent on the face and the spotting on the body.
Best Sites: Birds Hill PP; Oak Hammock Marsh; Hecla/Grindstone PP; Dog Lake; Lake Francis; Lyleton.

NORTHERN SHOVELER
Anas clypeata

In spring, it isn't uncommon to see small groups of male Northern Shovelers chasing around a single female, all the while proclaiming their ardour with nasal *took took took* calls. Unlike most dabbling ducks, male shovelers occupy their nesting territories throughout the incubation period, and female shovelers leave their nests frequently to partake in foraging excursions. • A large, spoon-like bill with comb-like structures allows this strangely handsome duck to strain small invertebrates from the water's surface or from the bottom of shallow ponds. The Northern Shoveler is often called a 'spoonbill,' and its scientific name *clypeata* is Latin for 'furnished with a shield.' Its green head makes it easy to confuse with a Mallard, but a closer look at the shoveler's bill quickly confirms its identity. Even when the bird is flying overhead, it's hard not to notice its remarkable bill.

ID: large, spatulate bill; blue forewing patch; green speculum. *Male:* green head; white breast; chestnut sides. *Female:* mottled brown overall; orange-tinged bill.
Size: *L* 46–51 cm.
Status: uncommon in the north and in central parts; common in the south; early April to October.
Habitat: temporary wetlands, sewage lagoons, sloughs, shallow marshes, bogs and lakes with muddy bottoms and emergent vegetation.
Nesting: in a shallow hollow on dry ground, usually within 50 m of water; female builds the nest with dry grass and down and incubates 10–12 pale buff-olive eggs for 21–28 days.

Feeding: dabbles in shallows; strains out plant and animal matter, especially aquatic crustaceans, insect larvae and seeds; rarely tips up.
Voice: generally quiet; males have a distinctive *took took took* spring courtship call; females occasionally utter a raspy chuckle or *quack*.
Similar Species: *Mallard* (p. 36): blue speculum bordered by white; lacks the pale blue forewing; male has a chestnut breast and white flanks. *Blue-winged Teal* (p. 37): much smaller bill; smaller overall; male has a white facial crescent and a spotted breast and sides.
Best Sites: Oak Hammock Marsh; Delta Marsh; Lyleton; Oak/Plum lakes; Minnedosa pothole region.

NORTHERN PINTAIL

Anas acuta

Elegant and graceful on the water and in the air, the male pintail's beauty and style are unsurpassed by most of Manitoba's birds. This bird's trademark is its long, tapering tail feathers—in Manitoba, only the Long-tailed Duck (formerly called the Oldsquaw) shares this pintail feature. • Migrating pintails are often seen in flocks of 20 to 40 birds, but where excellent habitat is available, some flocks have been known to consist of thousands of individuals. Northern Pintails arrive here in early spring, often around the same time as Mallards, but they leave earlier in the fall, usually before ice has formed on shallow wetlands. • In general, waterfowl numbers have increased substantially during the 1990s. However, pintail populations seem to have declined throughout much of their range.

ID: long, slender neck and pointed tail are distinctive; dark glossy bill. *Male:* chocolate brown head; long, tapering tail feathers; white of the breast extends up the sides of the neck; dusty grey body plumage; black and white hindquarters. *Female:* mottled light brown overall; grey bill; shorter, pointed tail. *In flight:* brownish speculum with a white trailing edge.

Size: *Male: L* 64–76 cm. *Female: L* 51–56 cm.

Status: fairly common in the central boreal forest; abundant in most parts; late March to mid-November.

Habitat: widespread; shallow wetlands, flooded fields and lake edges; also on arctic tundra.

Nesting: in a small depression of vegetation; nest of grass, leaves and moss is lined with down; female incubates 6–12 greenish-buff eggs for 22–25 days.

Feeding: tips up and dabbles in shallows for the seeds of sedges, willows and pondweeds; also eats aquatic invertebrates and larval amphibians; eats waste grain during migration.

Voice: *Male:* soft, double-toned whistle: *prrip prrip. Female:* rough *qua-ack.*

Similar Species: *Mallard* (p. 36) and *Gadwall:* females are chunkier and lack the tapering tail and the long, slender neck. *Blue-winged Teal* (p. 37): female is smaller; green speculum; blue forewing patch. *Long-tailed Duck:* shorter, black neck; black head; white eye patch.

Best Sites: Oak Hammock Marsh; Delta Marsh; Whitewater Lake; Lyleton; Churchill; Oak/Plum lakes.

GREEN-WINGED TEAL

Anas crecca

Green-winged Teals are usually seen in small, tight flocks, and they are among the smallest, speediest and most maneuverable of waterfowl. • Of all our dabbling or surface-feeding ducks, the Green-winged Teal shows the strongest association to tree-lined wetlands. Consequently, they are most common in northern parts of our province. • Teals and other ducks keep their nests hidden in large areas of undisturbed vegetation and in lightly to moderately grazed upland grass and brush. They are protective parents, and they cover their eggs with nest materials when they leave for brief foraging bouts. However, despite the parents' best efforts, many nests are inevitably discovered by predators, such as weasels, skunks, foxes, coyotes, raccoons and domestic cats. If hatched successfully, young Green-wings grow rapidly, possibly faster than any other North American duck.

ID: small bill; deep green and black speculum. *Male:* chestnut head; green swipe running back from each eye (seen in sunlight); white shoulder slash; creamy breast is spotted with black; pale grey sides. *Female:* mottled brown overall; green speculum; light belly.
Size: *L* 30–41 cm.
Status: common in the north and in central parts; uncommon to common in the south; late March to mid-November.
Habitat: wooded ponds, shallow lakes, wetlands, beaver ponds and meandering rivers.
Nesting: in tall, concealing vegetation near water; nest is built of grass and leaves and lined with down; female incubates 6–14 cream to pale buff eggs for 20–24 days.
Feeding: dabbles in shallow water for aquatic invertebrates, larval amphibians, sedge seeds and pondweeds.
Voice: *Male:* crisp whistle. *Female:* soft *quack.*
Similar Species: *American Wigeon* (p. 35): male lacks the white shoulder slash and the chestnut head. *Blue-winged Teal* (p. 37): blue forewing patch; paler underparts.
Best Sites: Hecla/Grindstone PP; Interlake area; Delta Marsh; Riding Mountain NP; Churchill.

CANVASBACK

Aythya valisineria

M ale Canvasbacks are handsome ducks—they have a rich, mahogany red head, red eyes and a bright, clean back that is as white as a sheet of canvas. Their white back, sloping forehead and bill are unmistakable field marks. • Canvasbacks are devoted deep divers, and they prefer to feed and nest in deepwater marshes, sloughs and in sheltered bays of larger lakes. • Like many ducks, female Canvasbacks often return to the area where they were raised. By contrast, evidence suggests that males show less fidelity to their early nesting grounds. • Canvasback nests are commonly parasitized by female Redheads, which also lay their eggs in other ducks' nests. • In recent years, the cultivation of many of Manitoba's sloughs has contributed to an overall decline in the Canvasback population. A number of wetland restoration projects in southern Manitoba are working to reverse this trend. • The scientific name *valisineria* refers to one of the Canvasback's favourite foods—wild celery (*Vallisneria americana*).

ID: long, sloping forehead and bill; dark grey bill. *Male:* canvas white back; dark red head and eyes; black breast and hindquarters. *Female:* duller brownish grey overall; brown eyes.

Size: *L* 48–60 cm; *W* 70–90 cm.

Status: a few are present in the north; rare to uncommon in central parts; fairly common in the south; early April to early November.

Habitat: open marshes and wetlands bordered by emergent vegetation.

Nesting: suspended above shallow water in dense stands of aquatic plants; may also nest on a muskrat house or on dry ground; basket nest is built of reeds and vegetation and is lined with down; female incubates 7–12 olive green eggs for up to 29 days.

Feeding: dives for roots, tubers and the basal stems of plants; occasionally eats aquatic invertebrates, seeds and clams.

Voice: *Male:* occasional coos and 'growls' during courtship. *Female:* low, soft, 'purring' *quack* or *kuck*; also 'growls.'

Similar Species: *Redhead:* rounded forehead; black-tipped, blue bill; male has a greyer back; female is browner overall with a light patch near the base of the bill.

Best Sites: Lake Francis; potholes in the Tiger Hills area; Turtle Mountain PP; Minnedosa pothole region.

LESSER SCAUP

Aythya affinis

The Lesser Scaup and its similar-looking relative, the Greater Scaup, are easy to spot—both birds are dark at each end and whitish in the middle. The Lesser Scaup is more abundant in migration, and it nests throughout most of the province, so it is the more familiar of the two species. The Ring-necked Duck is another similar-looking relative, and it can be distinguished by the white ring around its otherwise dark bill. The Lesser Scaup was once called the 'Little Blue-bill,' and the Greater Scaup was called the 'Big Blue-bill.' • Lesser Scaup prefer to nest along deepwater lakes where the aquatic vegetation grows to within a foot of the water's surface. • The Lesser Scaup's gregarious nature occasionally leads this bird into trouble—hunters often lure scaup into range with decoys.

ID: yellow eyes. *Male:* dark iridescent purplish head; black breast and hindquarters; dirty white sides; greyish back; bluish-grey, black-tipped bill. *Female:* dark brown overall; white patch encircles the base of the bill.
Size: *L* 38–46 cm.
Status: fairly common to common in most parts; uncommon in the north; early April to November; occasional in winter.
Habitat: *Nesting:* woodland and tundra ponds, wetlands and lake edges with grassy margins.
In migration: deep lakes, marshes and rivers.
Nesting: on the ground near water or over water on floating mats; a shallow scrape in concealing vegetation is lined with dry grass and down; female incubates 8–14 olive-buff eggs for 21–27 days; nests with more than 14 eggs generally include eggs from more than one female.
Feeding: dives underwater for aquatic vegetation and invertebrates, including mollusks, amphipods and insect larvae.
Voice: alarm call is a deep *scaup*. *Male:* soft, whistled *whee-oooh* in courtship. *Female:* purring *kwah*.
Similar Species: *Greater Scaup:* rounded head; slightly larger bill; longer, white wing edge; male has a dull, iridescent green head. *Ring-necked Duck:* male has a white shoulder slash, a black back and a white ring around the bill; female has dark eyes, a slight eye ring and a ring on the bill. *Redhead:* female has dark eyes and less white at the base of the bill.
Best Sites: Hecla/Grindstone PP; Turtle Mountain PP; Oak/Plum lakes; Riding Mountain NP; Churchill.

BUFFLEHEAD
Bucephala albeola

Beginner birdwatchers are often surprised to see a duck flying into a nest box or a tree cavity. In summer, Buffleheads lead a quiet life, choosing to breed, like goldeneyes, in secluded nest cavities. Long-term pair bonds are common among Buffleheads, and a pair will often return to the same nest site year after year. Once the female begins incubation, the male quickly disappears from the scene, migrating with other males to traditional moulting grounds. • The Bufflehead is actually a small goldeneye, as similarities in their profile, behaviour and scientific names will attest. • The common name refers to this duck's large head and sloped forehead, which are similar in shape to those of a buffalo.

ID: small, rounded duck; short grey bill; puffy head; short neck. *Male:* large bonnet-like white wedge on a dark iridescent green or purple head (often looks black); dark back; white neck, flanks and underparts. *Female and Immature:* dark brown head; white, oval ear patch; light brownish-grey to greyish-white underparts; small, white wing patch. *In flight:* large, white wing patch; rapid wingbeats.
Size: *L* 33–40 cm; *W* 50–60 cm.
Status: occasional in the north; fairly common to common in central parts; rare to common in the south; mid-April to mid-November.
Habitat: small coniferous or deciduous woodlands near ponds and wetlands.

Nesting: in a natural tree cavity or artificial nest box, usually near water; nest cavity is lined with down; female incubates 6–12 ivory-coloured eggs for 28–33 days.
Feeding: dives for aquatic invertebrates; also eats invertebrate larvae, seeds and small fish.
Voice: *Male:* hoarse, growling call. *Female:* harsh *quack*.
Similar Species: *Hooded Merganser* (p. 45): long, spike-like bill; dark sides; white head crest is outlined in black. *Common Goldeneye* (p. 44): males are larger and have a white patch between the eye and the bill.
Best Sites: Whiteshell PP; Tiger Hills; Turtle Mountain PP; Erickson-Rossburn area; Riding Mountain NP.

COMMON GOLDENEYE

Bucephala clangula

When in search of a nest site, Common Goldeneyes will hunt high and low for cavities in trees or elevated stumps. They will even explore chimneys, and where suitable sites are scarce, females may lay their eggs in other goldeneye nests (known as 'brood parasitism'). This sometimes results in clutches of over 30 eggs. Since female goldeneyes, like many other ducks, often return to the area where they were hatched, the extra eggs often belong to close relatives. If parasitism occurs early in the nesting cycle, a female may reduce the number of eggs she lays. Soon after hatching, the black and white ducklings jump out from the nest cavity, often falling a long distance to the ground below. • Goldeneyes are frequently called 'whistlers,' because the wind whistles through their wings when they fly.

ID: short neck; peaked, 'puffy' head; steep forehead; black wings with large, white patches; golden eyes. *Male:* dark, iridescent green head; round, white cheek patch; dark bill and back; white sides and belly. *Female:* chocolate brown head; brownish-grey overall with a lighter breast and belly; dark bill, tipped with yellow in spring and summer; white collar is not always visible. *Immature:* similar to the female, but lacks the white collar.
Size: *L* 41–51 cm.
Status: fairly common in the north; common in central parts; uncommon to common in the south; late March to mid-November; rare to locally uncommon in winter.
Habitat: *Nesting:* woodland marshes, ponds, lakes and rivers. *Non-nesting:* open water of lakes and rivers.

Nesting: in a tree cavity or nest box, usually close to water; nest cavity is lined with wood chips and down; female incubates 6–15 greyish-green eggs for 28–32 days.
Feeding: dives underwater for crustaceans, mollusks and aquatic insect larvae; may also eat tubers, leeches, frogs and small fish.
Voice: wings whistle in flight. *Male:* courtship calls are a nasal *peent* and a hoarse *kraaagh*. *Female:* harsh croak.
Similar Species: *Barrow's Goldeneye:* male has a large, white, crescent-shaped cheek patch and larger, white marks on the back; accidental in Manitoba. *Bufflehead* (p. 43): smaller; male a white head crest; female has a white, oval ear patch.
Best Sites: Nopiming PP; Hecla/Grindstone PP; Mantagao Lake WMA; Riding Mountain NP; Duck Mountain PP.

HOODED MERGANSER

Lophodytes cucullatus

The Hooded Merganser is one of Manitoba's most sought-after ducks. Most bird-watchers direct all their attention toward the handsome male, whose flashy headwear is certainly among the grooviest of all Manitoba birds. Much of the time his crest is held flat, but in moments of arousal or agitation, he unfolds his brilliant crest to attract a mate or signal approaching danger. • All mergansers have slim, saw-toothed bills for keeping a grasp on slippery prey. Before eating, Hoodies re-position their prey, using only their bill and slight tosses of the head, so that the fish can be swallowed headfirst. The smallest of the mergansers, Hoodies have a more diverse diet than their larger relatives. • The scientific name *Lophodytes* means 'crested diver.'

ID: crested head; dark, thin bill. *Male:* black head and back; bold white crest is outlined in black; white breast with 2 black slashes; rusty sides. *Female:* dusky brown body; shaggy, reddish-brown crest. *In flight:* small, white wing patches.

Size: *L* 41–48 cm.

Status: occasional in the north; uncommon in elsewhere; mid-March to early November.

Habitat: forest-edged ponds, lakes and rivers.

Nesting: in a tree or stump cavity near water; may also use nest boxes; rarely on the ground; cavity is lined with leaves, grass and down; female incubates 10–12 white eggs for 29–33 days; 'dump nests' are common.

Feeding: dives for small fish, caddisfly and dragonfly larvae, snails and amphibians.

Voice: low grunts and croaks. *Male:* frog-like *crrrrooo* in courtship display. *Female:* generally quiet; occasionally a harsh *gak* or a croaking *croo-croo-crook*.

Similar Species: *Bufflehead* (p. 43): chubbier; male has white sides and lacks the black outline to the crest and the black breast slashes. *Common Merganser* (p. 46) and *Red-breasted Merganser*: females are larger and greyer, have rufous-coloured heads and much longer, orange bills.

Best Sites: Whiteshell PP; Spruce Woods PP; Souris River; Little Saskatchewan River; Dauphin.

COMMON MERGANSER

Mergus merganser

Straining like a jumbo jet in take-off, the Common Merganser runs along the surface of the water, thrashing its wings and paddling its feet until it gains sufficient speed to become airborne. Once in the air, it flies low over the water like an arrow, making broad, sweeping turns to follow meandering shorelines. • Most Common Mergansers eat medium-sized fish, but some individuals occasionally catch one that exceeds 30 cm in length. A single, successful dive by one merganser may cause pandemonium, as nearby birds attempt to steal the catch before it is swallowed headfirst. • An early Manitoba naturalist once noted that Common Mergansers were never found on 'still water,' and that they preferred clear, unpolluted streams where fish were abundant. • In Manitoba, Common Mergansers nest along the forest-edged waterways of the Canadian Shield.

ID: large, elongated body. *Male:* long, whitish body; black back; glossy greenish-black head without a crest; blood red bill and feet; dark eyes. *Female:* grey body; rusty neck and crested head; clean white throat and breast; reddish bill and feet; orangish eyes. *In flight:* shallow wingbeats; arrow-like flight.

Size: *L* 56–69 cm.

Status: uncommon in the north; common in central parts; rare to common in the south; late March to mid-November; rare in winter.

Habitat: large, forest-lined rivers and deep lakes.

Nesting: in a tree cavity 4.5–6 m high; occasionally on the ground under a bush or log, on a cliff ledge or in a large nest box; usually near water; female incubates 8–11 pale buff eggs for 30–35 days.

Feeding: dives underwater (up to 9 m) for fish, usually whitefish, trout, suckers, perch and minnows; may eat amphibians or aquatic invertebrates.

Voice: *Male:* harsh *uig-a*, like a guitar twang. *Female:* harsh *karr karr*.

Similar Species: *Red-breasted Merganser:* male has a shaggy green head crest and a spotted, red breast; female has a white throat and foreneck. *Common Loon* (p. 20): white spotting on the back; dark bill; red eyes.

Best Sites: Nopiming PP; Riding Mountain NP; Hecla/Grindstone PP; Duck Mountain PP; Grass River PP.

RUDDY DUCK
Oxyura jamaicensis

Ruddy Ducks display their courtship rituals with comedic enthusiasm. In an attempt to attract a female, the brightly coloured male eagerly pumps his bright blue bill at increasing speed until he reaches the hilarious climax of a spasmodic jerk and sputter. • Female Ruddies commonly lay up to 10 eggs at a time—a remarkable feat, considering that their eggs are bigger than those of a Mallard, even though a Mallard is twice the size of a Ruddy Duck. Female Ruddy Ducks have a habit of occasionally laying their eggs in other ducks' nests. • Ruddy Ducks often seem reluctant to take flight. When they do, like most diving ducks, they patter across the water's surface for quite a distance before they become airborne. When on land, Ruddy Ducks are almost completely helpless.

breeding

ID: small, chubby duck; large bill and head; short neck; long tail (often cocked upward); greyish-white underparts. *Breeding male:* white cheeks; rusty red body; bright blue bill; black tail and crown. *Female:* brownish-grey overall; white cheek with a dark stripe; darker crown and back; greyish bill. *Non-breeding male:* like the female, but with a white cheek.
Size: *L* 38–41 cm.
Status: rare in central parts; fairly common in the south; mid-April to early November.
Habitat: shallow marshes with dense emergent vegetation and muddy bottoms.
Nesting: in emergent vegetation; may use an abandoned duck or coot nest, a muskrat lodge or an exposed log; platform nest of reeds is built over water and is lined with fine materials; female incubates 5–10 rough, whitish eggs for about 26 days; may parasitize other waterbird nests.
Feeding: dives to wetland bottoms for insect larvae, invertebrates, seeds and the leafy parts of aquatic plants.
Voice: *Male:* male courtship call is a sputtering *Chick-ik-ik-ik-k-k-k-kurrrrr;* 'buzzy' in flight.
Similar Species: *Other diving ducks* (pp. 41–46): *males lack the bright blue bill and the rusty red plumage; females lack the long, stiff tail and the dark facial stripe.*
Best Sites: Fort Whyte; Oak Hammock Marsh; Hecla/Grindstone PP; Delta Marsh; Riding Mountain PP.

OSPREY

Pandion haliaetus

Ospreys eat fish almost exclusively, and they are almost always found near water. Their primarily white undersides help them to blend into the sky as they soar on broad wings high above lakes in search of prey. Locked in a perilous headfirst dive toward its target, the Osprey thrusts its feet forward the instant before striking the water. Sometimes it will make a tremendous splash, and it will even disappear beneath the water's surface. Rising into the air and shaking its soggy feathers, the Osprey, if necessary, re-positions the fish to face forward for optimal aerodynamics. Opposable talons and spiny foot pads help the Osprey keep hold of its slippery prey. • On a typical day, Osprey parents feed their young 3 kg of fish. Although some females switch off with their mates during incubation, others are fed entirely by their male partners through courtship, incubation and brood-rearing.

ID: large raptor; dark upperparts; white underparts; head is largely white with a dark eye line; yellow eyes. *Male:* all-white throat. *Female:* fine, dark 'necklace.' *In flight:* long wings are held in a shallow M (held slightly bent at both joints instead of fully extended); dark 'wrist' patches.
Size: *L* 53–63 cm; *W* 1.4–1.8 m.
Status: uncommon in most parts; rare in the north; April to mid-September.
Habitat: lakes and slow-flowing rivers and streams.
Nesting: on treetops, usually near water; also on artificial platforms, utility poles or towers up to 27 m high; massive stick nest is reused over many years; mostly the female incubates 2–4 white to pinkish eggs for 32 or 33 days.
Feeding: fish, averaging 1 kg, make up almost all of the diet; may take some rodents, birds and other small vertebrates.
Voice: series of melodious ascending whistles: *chewk-chewk-chewk*; also an often-heard *kip-kip-kip*.
Similar Species: *Bald Eagle* (p. 49): larger; holds its wings flat when soaring; adult has a completely white head and tail on an otherwise dark body; immatures lack the white underparts and the dark 'wrist' patches.
Best Sites: Nopiming PP; Hecla/Grindstone PP; shorelines of Lake Winnipeg and Lake Winnipegosis; Grass River PP; Churchill.

BALD EAGLE
Haliaeetus leucocephalus

Bald Eagles are part of the sea eagle group, and they feed mainly on fish and carrion. In fall and winter, they often scavenge on moose and deer, and in summer, they occasionally attempt to steal prey from Ospreys, which often results in a spectacular aerial chase. • The Bald Eagle is a source of inspiration for anyone encountering this magnificent bird of prey. For hundreds of years, it has held a prominent place in the beliefs and sacred rituals of Manitoba's First Nations peoples. • A pair of Bald Eagles may mate for life, each year renewing their pair bond through courtship rituals and by adding new sticks and branches to a massive nest. • Competition among Bald Eagle nestlings usually results in the smallest and weakest dying from starvation or getting pushed out of the nest. During the 1980s, young Bald Eagles were taken from nests in Manitoba (where more than one young was present) and relocated to various U.S. states to replace previously extirpated populations.

immature

ID: white head and tail on an otherwise dark brown body; yellow bill and feet; adult plumage aquired in the 5th year. *Immature:* variable dark plumage with white patches and highlights; often shows white on the tail base and the underwing linings; eyes and bill gradually turn from dark to yellow.
Size: *L* 85–110 cm; *W* 1.8–2.3 m.
Status: occasional in the north; fairly common elsewhere; mid-March to early December; a few are present in winter.
Habitat: *Nesting:* large lakes, rivers, cooling ponds and open areas. *In migration:* major river valleys.
Nesting: in shoreline trees; occasionally on cliffs; sometimes far from water; huge stick nest, up to

2 m across, is reused for many years; pair incubates 1–3 white eggs for about 35 days.
Feeding: waterbirds, small mammals and fish captured at the water's surface; frequently feeds on carrion; pirates fish from Ospreys.
Voice: thin, weak squeal or gull-like cackle: *kleek-kik-kik-kik* or *kah-kah-kah*.
Similar Species: Adult is distinctive. *Golden Eagle:* adult is dark overall with a golden nape, a smaller bill and a shorter neck; immature has a prominent white patch on the primary flight feathers and the base of the tail. *Osprey* (p. 48): M-shaped wings in flight; dark 'wrist' patches; dark bill.
Best Sites: Whiteshell PP; shorelines of Lake Winnipeg and Lake Winnipegosis; Grass River PP; northern lakes and rivers.

NORTHERN HARRIER

Circus cyaneus

The Northern Harrier may be the easiest raptor to identify on the wing, because no other hawk routinely flies so close to the ground. When hunting, it cruises low over fields, meadows and marshes, grazing the tops of long blades of grass and cattails. Although the Harrier has excellent vision, its owl-like, parabolic facial disc allows it to hunt easily by sound. • The harrier's sky-diving courtship flight is an event worth seeing. The male performs a series of looping dives and barrel rolls in a bid to secure the attention of onlooking females. • The Northern Harrier was once known as the Marsh Hawk in North America, and it is still called the Hen Harrier in Europe.

Habitat: open country, including scrubby areas, hayfields, wet meadows, marshes and bogs.

Nesting: on the ground, usually in long grass, cattails or dense scrub; nest is lined with weeds, sticks and cattails; female incubates 4–7 bluish-white eggs for 30–32 days.

Feeding: hunts in low flights, often skimming just above the top of ground vegetation; eats small mammals, birds, amphibians, reptiles and large insects.

Voice: generally quiet; high-pitched *ke-ke-ke-ke-ke-ke* near its nest.

ID: distinctive white rump patch; long wings; long, narrow tail. *Male:* blue-grey to silvery-grey upperparts; white underparts; indistinct tail bands except for the dark subterminal band. *Female:* dark brown upperparts; streaky brown and buff underparts. *Immature:* rich reddish-brown underparts; dark tail bands; streaked breast, sides and flanks. *In flight:* wings held in a V.

Size: *L* 43–58 cm; *W* 97–122 cm.

Status: fairly common in most parts; uncommon in the central boreal forest; mid-March to early November; a few may be present in winter.

Similar Species: *Swainson's Hawk* (p. 53): dark bib; dark flight feathers contrast with the pale underbody and under-wing linings. *Rough-legged Hawk*: broader wings; dark 'wrist' patches; fan-like tail with a white base and a broad, dark subterminal band; dark belly band. *Red-tailed Hawk* (p. 54): lacks the white rump and the long, narrow tail.

Best Sites: Fort Whyte; Oak Hammock Marsh; Hecla/Grindstone PP; Lake Francis; Delta Marsh; Lyleton; Churchill.

SHARP-SHINNED HAWK

Accipiter striatus

If songbirds dream, the Sharp-shinned Hawk is sure to be the subject of their worst nightmares. This forest hawk hunts silently, using surprise and speed to ambush wary prey. Like all accipiters, 'Sharpies' have rounded wings and long, rudder-like tails, which give them the maneuverability to negotiate high-speed turns through forest foliage. These birds use their long legs and sharp talons to catch quarry in mid-air, and after a successful hunt, they usually perch on a 'plucking post,' grasping their prey in their razor-sharp talons. When not chasing down its next meal, this hawk flaps and glides through mixed forests, as it either scouts over the treetops or crosses small forest openings. • Sharp-shinned Hawks require large tracts of woodland to hunt and raise their families, so they are rarely seen in much of our province's southern prairie and parkland regions.

ID: small hawk; short, rounded wings; long, straight, heavily barred tail, squared at the tip; dark barring on the pale undertail and underwings. *Adult:* blue-grey back; red horizontal bars on the underparts; red eyes. *Immature:* brown upperparts; dark eyes; brown vertical streaking on the breast and belly. *In flight:* flap-and-glide flyer.
Size: *Male: L* 25–30 cm; *W* 51–61 cm. *Female: L* 30–36 cm; *W* 61–71 cm.
Status: uncommon; April to early October.
Habitat: *Nesting:* dense to semi-open forests and large woodlots; favours dense, deciduous or mixed forests and bogs. *In migration:* wooded rivers and valleys, farmsteads and urban woodlots, especially near birdfeeders.
Nesting: in trees along woodland edges and clearings; usually builds a new stick nest each year; sometimes remodels an abandoned crow, squirrel or magpie nest; nest is lined with bark strips and vegetation; female incubates 4 or 5 whitish eggs for up to 35 days.
Feeding: small birds, such as chickadees, finches and sparrows; rarely takes small mammals, amphibians and insects.
Voice: generally silent; intense, shrill *kik-kik-kik-kik* is occasionally issued.
Similar Species: *Cooper's Hawk:* usually larger; tail tip is more rounded and has a broader terminal band. *American Kestrel* (p. 55): pointed wings; 2 dark facial stripes. *Merlin* (p. 56): dark eyes; 1 dark facial stripe; brown streaking on the buff underparts; pointed wings; rapid wingbeats.
Best Sites: *Nesting:* Turtle Mountain PP; Riding Mountain NP; Grass River PP. *In migration:* widespread.

NORTHERN GOSHAWK
Accipiter gentilis

Northern Goshawks are agile and powerful predators. They are able to negotiate lightning-fast turns through dense forest, and they will prey on any animal they can overtake. Goshawks have even been known to chase their quarry on foot through thick underbrush should elusive prey disappear under the cover of dense thickets. • The male goshawk is smaller than the female, and he is also more agile. He does most of the hunting while the female tends to her incubation and brood-rearing duties. Female goshawks are devoted parents, often boldly attacking intruders that venture too close to an active nest. • When northern prey populations crash—an event that tends to occur about every 10 years— large numbers of Northern Goshawks move into southern Manitoba in search of food, usually during the winter months (known as a 'winter irruption').

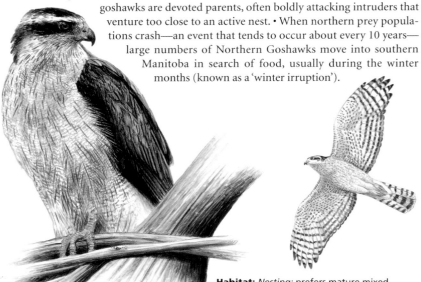

ID: large hawk; rounded wings; long, banded tail with a white, terminal band; white eyebrow stripe. *Adult:* red eyes; dark crown; blue-grey back; fine, grey, vertical streaking on the pale breast and belly; grey barring on the pale undertail and underwings. *Immature:* yellow eyes; brown overall; brown streaking on the whitish breast and belly; irregular brown barring on the pale undertail and underwings; pale eyebrow stripe is evident.
Size: *Male: L* 53–58 cm; *W* 1–1.1 m. *Female: L* 58–64 cm; *W* 1.1–1.2 m.
Status: rare in the north and in the extreme south; uncommon elsewhere; mid-March to April and from September to October; rare to uncommon in the south; November to mid-March.

Habitat: *Nesting:* prefers mature mixed woodlands; also found in extensive deciduous forests. *Non-nesting:* forest edges, semi-open parklands and farmlands.
Nesting: in a deciduous tree in deep woods; large, bulky stick platform nest is often reused for several years; female incubates 2–5 bluish-white eggs for 35 or 36 days.
Feeding: eats grouse, rabbits, ground and tree squirrels; may take Rock Doves in winter.
Voice: generally silent; adults utter a loud and fast *kak-kak-kak-kak* or *kuk-kuk-kuk-kuk* (heavier than the call of the Cooper's Hawk or the Sharp-shinned Hawk) during the nesting season.
Similar Species: *Cooper's Hawk* and *Sharp-shinned Hawk* (p. 51): smaller; adults have reddish breast bars and no white eyebrow stripe. *Buteo hawks* (pp. 53–54): shorter tails; broader wings. *Gyrfalcon:* pointed wings; dark eyes with a 'tearstreak.'
Best Sites: Whiteshell PP; Duck Mountain PP; Riding Mountain NP; Grass River PP.

SWAINSON'S HAWK

Buteo swainsoni

While the Red-tailed Hawk can dominate the skies over much of our province, the Swainson's Hawk takes center stage where open country far exceeds forests, especially in grassy expanses where ground squirrels are abundant. A nesting pair of Swainson's Hawks may catch up to 300 ground squirrels in a single summer. • Twice each year, Swainson's Hawks undertake one of the longest migrations of any Manitoba raptor, wintering as far as South America. Recently, toxic insecticides used in Argentina to control grasshoppers (a major source of food for these hawks in winter) have killed large numbers of Swainson's Hawks, reminding us that the conservation of migratory species requires international cooperation. • Swainson's Hawks may reuse a nest from year to year, construct a new one or build on top of an old magpie nest.

light morph

dark morph

ID: long, narrow wings; fan-shaped tail. *Light morph:* dark bib; white wing linings contrast with the dark flight feathers; white belly; finely barred tail; white uppertail coverts. *Dark morph:* brown overall; dark wing linings blend with the brown flight feathers. *In flight:* wings are held in a shallow V.
Size: *L* 48–51 cm; *W* 1.3 m (female is slightly larger).
Status: fairly common; mid-April to mid-September.
Habitat: open fields and grasslands with scattered trees or large shrubs for nesting.
Nesting: in a tree or shrub adjacent to open habitat; rarely on cliffs; nest is made of sticks, twigs and forbs and is lined with bark and fresh leaves; pair incubates 2–4 brown-spotted, whitish eggs for 28–35 days.

Feeding: dives to the ground for voles, mice and ground squirrels; also eats large numbers of grasshoppers and other insects; eats some snakes, small birds and rabbits.
Voice: typical call, *keeeeeeer*, is higher pitched than the Red-tailed Hawk's call.
Similar Species: *Red-tailed Hawk* (p. 54): wings are held flat in flight; more rounded wing tips; dark leading edge on the underwing; dark belly band. *Other buteos:* flight feathers are lighter than the wing linings; all lack the dark bib.
Best Sites: Oak Hammock Marsh; Brandon Hills; Lyleton; Poverty Plains; open country in SW Manitoba.

RED-TAILED HAWK

Buteo jamaicensis

Red-tails are the most commonly seen hawks throughout much of Manitoba. They are most often identified by their brick-red tails, but some colour morphs have a whitish tail and others are completely dark throughout. It helps to know other distinguishing Red-tail features, such as the dark, streaky band across the bird's abdomen and the dark leading edge on the underside of the wings, but even these features are not always present. • Like other soaring hawks, Red-tails use their binocular-like vision to spot prey from great distances. They also hunt from fenceposts, exposed tree limbs and utility poles overlooking open fields and roadsides. • Strychnine and other chemicals intended to kill rodents and insects often end up killing Red-tailed Hawks and other birds of prey that naturally keep the number of insects in check.

ID: red tail; streaky, dark brown abdominal 'belt'; dark brown head. *Immature:* extremely variable; greyish tail is generally barred. *In flight:* fan-shaped tail; dark leading edge on the underside of the wings is distinctive when present.
Size: *Male: L* 48–58 cm; *W* 1.2–1.5 m. *Female: L* 51–65 cm; *W* 1.2–1.5 m.
Status: occasional in the north; uncommon in the central boreal forest; common in the south; mid-March to early November; occasionally present in winter.
Habitat: semi-open country with some trees to forested terrain with openings, including roadsides and fields near woodlots, hedgerows and open mixed forests.
Nesting: usually high in a deciduous tree adjacent to open areas; rarely on cliffs or in conifers; often adds to the bulky stick nest each year; pair incubates 2–4 brown-spotted, whitish eggs; female raises the young.

Feeding: scans for food while perched or soaring; takes primarily rodents; also takes some insects, birds, amphibians, reptiles and small rabbits.
Voice: powerful, descending scream: *Keeearrrr.*
Similar Species: *Rough-legged Hawk:* white tail base; dark underwing 'wrist' patches; broad, dark terminal tail band. *Broad-winged Hawk:* broad, banded tail; broader wings with pointed tips; lacks the dark 'belt.' *Swainson's Hawk (p. 53):* dark bib; dark flight feathers and pale underwing linings; holds its wings in a shallow V; more pointed wing tips.
Best Sites: Birds Hill PP; Dog Lake; Delta Marsh; Spruce Woods PP; Turtle Mountain PP; Riding Mountain NP.

AMERICAN KESTREL

Falco sparverius

The American Kestrel is the smallest and most common of Manitoba's falcons. The colourful male is striking with his blue crown and wings and rusty red cap, back and tail. • A kestrel perched on a telephone wire or fencepost along an open field is a familiar sight throughout much of our province, especially in southern parts. It is also not uncommon to see a kestrel hovering low over a ditch or meadow with its tail flared and wings beating into a blur as it searches for ground-dwelling prey. • American Kestrels were once called 'Sparrow Hawks,' even though their diet primarily consists of insects and small rodents. • The American Kestrel is unique among Manitoba's raptors, because it typically nests in tree cavities and nest boxes.

ID: small, colourful falcon; 2 distinctive dark facial stripes. *Male:* rusty back; blue-grey wings; blue-grey crown with a rusty cap; lightly spotted underparts. *Female:* rusty back, wings and breast streaking. *In flight:* frequently hovers; long, rusty tail.
Size: *L* 23–30 cm; *W* 50–62 cm.
Status: uncommon in the north; fairly common in central parts; fairly common to common in the south; mid-March to October; a few are present in winter.
Habitat: open or partly open habitats with scattered trees; hunts along roadside ditches, grasslands and croplands.
Nesting: in a cavity or nest box; rarely on a building or cliff; little nest material is added; pair

incubates 4–7 white or pinkish eggs blotched with reddish-brown for about 30 days.
Feeding: swoops from a perch or from a hovering position; mainly eats insects and small rodents; may take some small birds, reptiles and amphibians.
Voice: high-pitched, rapid *killy-killy-killy* or *klee-klee-klee*; female's voice is lower pitched.
Similar Species: *Merlin* (p. 56): lacks the double facial stripes; does not hover; flight is more direct; less colourful. *Sharp-shinned Hawk* (p. 51): short, rounded wings; red barring on the underparts; lacks the facial stripes; flap-and-glide flight style.
Best Sites: Pinawa area; Fort Whyte; Interlake area; Spruce Woods PP; Riding Mountain NP; Duck Mountain PP.

MERLIN

Falco columbarius

The main weapons of all falcons are speed, surprise and sharp talons. The Merlin's sleek body, long, narrow tail and pointed wings increase its aerodynamic efficiency for high-speed songbird pursuits. • Most Merlins migrate to Central and South America each fall, but a few remain in our province over winter, enticed by mild urban climates and an abundance of overwintering songbirds at backyard feeders. • Merlins are often noisy nesters, and the appearance of a nesting pair in your neighbourhood may initially cause concern. Once settled in, however, Merlins are sure to add action, drama and ecological balance to your community. Rural cemeteries and parks with mature spruce trees are good places to look for these birds. • The Merlin was formerly known as the Pigeon Hawk, and the scientific name *columbarius* comes from the Latin for 'pigeon,' which it sometimes resembles in flight.

ID: heavily banded tail; heavily streaked underparts; 1 indistinct facial stripe; long, narrow wings and tail. *Male:* blue-grey back and crown; grey tail with black bands. *Female* and *Immature:* brown back and crown. *In flight:* very rapid, shallow wingbeats.
Size: *L* 25–35 cm; *W* 60–68 cm.
Status: uncommon in most parts; rare in the north; late March to early November; rare in winter.
Habitat: *Nesting:* open mixed and coniferous forests adjacent to open hunting grounds; suburban areas and rural cemeteries with a scattering of large conifers. *In migration:* open fields and lakeshores.
Nesting: often in a conifer tree; in a treeless area in a crevice or on a cliff ledge; usually reuses abandoned raptor, crow, magpie, jay or squirrel nests; pair incubates

4–7 white eggs, with reddish-brown markings, for 28–31 days.
Feeding: hunts smaller birds in flight; also eats some rodents and large insects; rarely takes birds as large as a Rock Dove.
Voice: loud, noisy, cackling cry: *kek-kek-kek-kek-kek* or *ki-ki-ki-ki*; calls in flight or while perched, often around the nest.
Similar Species: *American Kestrel* (p. 55): prominent facial stripes; more colourful; often hovers. *Peregrine Falcon:* larger; prominent dark helmet; black flecking on the pale undersides. *Sharp-shinned Hawk* (p. 51) and *Cooper's Hawk:* short, rounded wings; reddish barring on the breast and belly. *Rock Dove* (p. 76): broader wings in flight; shorter tail; often glides with its wings held in a V.
Best Sites: Assiniboine Park; Interlake area; Brandon; Riding Mountain NP; Churchill; Wapusk NP.

GRAY PARTRIDGE

Perdix perdix

Throughout much of the year, Gray Partridges are probably best seen 'gravelling up' along quiet country roads. Like other seed-eating birds, they regularly swallow bits of gravel to help crush the hard seeds they feed on. The gravel accumulates in the bird's gizzard, a muscular pouch of the digestive system. • In cold weather, Gray Partridges huddle together in a circle with each bird facing outward. At the slightest sign of danger, the birds explode into the air and move to safer ground. Although Gray Partridges are relatively hardy birds, many perish in harsh weather, and some birds become trapped under layers of hardened snow while taking refuge from the cold. • A small number of Gray Partridges were introduced into Manitoba during the 1920s, but most of the birds that we see in our province today originate from individuals that migrated here from neighbouring states and provinces. • This Eurasian bird was once known as the Hungarian Partridge; coveys of Gray Partridges are still called 'huns' by many hunters and bird enthusiasts.

ID: small, rounded, greyish bird; short tail; chestnut outer tail feathers; chestnut barring on the flanks; orange-brown face and throat; grey breast; mottled brown back; bare yellowish legs. *Male:* dark chestnut brown patch on the white belly. *Female:* lacks the dark belly patch; paler face and throat.
Size: *L* 28–36 cm.
Status: numbers fluctuate greatly; uncommon and local in the central boreal forest; fairly common to common in the south; year-round.
Habitat: grassy ditches, weedy fields and agricultural croplands (except alfalfa), often near hedgerows, farmsteads or other cover.
Nesting: on the ground; in hayfields, pastures and overgrown fencelines and field margins; a scratched-out depression is lined with grass; female incubates 15–20 olive-coloured eggs for about 24 days.
Feeding: gleans fields for waste grain and seeds; may also eat leaves, buds and large insects; often feeds among livestock manure piles in winter; forages at dawn and dusk during summer.
Voice: at dawn and dusk; sounds like a rusty gate hinge: *kee-uck* or *scirl*; call is *kuta-kut-kut-kut* when excited; also utters a loud *kar-wit kar-wit*.
Similar Species: *Ruffed Grouse* (p. 58): lacks the rusty face and the outer tail feathers.
Best Sites: outskirts of Winnipeg; Lyleton; farmsteads, field edges and shelterbelts in extreme SW Manitoba.

57

RUFFED GROUSE

Bonasa umbellus

When a male Ruffed Grouse is displaying nearby, he makes a sound that is felt more than heard. Each spring, the male Ruffed Grouse proclaims his territory, strutting along a fallen log with his tail fanned wide and his neck feathers ruffed, beating the air with accelerating wing strokes. 'Drumming' is primarily restricted to spring, but Ruffed Grouse may also drum for a few weeks in fall. • During winter, the feather bristles on the toes of these birds elongate, providing them with temporary snowshoes. • The Ruffed Grouse inhabits a wide variety of woodland habitats, ranging from small deciduous woodlots to vast expanses of mixedwood forest. It is the most common and widespread grouse in Manitoba. • Ruffed Grouse are an important source of food for many predators, including the Northern Goshawk. When Ruffed Grouse numbers crash, goshawk numbers follow a similar trend.

grey morph

♂

ID: small head crest; mottled grey-brown overall; black feathers on the sides of the lower neck (visible when fluffed out in courtship); fan-shaped, grey-barred tail with a distinctive dark subterminal band and a white tip. *Female:* incomplete subterminal tail band.

Size: *L* 38–48 cm; *W* 56–64 cm.

Status: fairly common to common; highly cyclical fluctuations; year-round.

Habitat: deciduous and mixed forests and woodlands with a dense, brushy understorey; favours young second-growth stands with birch and poplar.

Nesting: in a shallow scrape among leaf litter; often beside a boulder, shrub, fallen log or tree; nest is lined with feathers; female incubates 9–15 buff-coloured eggs for about 24 days.

Feeding: omnivorous diet includes seeds, buds, flowers, berries, catkins, leaves, insects, spiders and snails.

Voice: *Male:* deep 'drumming' courtship call suggests an accelerating motor: *bup...bup...bup...bup, bup, up, r-rrrrrr.* *Female:* clucks and 'hisses' around her chicks.

Similar Species: *Spruce Grouse* (p. 59): lacks the head crest and the white tip and barring on the tail; male has red eye combs. *Sharp-tailed Grouse* (p. 60): lacks the fan-shaped tail and the black feathers on the lower neck. *Willow Ptarmigan:* summer birds show white in the wings and legs.

Best Sites: Whiteshell PP; Birds Hill PP; Interlake area; Spruce Woods PP; Turtle Mountain PP; Riding Mountain PP.

SPRUCE GROUSE

Falcipennis canadensis

Spruce Grouse trust their camouflaged plumage even in open areas—they are often called 'fool hens'—and they often allow people to approach within metres. Most of the time, however, staying still seems to work, and more Spruce Grouse probably escape our detection than we notice. Setting out to find a Spruce Grouse is nowhere as easy as bumping into one by accident. • This secretive grouse spends most of its time in stands of black spruce and young, upland pine forests searching for seasonally available food, such as blueberries, cranberries, spruce buds and insects. • Spruce Grouse are most conspicuous in late April and early May, when the females issue their vehement calls, and the males suddenly surface in open areas along trails, roads and campgrounds.

grey morph

ID: black, unbarred tail with a chestnut tip; mottled grey, brown and black overall; feathered legs. *Male:* red comb over the eye; black throat, neck and breast; dark back; white-tipped undertail, lower neck and belly feathers. *Female:* brownish overall; mottled and barred underparts.
Size: *L* 38–44 cm.
Status: rare in the north; uncommon in the central boreal forest; rare and local in the south; year-round.
Habitat: moist, conifer-dominated forest, usually with a dense understorey; sometimes disperses into deciduous forests.
Nesting: on the forest floor; in a well-hidden, shallow scrape lined

with grass and conifer needles; female incubates 7–12 buff eggs for about 24 days.
Feeding: live buds and needles of spruce, pine and fir trees; also eats berries, seeds and a few insects in summer.
Voice: very low, guttural *krrrk krrrk krrrk.*
Similar Species: *Ruffed Grouse* (p. 58): head is crested; white-tipped tail has a broad, dark subterminal band; lacks the black throat and breast. *Willow Ptarmigan:* summer birds show white in the wings and legs. *Sharp-tailed Grouse* (p. 60): thinner, sharper tail; white throat; yellow eye combs.
Best Sites: Whiteshell PP; Spur Woods; Hecla/Grindstone PP; Duck Mountain PP; Grass River PP.

SHARP-TAILED GROUSE

Tympanuchus phasianellus

In late April and early May, male Sharp-tailed Grouse convene upon grassy knolls, shrubby forest clearings and muskeg bogs to perform courtship dances. With wings drooping at their sides, their long, thin tails pointed skyward and their purplish-pink air sacs inflated, the males furiously pummel the ground with their feet, vigourously cooing and cackling to attract females. As the males dance, they release air through their mouths from the inflated neck sacs to produce a cooing sound that can be heard for several hundred yards. Each male defends a small stage within the 'lek,' and the centre position features the dominant males, who are generally the best dancers. • Outside of the courtship season, Sharp-tailed Grouse remain inconspicuous and can be difficult to find.

ID: mottled brown and black neck, breast and upperparts; dark crescents on the white belly; white undertail coverts and outer tail feathers; long, central tail feathers; yellow eye combs; white throat; feathered legs. *Male:* purple-pink air sacs on the neck are inflated during the courtship display.
Size: *L* 40–48 cm; *W* 56–64 cm.
Status: rare to locally uncommon in the north; uncommon in central parts; locally common in the south; year-round.
Habitat: grasslands and lightly grazed pastures with patches of snowberry and wild rose, open bogs, fens and forest clearings.
Nesting: on the ground; usually under cover near the lek; in a depression lined with grass and feathers; female incubates 10–13

light brown eggs dotted with reddish brown for about 24 days.
Feeding: eats buds, seeds, flowers, green shoots and berries; also eats insects.
Voice: male gives a mournful *coo-oo* call and a cackling *cac-cac-cac-cac* during courtship.
Similar Species: *Ruffed Grouse* (p. 58): slight head crest; broad, fan-shaped tail with a broad, dark subterminal band; black patches on the neck. *Ring-necked Pheasant:* unfeathered legs; paler markings on the underparts; female has a longer tail. *Spruce Grouse* (p. 59): black, fan-shaped tail; black or mottled throat; male has red eye combs. *Willow Ptarmigan:* summer birds show white in the wings and legs.
Best Sites: Tall Grass Prairie Preserve; Narcisse; Shoal Lakes; Spruce Woods PP; Mixed-grass Prairie Preserve.

SORA
Porzana carolina

Two ascending whistles followed by a loud, descending 'whinny' abruptly announce the presence of the often undetectable Sora. Although it is the most common and widespread rail in North America, the Sora is seldom seen by birders. Its elusive habits and preference for dense marshlands force most would-be observers typically to settle for a quick look at this small bird. • Soras are odd-looking, chicken-like birds. Their large feet, which help them rest atop thin mats of floating plant material, add to their strange appearance. • If you've ever questioned the expression 'thin as a rail,' you might wonder how it applies to this relatively plump-bodied member of the rail family. Like all rails, soras can laterally compress their bodies, so they are masters at squeezing through tightly packed stands of bulrushes and cattails.

breeding

ID: short, yellow bill; black patch on the throat and the front of the face; grey neck and breast; short, cocked tail; long, greenish legs. *Immature:* brown overall; no black patch.
Size: *L* 20–25 cm; *W* 30–36 cm.
Status: fairly common in the north; common elsewhere; late April to early October.
Habitat: marshes and sloughs with abundant emergent vegetation.
Nesting: usually over water under concealing vegetation, but occasionally in a moist meadow; basket nest is made of reeds and aquatic vegetation; pair incubates 8–12 buffy-brown eggs for up to 20 days.

Feeding: seeds, plants, aquatic insects and mollusks.
Voice: alarm call is a sharp *keek*; courtship song is a plaintive *ker-wee*, often followed by a descending 'whinny.'
Similar Species: *Virginia Rail:* long, down-curved, reddish bill; chestnut wing patch; rusty breast; call is a telegraph-like *kik, kik, ki-dik, ki-dik, ki-dik, ki-dik. Yellow Rail:* smaller; upperparts are streaked black and tawny; white throat; white trailing edges of the wings are seen in flight; call is like two stones being clicked together: *tik, tik, tik-tik-tik.*
Best Sites: Birds Hill PP; Oak Hammock Marsh; Hecla/Grindstone PP; Delta Marsh; Minnedosa pothole region; Churchill.

AMERICAN COOT

Fulica americana

The coot is truly an all-terrain bird: in its quest for food, it dives and dabbles like a duck, grazes confidently on land and swims about skillfully with its lobed feet. • Coots are aggressive and territorial throughout the nesting season. When a dispute arises, they flail their wings and raise their tails, displaying prominent white undertail patches. If posturing fails to intimidate, rivals strike each other with their bills and even attempt to hold their opponent underwater. As the nesting season wanes, coots become less competitive and band together in large groups in preparation for fall migration. Newly hatched coots are easily recognized by their distinctive reddish-orange down and bald, red crown. • Coots are colloquially known as 'Mud Hens.'

ID: grey-black overall; white bill extends onto the forehead; red forehead spot; long, green-yellow legs; lobed toes; white patches under the tail; red eyes. *Immature:* lighter overall; darker bill and legs; less prominent forehead shield.

Size: *L* 33–40 cm; *W* 58–70 cm.

Status: rare in the north; fairly common in central parts; abundant in the south; early April to early November.

Habitat: shallow marshes, ponds and semi-permanent wetlands with open water and emergent vegetation; also sewage lagoons.

Nesting: in emergent vegetation usually over water; floating or anchored nest is made of reeds and aquatic vegetation; pair incubates 8–12 brown-spotted, pinkish-buff eggs for about 24 days.

Feeding: eats insects, snails, worms, tadpoles and fish; also eats aquatic and terrestrial vegetation

Voice: calls frequently in summer: *kuk-kuk-kuk-kuk-kuk*; also *kakakakaka* and a variety of croaks, cackles and grunts.

Similar Species: *Ducks* (pp. 34–47): all lack the extended white bill and the uniform, blackish body colour. *Grebes* (pp. 21–24): lack the white forehead shield and the all-dark plumage. *Sora* (p. 61): yellow bill; tawny upperparts.

Best Sites: Pinawa area; Fort Whyte; Oak Hammock Marsh; Turtle Mountain PP; Minnedosa pothole region.

SANDHILL CRANE

Grus canadensis

Deep, resonant, rattling calls announce the approach of a flock of migrating Sandhill Cranes. These migrations can entertain a birder for an entire morning, as flock after flock pass overhead. Cranes can sail effortlessly for hours using thermal updrafts, and they sometimes circle and glide at such great heights that they can scarcely be seen. In spring, they occasionally touch down on open fields to feed or perform courtship displays. Their courtship rituals involve calling, bobbing, bowing, tossing grass, running with their wings extended and making spectacular leaps into the air with partially raised wings. During migration, large numbers of Sandhill Cranes can be viewed at staging areas, such as Whitewater Lake, Delta Marsh and Oak Hammock Marsh.

• Sandhill Cranes are sensitive nesters, so they prefer to raise their young in areas that are isolated from human disturbance. Before the prairies gave way to human settlement and agriculture, Sandhill Cranes nested throughout much of southern Manitoba.

ID: very large, grey bird; plumage is often stained rusty red; long legs and neck; naked, red crown; long, straight bill; 'bustle' of shaggy feathers hangs over the rump of a standing bird. *Immature:* lacks the red crown; reddish-brown plumage may appear patchy. *In flight:* fully extended neck and legs; glides, soars and circles in flocks.
Size: *L* 85–120 cm; *W* 1.8–2.1 m.
Status: fairly common to common in the north and in central parts; uncommon to common in the south; early April to mid-October.
Habitat: *Nesting:* isolated, open marshes, fens and bogs lined with trees or shrubs and coastal tundra. *In migration:* agricultural fields and shorelines.

Nesting: in water or along undisturbed shorelines; nest is a large mound of sticks, reeds and aquatic vegetation; pair incubates 2 large, buff-olive eggs for 29–32 days.
Feeding: opportunistic; takes insects, soft-bodied invertebrates, waste grain, shoots, tubers and even small mammals and eggs.
Voice: loud, resonant, rattling: *gu-rrroo gu-rrroo gurrroo*.
Similar Species: *Great Blue Heron* (p. 28): crooked neck in flight; lacks the tufted tail and the red forehead patch. *Whooping Crane:* all-white plumage with black flight feathers.
Best Sites: *Nesting:* Whiteshell PP; Churchill; Interlake area. *In migration:* Oak Hammock Marsh; Delta Marsh.

63

KILLDEER

Charadrius vociferus

The ubiquitous Killdeer is often the first shorebird a beginning birdwatcher will learn to identify. It has adapted well to urbanization, and it finds roadside ditches, gravel driveways, golf courses and abandoned industrial areas as much to its liking as shorelines. Its colours and markings are quite striking, yet it can blend into its surroundings so well that it will often go unnoticed. Its boisterous calls, however, are so distinctive and incessant that you can't help but spot this bird. • If you happen to wander too close to a Killdeer nest, the parents will try to lure you away, issuing loud alarm calls and feigning a broken wing. Killdeers are well known for their broken wing act.

ID: long, dark yellow legs; white breast with 2 black bands; brown upperparts; white collar and underparts; white eyebrow; tail projects beyond the wing tips; black forehead band; rusty rump. *Immature:* downy; only 1 breast band.
Size: *L* 22–28 cm; *W* 48–53 cm.
Status: uncommon in the north; fairly common in central parts; abundant in the south; late March to mid-October.
Habitat: various open areas including gravel parking lots and roadsides, lakeshores, sandy beaches, mudflats, streambeds, wet meadows and grasslands.

Nesting: on open ground; in a shallow usually unlined depression; pair incubates 4 speckled, buff eggs for 28 days; occasionally has 2 broods per year.
Feeding: run-and-stop feeder; mainly eats insects; also takes spiders, snails and earthworms.
Voice: loud and distinctive *kill-dee kill-dee kill-deer* and variations; also a plaintive, rising *dee-dee-dee-dee* and trill.
Similar Species: *Semipalmated Plover:* smaller; only 1 breast band. *Piping Plover:* smaller; much lighter upperparts; 1 breast band.
Best Sites: extremely widespread; almost any open or disturbed area.

AMERICAN AVOCET

Recurvirostra americana

An American Avocet in full breeding plumage is among the most elegant birds in North America. To some birders, its slender, curving features, graceful movements and striking colours are unmatched. • This shorebird is easily identified by its long legs, its bold black and white wings in flight (a feature shared only by the Willet) and its habit of whisking its thin, long, upturned bill back and forth through shallow water when feeding. The avocet does such a good job of stirring up insects and small crustaceans that Wilson's Phalaropes will follow closely behind it while it feeds. • Avocets often form loose colonies, and two females may sometimes share the same nest. • Most avocets observed after August have had their colourful peachy plumage replaced by pale winter colours.

breeding

♂

ID: long, upturned, black bill; long, pale blue legs; black wings with wide white patches; white underparts; female's bill is slightly more upturned and shorter than the male's. *Breeding:* peachy tan head, neck and breast; white eye ring. *Non-breeding:* pale grey head, neck and breast. *In flight:* long legs and neck; boldly striped black and white wings.
Size: *L* 42–48 cm; *W* 68–96 cm.
Status: uncommon; late April to early September.
Habitat: exposed, sparsely vegetated shorelines, saline sloughs, permanent lake mudflats and semi-permanent wetland mudflats.
Nesting: colonial; on sparsely vegetated islands, mudflats or cultivated fields, always near water; in a shallow depression or a raised mound sparsely lined with vegetation; pair incubates 4 brown-spotted, olive-buff eggs for up to 29 days.
Feeding: sweeps its bill along or beneath the water's surface for crustaceans, aquatic insects and larvae; eats some aquatic vegetation and seeds.
Voice: harsh, shrill *wheek* or *kleet* is excitedly repeated near the nest.
Similar Species: *Willet:* greyish overall, including the back; straight bill. *Marbled Godwit:* brownish overall; thicker, long, bicoloured, slightly upturned bill.
Best Sites: Oak Hammock Marsh; Delta Marsh; Hecla/Grindstone PP; Lyleton; Turtle Mountain PP.

SPOTTED SANDPIPER

Actitis macularia

I t wasn't until 1972 that the unexpected truths about the Spotted Sandpiper's breeding activities were realized. Like the phalaropes, female Spotted Sandpipers defend territories and mate with more than one male in a single breeding season. This unusual behaviour, known as polyandry (meaning 'many men' in Greek), is found in only about one percent of all bird species. • Although its breast spots aren't noticeable from a distance, its stiff-winged, quivering flight pattern and tendency to burst from shore are easily recognizable. Like the Solitary Sandpiper, it is also known for its continuous teetering behaviour as it forages. • Spotted Sandpipers are rarely found in flocks.

breeding

ID: teeters almost continuously. *Breeding:* white underparts with heavy black spotting; yellow-orange legs; yellowish, black-tipped bill; white eyebrow stripe. *Non-nesting* and *Juvenile:* pure white breast, foreneck and throat; brown bill; dull yellow legs. *In flight:* flies close to the water's surface with very rapid, shallow wingbeats; white upperwing stripe.
Size: *L* 18–20 cm.
Status: uncommon in the north; fairly common elsewhere; May to late September.
Habitat: shorelines, gravel beaches, ponds, marshes, rivers, streams and sewage lagoons; occasionally in cultivated fields.
Nesting: usually near water; often

under overhanging vegetation among logs or pebbles; in a shallow depression lined with grass and moss; male incubates 4 eggs for 20–22 days and raises the young.
Feeding: picks and gleans along shorelines for terrestrial and aquatic invertebrates; also snatches flying insects from the air.
Voice: sharp, crisp *eat-wheat, eat-wheat,* or a rapidly repeated *wheat-wheat-wheat-wheat.*
Similar Species: *Solitary Sandpiper:* complete eye ring; greenish legs; lacks the breast spotting. *Other sandpipers:* all lack the breast spotting; most have black bills and legs.
Best Sites: Whiteshell PP; Hecla/Grindstone PP; Spruce Woods PP; Turtle Mountain PP; Duck Mountain PP.

MARBLED GODWIT

Limosa fedoa

The Marbled Godwit uses its long bill to probe deep into soil and mud. The tip of its bill is sensitive to underground movements, so this bird is adept at locating and extracting worms and mollusks. The dark end of the godwit's bill may also give the tip extra strength, because the black pigment, like melanin, hardens the structure of both bills and feathers. • Marbled Godwits are found primarily in southern parts of our province. They draw attention to themselves with their loud, incessant calls, so they are often easy birds to find.

breeding

ID: long, slightly upturned bill is dark with a yellowish base; long neck; mottled buff-brown plumage is darkest on the upperparts; long, black-blue legs. *In flight:* cinnamon wing linings.

Size: *L* 40–50 cm; *W* 80 cm.

Status: rare in the central boreal forest; fairly common in the southeast; common in the southwest; mid-April to mid-September.

Habitat: *Nesting:* marshes, shoreline plains and remnant prairie. *In migration:* flooded fields, wet meadows, marshes, mudflats and lakeshores.

Nesting: often in loose colonies; on dry ground in short grass, usually near water; in a slight depression lined with dry grass;

may have a canopy; pair incubates 4 brown-spotted, olive-brown eggs for 21–23 days.

Feeding: probes deeply in soft substrates for worms, insect larvae, crustaceans and mollusks; picks insects from grass.

Voice: loud squawks: *co-rect co-rect* or *god-wit god-wit*; also *raddica-raddica-raddica*.

Similar Species: *Hudsonian Godwit:* smaller; chestnut red neck and underparts; white rump. *Greater Yellowlegs:* shorter, all-dark bill; long, bright yellow legs. *Dowitchers:* smaller; straight, all-dark bill; white rump wedge; yellow-green legs. *Long-billed Curlew:* long, downcurved bill; accidental in Manitoba.

Best Sites: Oak Hammock Marsh; Dog Lake; Delta Marsh; Oak/Plum lakes; pastures and haylands in extreme SW Manitoba.

LEAST SANDPIPER

Calidris minutilla

The Least Sandpiper is the smallest of the 'peep' sandpipers, which are similar-looking sandpipers in the genus *Calidris*. Members of this group are difficult to identify, so taking note of leg colour and bill shape and length will help you distinguish them. • 'Peeps' commonly migrate in large, mixed-species flocks. Flying in close formation, they wheel and turn in unison. Alighting on a shoreline, they quickly scatter, feeding with quick, fidgety movements. • Like most other sandpipers, the Least Sandpiper migrates almost the entire length of the globe twice each year, from the Arctic to the southern tip of South America and back again. • Because arctic summers are short, shorebirds must optimize their breeding efforts. Least Sandpiper eggs are large compared to the eggs of other sandpipers, and the entire clutch might weigh over half the weight of the female. The young hatch in an advanced state of development, getting an early start on preparations for the fall migration.

breeding

ID: slender, black bill; yellowish legs; dark, mottled back; buff-brown breast, head and nape; light breast streaking. *Immature:* like the adult, but with a faintly streaked breast.
Size: *L* 13–17 cm.
Status: common in the north; May to September; fairly common to common elsewhere late; April to mid-June and from early July to mid-September.
Habitat: *Nesting:* mossy tundra, sedge or grass bogs and marshes. *In migration:* sandy beaches, lakeshores, ditches, sewage lagoons, mudflats and wetland edges.
Nesting: on a dry, grassy mound surrounded by wet ground; in a shallow depression lined with grass, leaves and moss; pair incubates 4 brown-blotched, pale buff eggs for about 20 days.
Feeding: probes or pecks for insects, crustaceans, small mollusks and seeds.
Voice: high-pitched, drawn out *kreeet, kree-eet.*
Similar Species: *Semipalmated Sandpiper:* black legs; lighter upperparts; tinge of rufous on the crown, ear patch and scapulars. *Other peeps:* all are larger, have slightly stouter bills and dark legs.
Best Sites: *Nesting:* Churchill; Wapusk NP. *In migration:* widespread along shorelines, mudflats and flooded fields.

COMMON SNIPE

Gallinago gallinago

Visit any wetland at dusk during spring or early summer and there is a good chance you will hear the eerie, hollow, winnowing sound of courting Common Snipes. Specialized outer tail feathers vibrate rapidly in the air as the birds perform headfirst dives high above the wetlands in which potential mates are waiting and watching. In between courtship flights, male snipes are commonly seen scanning their territory from atop a fencepost. • Outside of the courting season, this well-camouflaged bird is shy and secretive. Only when an intruder approaches too closely will a snipe flush from cover, exploding into the air, performing a series of zig-zag maneuvers and often emitting loud *scaip* calls. • The snipe's long bill is extremely flexible, and it is sensitive to the movement of earthworms and larval insects buried deep within the mud. Its long, spiked tongue moves food to the back of the mouth so that it can be swallowed.

ID: extremely long, straight bill; short legs; heavily striped head and back; dark barring on the sides and flanks; unmarked white belly. *In flight:* zig-zag flight pattern; short, orange tail is obvious.

Size: *L* 26–29 cm; *W* 44–50 cm.

Status: common; mid-April to October.

Habitat: marshes, sedge meadows, grassy margins of creeks and sloughs, poorly drained floodplains, bogs and fens.

Nesting: in dry grass, often under vegetation; often on a raised hummock in marshes and fens; nest is made of grass, moss and leaves; female incubates 4 darkly spotted olive-buff eggs for about 20 days.

Feeding: probes soft substrates for larvae, earthworms and other soft-bodied invertebrates; also eats mollusks, crustaceans, spiders, small amphibians and some seeds.

Voice: accelerating aerial courtship display sound is a winnowing *woo-woo-woo-woo-woo-woo*; often sings *wheat wheat wheat* or *chip-a, chip-a, chip-a*; *scaip* alarm call.

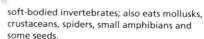

Similar Species: *Dowitchers:* lack the heavy striping on the head, back, neck and breast; longer legs; reddish underparts in spring; usually travel in flocks. *Marbled Godwit* (p. 67): much larger; slightly upturned bill; much longer legs. *American Woodcock:* unmarked buff underparts; yellowish bill; light bars on the black crown and hindneck.

Best Sites: Whiteshell PP; Oak Hammock Marsh; Delta Marsh; Minnedosa pothole region; Riding Mountain NP.

WILSON'S PHALAROPE

Phalaropus tricolour

Besides its bright colours, which are unusual for a shorebird, the Wilson's Phalarope is known for its peculiar mating strategy. Phalaropes practise polyandry, in which females mate with several males. After laying a clutch, the female usually abandons her partner, leaving him to incubate the eggs and tend the young. She may either continue to 'play the field' or act as a lookout for one of her males. Naturally, this reversal of traditional gender roles also includes a reversal of plumage characteristics—females are more brightly coloured than their male counterparts, whose pale plumage allows them to remain inconspicuous while sitting on their nest. • The Wilson's Phalarope is the only member of the phalarope clan that breeds in southern Manitoba. During migration, it far outnumbers its two close relatives, the Red-necked Phalarope and the Red Phalarope. All three phalaropes share a unique feeding style: in shallow water, they spin rapidly in tight circles, using their feet to create small water funnels that stir up prey.

breeding

ID: dark, needle-like bill; white eyebrow; light underparts; black legs. *Breeding female:* very defined colours; grey cap; chestnut throat; black eye line extends down the neck. *Breeding male:* duller overall; dark cap.
Size: *L* 21–24 cm; *W* 36–40 cm.
Status: occasional in the north; uncommon in central parts; common in the south; early May to mid-September.
Habitat: *Nesting:* marshes, wet meadows and margins of sewage lagoons. *In migration:* lakeshores, marshes and sewage lagoons.
Nesting: on the ground, often near water; in a depression lined with grass and other vegetation; nest is often well concealed; male incubates 4 brown-spotted, buff eggs for about 20 days; male rears the young.

Feeding: whirls in tight circles in water to stir up prey, then picks out aquatic insects, worms and small crustaceans; makes short jabs on land to pick up insects, crustaceans and some seeds.
Voice: deep, grunting *work work* or *wu wu wu*, given on the nesting grounds.
Similar Species: *Red-necked Phalarope:* red stripe down the side of the neck; wing stripes are obvious in flight. *Red Phalarope:* all-reddish neck, breast and underparts; wing stripes; rarely seen inland. *Lesser Yellowlegs:* larger; yellow legs; streaked neck; mottled upperparts.
Best Sites: Oak Hammock Marsh; Hecla/Grindstone PP; Delta Marsh; Lyleton; Oak/Plum lakes.

FRANKLIN'S GULL

Larus pipixcan

Although we refer to the Franklin's Gull as a 'sea gull,' this bird spends much of its life away from saltwater. It is a common prairie gull that nests on inland lakes, and only in winter is it found along coastlines. • The Franklin's Gull is often called the 'Prairie Dove,' because of its dove-like profile and gentle disposition. In the late 1800s, it went by the name 'Rosy Gull,' because of the pinkish tinge on its breast. • Franklin's Gulls are commonly seen following tractors across agricultural fields, skilfully snatching up insects from the tractor's path. Small groups frequently return to their nesting colony to feed their young, and they are continually replaced by others arriving to feed.

breeding

ID: grey mantle; broken, white eye ring; white underparts. *Breeding:* black head; orange-red bill and legs; breast may have a pinkish tinge. *Non-breeding:* white head; dark patch on the back of the head. *In flight:* black crescent on the white wing tips.
Size: *L* 33–38 cm; *W* 90 cm.
Status: common in central parts; abundant in the south; early April to early October.
Habitat: agricultural fields, marshy lakes, landfills and large river and lake shorelines.
Nesting: colonial; on a floating platform of reeds; nest is made of coarse marsh vegetation and lined with fine grass and plant down; pair incubates 2–4 greenish-buff eggs for 24 days.

Feeding: opportunistic; gleans fields for grasshoppers and other insects; often catches insects in mid-air; also eats small fish and some crustaceans.
Voice: mewing, shrill *weeeh-ah weeeeh-ah* while feeding and in migration; also a shrill *kuk-kuk-kuk.*
Similar Species: *Bonaparte's Gull:* adult has a black bill; conspicuous white wedge on the forewing. *Little Gull:* paler mantle; lacks the black crescent on the wing tips; breeding adult lacks the broken white eye ring and the white nape; non-breeding adult lacks the black face mask; rare in Manitoba. *Sabine's Gull:* large black, white and grey triangles on the upperwings; dark bill with a yellow tip.
Best Sites: Birds Hill PP; Oak Hammock Marsh; Hecla/Grindstone PP; Delta Marsh; Oak/Plum lakes; Riding Mountain NP.

RING-BILLED GULL

Larus delawarensis

Ring-billed Gulls are common gulls in southern Manitoba, gathering in great numbers to scavenge in landfills and sewage reservoirs. They have become pests in some urban settings, and parks, beaches, golf courses and parking lots are often inundated with marauding birds looking for food handouts. Ring-bills are also found in rural settings, where large numbers gather in agricultural fields. • Ring-billed Gulls nest in mixed-species colonies on isolated islands in large inland lakes, where their nests are protected from predators, such as skunks, foxes and coyotes. They often eat other birds' eggs, and they are also predators of hatchling ducks and shorebirds. • Ring-billed Gulls do not attain their adult plumage or reproduce until they are at least three years of age.

breeding

ID: medium-sized gull; white head; yellow bill and legs; black ring around the bill tip; pale grey mantle; yellow eyes; white underparts. *Immature:* variable amounts of grey and/or brown on the back and wings; brown flecking on the head, neck, breast, sides and flanks. *First-year:* black-tipped, white tail is distinctive. *In flight:* white-spotted, black wing tips.
Size: *L* 45–50 cm; *W* 120 cm (male is slightly larger).
Status: uncommon in the north; fairly common in central parts; abundant in the south; late March to early November;
Habitat: *Nesting:* on small, barren islands. *In migration:* lakes, rivers, landfills, parks, parking lots and cultivated fields.
Nesting: colonial; on the ground in a shallow scrape lined with reeds, debris, grass and sticks; pair incubates

2–4 buff-white eggs for 26 or 27 days.
Feeding: gleans the ground for garbage, spiders, insects, rodents, earthworms, grubs and some waste grain; scavenges for carrion; surface-tips for aquatic invertebrates and fish while swimming; will take mice, eggs and young birds.
Voice: high-pitched *kakakaka-akakaka*; also a low, laughing *yook-yook-yook*.
Similar Species: *California Gull:* much larger; no bill ring; black and red spot near the tip of the lower mandible; dark eyes. *Herring* (p. 73), *Thayer's* and *Glaucous gulls:* larger; adults have pinkish legs, a red spot near the tip of the lower mandible and lack the bill ring. *Mew Gull:* dark eyes; darker mantle; lacks the bill ring; adults have less black on the wing tips; rare in Manitoba.
Best Sites: Whiteshell PP; Lake Manitoba, Winnipeg and Winnipegosis; Oak Hammock Marsh.

HERRING GULL

Larus argentatus

Herring Gulls are skilled hunters—they eat insects, mollusks, frogs and mice—and they are also opportunistic birds that scavenge at landfills. On occasion, they will pirate food from other birds and prey on nestlings. In Manitoba, they are usually seen over larger lakes, searching the shorelines for carrion that has washed up in the waves. • Like many large gulls, Herrings have a small red spot on their lower mandible that serves as a target for nestling young. When a downy chick pecks at this spot, the parent recognizes the cue and regurgitates its meal. Soon after hatching, the young gather in groups or 'creches,' where they are watched over by other adults. The parents are then able to search for food, which is often some distance from the colony, while their young are guarded.

breeding

ID: large gull; yellow bill; red spot on the lower mandible; light eyes; light grey mantle; pink legs. *Immature:* variably mottled brown; may show a black ring around the bill; takes 4 years to attain full adult plumage. *In flight:* white-spotted, black wing tips.
Size: *L* 56–66 cm; *W* 1.3–1.4 m.
Status: abundant in the north; common elsewhere; mid-March to mid-November.
Habitat: *Nesting:* undisturbed islands, peninsulas and cliffs. *In migration:* large lakes, wetlands, rivers, landfills and urban areas.
Nesting: colonial; often with pelicans, cormorants and other gulls; on islands or open beaches; on the ground in a shallow scrape lined with plants, debris and sticks; pair incubates 2–4 darkly blotched, olive eggs for 25–28 days.
Feeding: generalist; fish, aquatic invertebrates, insects, worms, garbage and the eggs and young of other birds.
Voice: loud *hi-yah, hi-yah* or *yuk-yuk-yuk-yuk*; bugle-like *kleew-kleew*; also an alarmed *kak-kak-kak*.
Similar Species: *California Gull:* much smaller; dark eyes; yellowish legs; black and red spot on the lower mandible. *Ring-billed Gull* (p. 72): much smaller; black bill ring; yellow legs. *Thayer's Gull* and *Glaucous Gull:* lack the black in the wings; paler mantle.
Best Sites: Pinawa area; Fort Whyte; islands in lakes Manitoba, Winnipeg and Winnipegosis; Churchill.

COMMON TERN

Sterna hirundo

Common Terns are found throughout most of Manitoba, and they are most predominant on our large lakes in summer. They are absent only along Hudson Bay and in extreme northern parts of the province, where they are replaced by similar-looking Arctic Terns. In some of the smaller marshes throughout southwestern Manitoba, they relinquish their prominent status to Forster's Terns. • When hunting, this tern hovers briefly over its intended target, then plunges into the water. Its dive may take it underwater momentarily, and it often pops to the surface carrying a minnow or other small fish in its bill. • Unlike gulls, the Common Tern does not scavenge for its meals. It feeds mostly on small, freshwater fish, and its spring arrival coincides with the disappearance of ice from our lakes. • The Common Tern's graceful flight over lakes and oceans once inspired the name 'Sea Swallow.'

breeding

ID: *Breeding:* black cap; white underparts; pearl grey mantle; red, black-tipped bill; red legs; white rump; white tail with grey outer edges. *Non-breeding:* black nape; lacks the black cap. *In flight:* shallowly forked tail; long, pointed wings; darker wedge near the upperwing tips.
Size: *L* 33–41 cm; *W* 76 cm.
Status: rare in the north; fairly common to common elsewhere; May to September.
Habitat: *Nesting:* islands, breakwaters and beaches. *In migration:* large lakes, open wetlands and slow-moving rivers.
Nesting: colonial; in open areas without vegetation; nest scrape is lined with pebbles, vegetation,

debris or shells; pair incubates 1–3 variably marked brown eggs for 21–30 days.
Feeding: hovers over the water and plunges headfirst after small fish; also takes insects and aquatic invertebrates.
Voice: drawn-out *keee-arrrr* with a downward inflection; also *kik-kik-kik* and *kirri-kirri*.
Similar Species: *Forster's Tern:* grey tail with white outer edges; upper primaries have a silvery look. *Arctic Tern:* all-red bill; deeply forked tail; upper primaries lack the dark grey wedge; greyer underparts. *Caspian Tern:* much larger overall; much heavier red-orange bill.
Best Sites: islands in lakes Manitoba, Winnipeg and Winnipegosis; Dog Lake; Oak Lake; Pelican Lake; Duck Mountain PP.

BLACK TERN

Chlidonias niger

Wheeling about in foraging flights, Black Terns pick small minnows from the water's surface and catch flying insects in mid-air. Even on stormy days, these acrobats slice through the air with grace. • Black Terns are finicky nesters, refusing to return to areas that show slight changes in the water level or density of emergent vegetation. • Black Terns often nest in association with Forster's Terns. Their nesting colonies are noisy, and an intruder is sure to be met by a barrage of squawks and aerial dive-bomb attacks. • Black Terns were once abundant summer visitors to large sloughs throughout Manitoba, but their numbers have been in decline. In fact, recent breeding bird surveys have revealed that their numbers are in decline throughout much of North America.

breeding

ID: *Breeding:* black head and underparts; grey back, tail and wings; white undertail coverts; black bill; reddish-black legs. *Non-breeding:* white forehead and underparts; moulting fall birds may be mottled with brown. *In flight:* long, pointed wings; shallowly forked tail.
Size: *L* 23–25 cm; *W* 61 cm.
Status: locally fairly common in the north; fairly common in central parts; common in the south; early May to early September.
Habitat: shallow, freshwater marshes, wet meadows, lake edges and sewage ponds with emergent vegetation.
Nesting: in loose colonies; in emergent vegetation, usually over water; nest of dead plant material is built on floating vegetation, a muddy mound or a muskrat lodge; pair incubates 2–4 blotched dark olive-buff eggs for about 22 days.
Feeding: snatches insects from the air, from tall grass and from the water's surface; often follows farm machinery; also takes small fish.
Voice: shrill, metallic *kik-kik-kik-kik-kik*; typical alarm call is *kreea*.
Similar Species: *Other terns:* all are light in colour, not dark.
Best Sites: Rat River WMA; Oak Hammock Marsh; Mantagao Lake WMA; Delta Marsh; Whitewater Lake; Duck Mountain PP.

ROCK DOVE

Columba livia

The Rock Dove was introduced to North America in the 17th century, and it has since become the familiar 'pigeon' of most cities, towns, parks and farmyards. Most Rock Doves seem content to nest among human dwellings, but 'wilder' members of this species can occasionally be seen nesting on tall cliffs. • Rock Doves are believed to have been domesticated from Eurasian birds in about 4500 B.C. as a source of meat. Since then, they have been used as message couriers—both Caesar and Napoleon used them—as scientific subjects and even as pets. Much of our understanding of bird migration, endocrinology and sensory perception derives from experiments involving Rock Doves. • These birds reproduce quickly—they reach reproductive maturity within six months of hatching and nest anytime of the year. Like other members of the pigeon family, Rock Doves are fed 'pigeon milk' by their parents, a liquid that is produced in the lining of the bird's crop.

ID: colour is typically blue-grey, but highly variable (domestic or feral birds may be red, white or tan); 2 black wing bars; white rump; orange feet; dark-tipped tail.
In flight: claps its wings on take-off; holds its wings in a deep V while gliding.
Size: *L* 33–36 cm; male is usually larger.
Status: occasional in the north; uncommon in central parts; abundant in the south; year-round.
Habitat: urban areas, railway yards, farmyards and grain elevators; high cliffs are used by some.

Nesting: on the ledges of barns, bridges, buildings and towers; rarely on cliffs; flimsy nest is made of sticks, grass and assorted vegetation; pair incubates 1 or 2 unmarked white eggs for about 18 days.
Feeding: gleans the ground for waste grain, seeds and fruits; occasionally eats insects.
Voice: soft, gurgling *coorrr-coorrr-coorrr.*
Similar Species: *Merlin* (p. 56): not as heavy bodied; longer tail; does not hold its wings in a V; wings do not clap on take-off.
Best Sites: widespread in towns, cities, urban or suburban parks, farms or grain elevators.

MOURNING DOVE

Zenaida macroura

In Ernest Thompson Seton's 1891 publication, *Birds of Manitoba*, the Mourning Dove was listed as a rare summer resident throughout much of southern Manitoba. In 1893, however, Seton upgraded its status, noting that the disappearance of the Passenger Pigeon, which was last seen in any numbers in Manitoba in 1878, had been followed closely by the appearance of the Common [Mourning] Dove. Today, the soft cooing call of the Mourning Dove is a common sound heard filtering through southern and central Manitoba woodlands, farmlands and suburban parks and gardens. • This bird is named for its plaintive, mournful calls, which novice birdwatchers sometimes mistake for the sound of a hooting owl. • Despite its fragile appearance, the Mourning Dove is a swift, direct flyer, capable of eluding many winged predators. In courtship or territorial displays, its wings often produce a distinctive whistle as it cuts through the air at high speed. • Although it is illegal to hunt Mourning Doves, this bird is the most widely hunted and harvested of all North American gamebirds.

ID: buffy grey-brown plumage; small head; long, white-edged, pointed tail; sleek body; dark, shiny patch below the ear; dull red legs; dark bill; pale rosy underparts; nods its head while walking.

Size: *L* 28–33 cm; *W* 43–48 cm.

Status: fairly common in central parts; abundant in the south; April to mid-October; a few may be present in winter.

Habitat: open woodlands, forest edges, hedgerows, farmyards, suburban areas and open parks.

Nesting: in the fork of a tree or shrub; rarely on the ground; fragile, shallow platform nest is made of twigs, weeds and grasses; pair incubates 2 white eggs for 14 days.

Feeding: gleans the ground and vegetation for seeds, waste grain, berries or insects; may be seen in winter at feeders or feedlots.

Voice: mournful, soft *co-ooooooh coo-coo-coo*.

Similar Species: *Rock Dove* (p. 76): stockier; more colourful; white rump; shorter, fanned tail; iridescent neck. *Black-billed Cuckoo:* larger, curved bill; larger head; red eyes; long tail with a broad, rounded tip; brown upperparts, white underparts.

Best Sites: widespread in open woodlands, parks, farmland and suburbs.

EASTERN SCREECH-OWL

Otus asio

The tiny Eastern Screech-Owl is at best an uncommon resident in southern Manitoba. It inhabits deciduous woodlands south of the Canadian Shield, and its presence is rarely detected by humans. Most screech-owls sleep away the daylight hours perched in large coniferous trees or snuggled safely inside a tree cavity or nest box. The sounds of mobbing chickadees or squawking gangs of Blue Jays will occasionally alert you to the presence of a screech-owl during daylight hours. More commonly, you will find this owl by listening for the male's eerie, horse-like 'whinny' courtship call. Riparian woodlands are good places to visit if you're interested in seeing an Eastern Screech-Owl, and old, cavity-ridden cottonwoods are some of its favourite haunts. • Despite its small size, the Eastern Screech-Owl is a formidable hunter.

grey morph

ID: the only small owl with ear tufts; pale facial disc; reddish or greyish overall; dark vertical breast streaking; yellow eyes; pale greyish bill.
Size: *L* 20–23 cm; *W* 50–55 cm (female is slightly larger).
Status: rare to uncommon; year-round.
Habitat: riparian woodlands, open, mature deciduous forests, urban parks, orchards and shade trees with natural cavities.
Nesting: in a natural cavity or artificial nest box; no lining is added; female incubates 3–8 white eggs for about 26 days.

Feeding: small mammals, birds and insects, including moths in flight; feeds at dusk and at night.
Voice: eerie, horse-like 'whinny' that descends in pitch and speeds up to a tremolo.
Similar Species: *Northern Saw-whet Owl* and *Boreal Owl:* lack the ear tufts; longer, bolder, reddish or brownish vertical streaks on the white breast. *Long-eared Owl:* much longer, slimmer body; large, closer-set ear tufts. *Great Horned Owl* (p. 79): much larger; lacks the vertical breast streaks.
Best Sites: Assiniboine Park; Spruce Woods PP; Crescent Lake; near farm buildings in SW Manitoba in winter.

GREAT HORNED OWL

Bubo virginianus

The familiar *hoo-hoo-hoooo hoo-hoo* that resounds through campgrounds, suburban parks, woodlot-edges and farmyards is the call of the adaptable and superbly camouflaged Great Horned Owl. During daylight hours, it sits motionless, blending perfectly with its woodland background. It hunts primarily at night, using its acute hearing, powerful talons and human-sized eyes to hunt for an astonishingly wide diversity of prey, including birds, amphibians, ground squirrels and waterfowl. Its poorly developed sense of smell might explain why the Great Horned Owl is one of the few predators that consistently preys on skunks. • Great Horned Owls begin their courtship as early as January, at which time their hooting calls make them quite conspicuous. By February and March, they are already incubating their eggs, and by the time the last migratory birds have moved into Manitoba, Great Horned owlets have already fledged.

ID: large owl; prominent ear tufts are set wide apart on the head; yellow eyes; fine, horizontal barring on the breast; facial disc is outlined in black; white chin; overall colour varies from light grey to dark brown.
Size: *L* 46–64 cm; *W* 90–150 cm.
Status: rare in the north; common elsewhere; year-round.
Habitat: deciduous or coniferous forests, scattered trees in agricultural areas, riparian woodlands and suburban parks; widespread among fragmented or open woodlands; absent from large areas of continuous forest.
Nesting: in the abandoned stick nest of a crow, raven or hawk; rarely in abandoned buildings; little material is added to the nest; mostly the female incubates 2–6 dull whitish eggs for about 33 days; nests as early as February.

Feeding: nocturnal; may also hunt at dusk and dawn, or by day in winter; usually swoops from a perch; eats small mammals, birds, snakes and amphibians.
Voice: 4–6 deep, resonant hoots: *huu-hu-hu hooo-hooo* or *eat-my-food, I'll-eat you*; female's hoots are faster and higher-pitched.
Similar Species: *Long-eared Owl:* much smaller; tall and thin body and head; vertical breast streaks; ear tufts are close-set. *Eastern Screech-Owl* (p. 78): much smaller; vertical breast streaks. *Other large owls:* lack the prominent ear tufts.
Best Sites:; Pinawa area; Mantagao Lake WMA; Delta Marsh; Spruce Woods PP; Turtle Mountain PP; Duck Mountain PP.

SNOWY OWL

Nyctea scandiaca

When the mercury drops and the landscape hardens in winter's grip, ghostly white Snowy Owls appear atop trees, fenceposts and utility poles. On windy days, these owls prefer to remain on the ground, where they blend perfectly against the snow-covered landscape. • Snowy Owl numbers fluctuate markedly from year to year in southern Manitoba. When lemmings are scarce in the Arctic, Snowy Owls may forego nesting and venture south in search of food. In years when lemmings are plentiful, a pair of Snowy Owls may raise nine or more young—the youngest often hatching when the eldest is near fledging age—and may remain in the Arctic over winter. Banding studies have revealed that females often return to the same winter territory and may be found on the same perch year after year. The males, on the other hand, are less predictable.

♀

ID: mostly white with varying amounts of dark flecking; white face and throat; yellow eyes; black bill and talons; rounded head with no ear tufts. *Male:* very little dark flecking. *Female:* prominent dark barring or flecking on the breast and upperparts. *Immature:* heavier barring than an adult female.

Size: *L* 50–70 cm; *W* 1.4–1.7 m (female is noticeably larger).

Status: uncommon in the north and in central parts; fairly common in the south; late October to late April; rare and erratic in summer.

Habitat: *Nesting:* on tundra. *Non-nesting:* in open country, including tundra, large forest clearings and fields.

Nesting: on a raised ridge, outcrop or hummock; in a slight depression sparsely lined with grass and feathers; female incubates 3–9 white eggs for about 33 days.

Feeding: usually hunts during daylight hours; eats lemmings and voles in summer and mice, voles, grouse, hares and weasels in winter.

Voice: quiet during winter; barking *krow-ow* or repeated *rick* call on nesting grounds.

Similar Species: *Great Grey Owl* (p. 82): grey plumage. *Great Horned Owl* (p. 79): prominent ear tufts; usually brown-grey overall; lacks the white face. *Short-eared Owl* (p. 83): brownish breast streaking and upperparts; black eye sockets; dark 'wrist' crescents.

Best Sites: *Nesting:* Churchill; Wapusk NP. *Non-nesting:* Oak Hammock Marsh; Winnipeg International Airport; field margins in southern Manitoba.

BURROWING OWL

Athene cunicularia

Burrowing Owls were once common birds in Manitoba, but their numbers have declined significantly in recent years. The Burrowing Owl is the only owl in North America that nests in underground burrows, and the extermination of burrowing mammals in our province has greatly reduced the number of suitable owl nesting sites. Other factors for their decline include poisonings, collisions with vehicles, the use of agricultural chemicals and the conversion of native grasslands to croplands and residential areas. A few nesting pairs persist in Manitoba, mostly in the southwestern part of the province. Fortunately, some landowners have agreed to protect Burrowing Owl habitat and some even support the introduction of artificial burrows to attract these birds to areas where ground squirrels are rare or absent. • During the day, these ground-dwelling birds can be seen atop fenceposts or rocks in open grassland habitat. When they perch at the entrance to their burrows, they look very similar to the ground squirrels with which they closely associate.

ID: long legs; short tail; rounded head; no ear tufts; white around the eyes; yellow bill; bold, white 'chin' stripe; horizontal barring on the underparts; brown upperparts are flecked with white. *Immature:* brownish band across the breast; pale, unbarred underparts.

Size: *L* 23–28 cm; *W* 50–60 cm.

Status: very rare and localized; mid-April to early October.

Habitat: open, short-grass haylands, pastures and prairies; occasionally on lawns and golf courses.

Nesting: singly or in loose colonies; in an abandoned natural or artificial burrow; nest is lined with bits of dry manure, food debris, feathers and fine grass; female incubates 5–11 white eggs.

Feeding: eats mostly ground insects, such as grasshoppers, beetles and crickets; also eats small rodents, some birds, amphibians and reptiles.

Voice: call is a harsh *chuk*; chattering *quick-quick-quick*; rattlesnake-like warning call when inside its burrow. *Male: coo-hooo* courtship call is higher than, but similar to, the Mourning Dove's coo.

Similar Species: *Short-eared Owl* (p. 83): heavy vertical streaks on the underparts; small ear tufts; long wings with dark 'wrist' marks; black eye sockets; doesn't nest in burrows. *Northern Saw-whet Owl:* bold, vertical reddish streaks on the underparts; short legs.

Best Sites: mostly restricted to extreme SW Manitoba.

GREAT GRAY OWL

Strix nebulosa

Before your eyes, a large, phantom-like owl glides down from a perch, hovers briefly, then plunges headfirst into a snowbank to acquire a meal. With a face designed like a satellite dish, the Great Gray Owl is able to detect and locate the quietest forest floor scurry or woodland twitch. Even the faint sound of a tiny rodent covered by 60 cm of snow can be detected by this owl. The Great Gray's facial discs funnel sound waves into its asymmetrically placed ears, enabling it, through triangulation, to pinpoint the precise location of its prey. • Although this magnificent bird is the largest of the North American owls, it is outweighed by as much as 15 percent by the Snowy Owl and the Great Horned Owl. • The Great Gray Owl is Manitoba's provincial bird, and it has been dubbed 'the phantom of the northern forest' by Robert Nero, our province's Great Gray Owl expert.

ID: dusky grey overall; heavy vertical streaks on the underparts; large, rounded head; no ear tufts; yellow eyes and bill; well-defined concentric rings in the facial disk; black and white forms a 'bow tie'; long tail.
Size: *L* 60–84 cm; *W* 1.4–1.5 m (female is slightly larger).
Status: rare in the south outside of the boreal forest; uncommon elsewhere; year-round.
Habitat: *Nesting:* undisturbed, dense spruce or poplar stands adjacent to open muskeg, fens, bogs or meadows. *Non-nesting:* clearings of boreal forest and along roadsides, bogs and open meadows.
Nesting: usually near spruce bogs or muskeg; in an abandoned hawk, raven or eagle nest; also uses tall tree stumps or artificial platforms; female incubates 2–5 white eggs for up to 36 days.
Feeding: hunts at dawn and dusk; eats mostly voles, mice, lemmings and shrews.
Voice: a deep, booming *whoo-hoo-hoo*; also a series of widely spaced, deep *whooo* notes.
Similar Species: *Barred Owl:* dark eyes; horizontal rather than vertical barring on the upper breast; lacks the white 'bow tie.' *Great Horned Owl* (p. 79): large ear tufts; dark bill. *Short-eared Owl* (p. 83): much smaller; black eye sockets; dark bill; black 'wrist' crescents.
Best Sites: Pinawa area; Nopiming PP; Spur Woods WMA; Hecla/Grindstone PP; Riding Mountain NP; Grass River PP.

SHORT-EARED OWL

Asio flammeus

The Short-eared Owl flies so characteristically that after a first encounter with this bird it will be easy to identify one in flight from quite a distance. It looks almost headless in flight, and it beats its long wings slowly and deeply as it courses erratically low over meadows and fields. • In spring, short-ears perform dramatic courtship dances that involve calling, soaring and an occasional swoop accompanied by a loud clapping of the bird's wings. They do not 'hoot' like forest-dwelling owls, because visual displays are more effective for communicating in open environments. • The large eyes of owls are fixed in place, so to look up, down or to the side, they must move their entire heads. Of course, owls have adapted wonderfully to this situation, and they can swivel their necks 180 degrees. • All owls, as well as many other birds, such as herons, gulls, crows and hawks, cough up 'pellets'—the indigestible parts of their prey, such as bones, feathers and fur. • As with many other birds of prey, Short-eared Owl populations grow and decline over many years in response to prey availability.

ID: yellow eyes set in black sockets; heavy, dark vertical streaking on the pale buff belly; straw-coloured upperparts; short ear tufts are often hidden. *In flight:* dark 'wrist' crescents; buff upperwing patches; irregular, 'flopping' flight pattern; deep wingbeats; long wings.
Size: *L* 33–43 cm; *W* 1–1.2 m (female is slightly larger).
Status: highly erratic from year to year; fairly common throughout most parts; uncommon in central Manitoba; late March to mid-November; rare in winter.
Habitat: open areas, including grasslands, wet meadows, marshes, airports, muskeg and tundra.

Nesting: on the ground; in a slight depression sparsely lined with grass; female incubates 4–12 white eggs for up to 37 days.
Feeding: usually hunts at dawn and dusk; eats mainly voles and other small rodents; some insects, small birds and amphibians are taken.
Voice: generally quiet; produces a soft *toot-toot-toot* during the nesting season; also sneezy 'barks' like a dog: *Kee-yow, wow* or *waow.*
Similar Species: *Burrowing Owl* (p. 81): smaller; much longer legs; brown, horizontal barring on the white underparts; bold, white chin stripe; white-spotted upperparts. *Great Horned Owl* (p. 79) and *Long-eared Owl:* long ear tufts; rarely hunt during the day.
Best Sites: Whiteshell PP; Oak Hammock Marsh; Delta Marsh; Churchill; Wapusk NP.

COMMON NIGHTHAWK

Chordeiles minor

Each May and June, male nighthawks fly high above forest clearings, fields and lakeshores, snatching up insects and gaining elevation in preparation for the climax of their noisy aerial dance. From great heights, males dive swiftly, thrusting their wings forward in a final braking action as they strain to pull out of the steep dive. This quick thrust of the wings produces a deep, hollow *vroom* that attracts female nighthawks. • Like other members of the nightjar family, the Common Nighthawk has a large head and eyes, tiny bill and a wide, gaping mouth surrounded by feather shafts that funnel insects into its mouth as it flies. • Nighthawks are generally less nocturnal than other nightjars, but they still spend most of the daylight hours resting on a tree limb or on the ground. If approached, a nighthawk will remain motionless, seemingly aware that its cryptic plumage is its best protection.

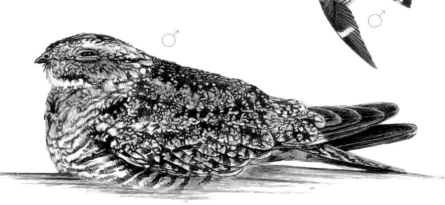

ID: cryptic, mottled light and dark plumage; barred underparts. *Male:* white throat and undertail stripe. *Female:* buff throat. *In flight:* bold, white 'wrist' patches on the long, pointed wings; shallowly forked, barred tail; erratic flight pattern.
Size: *L* 22–25 cm.
Status: occasional in the north; uncommon in central parts; fairly common in the south; mid-May to mid-September.
Habitat: open and semi-open habitats, such as forest openings, weedy meadows, barren islands, lakeshores, gravel pits, rooftops and abandoned parking lots.
Nesting: on bare ground; on sand or gravel or on a rooftop; may use

a stump or an abandoned robin's nest; pair incubates 2 olive white eggs for about 19 days.
Feeding: eats primarily at dawn and dusk, but will eat during the day and night; catches insects in flight; eats mosquitoes, moths and other flying insects.
Voice: frequently repeated, nasal *peent peent*; also makes a deep, booming *vroom* with its wings during courtship flights.
Similar Species: *Whip-poor-will:* less common; lacks the white 'wrist' patches; shorter wings; rounded tail and wing tips; calls its own name.
Best Sites: Fort Whyte; Birds Hill PP; Hecla/Grindstone PP; Mantagao Lake WMA; Spruce Woods PP; Duck Mountain PP.

CHIMNEY SWIFT

Chaetura pelagica

Chimney Swifts are the frequent flyers of the bird world—they feed, drink, bathe, collect nesting material and even mate while in flight. They spend much of their time scooping up flying insects high over Manitoba's cities and towns, and only the business of nesting and rest keeps them off their wings. • Chimney Swifts use saliva to glue their nests to vertical surfaces, and roosting birds use their sharp claws to cling to cracks in cliffs and the sides of buildings. Chimney Swifts once relied on natural tree cavities and woodpecker excavations for nest sites, but in recent times they have adapted to living in brick chimneys and other artificial structures. During migration, it is not uncommon to see thousands of swifts roosting in a single chimney. • Studies have revealed that male and female Chimney Swifts may occasionally take more than one mate, but the frequency of such situations is unknown. In nesting colonies, breeding pairs often have one or more helpers that assist in feeding the young and incubating the eggs. • Swifts are distinguished by their rapid 'twinkling' flight style and their narrow wings, which are often stiffly bowed in the shape of a boomerang.

ID: dark greyish-brown overall; slim body; long, thin, pointed wings; squared tail. *In flight:* rapid wingbeats; boomerang-shaped profile; erratic flight pattern.
Size: *L* 11–14 cm; *W* 30–32 cm.
Status: rare in central parts; locally common in the south; May to early September.
Habitat: nests and roosts in chimneys in cities and towns; may nest in cliffs or tree cavities.
Nesting: colonial; in the interior of a chimney or tree cavity; half-saucer nest of short, dead twigs is glued with saliva to a vertical wall; pair incubates 4–6 white eggs for about 19 days.
Feeding: flying insects are swallowed whole during continuous flight.
Voice: rapid chattering call given in flight: *chitter-chitter-chitter*; also gives a rapid series of *chip* notes.
Similar Species: *Swallows* (pp. 108–11): broader, shorter wings; smoother flight pattern; most have a forked or notched tail.
Best Sites: Steinbach; Winnipeg; Morden; Portage la Prairie; Brandon; Dauphin; large tree snags in Riding Mountain NP.

RUBY-THROATED HUMMINGBIRD

Archilochus colubris

R uby-throated Hummingbirds span the ecological gap between birds and bees—they feed on the sweet, energy-rich nectar that flowers provide in exchange for pollination. Many avid gardeners and birders have long understood the nature of this co-dependence and have planted native nectar-producing plants in their yards in hopes of attracting these delightful birds. Non-gardeners can attract hummingbirds by setting out specially designed hummingbird feeders filled with sweetened water (one part sugar to four parts water). • Weighing only about as much as a quarter, hummingbirds are capable of speeds of up to 100 km/h. When hovering or in flight, they beat their wings 55 to 75 times a second, and their hearts can beat up to 1200 times a minute. • To save energy at night and during periods of food shortage, these tiny birds enter a torpid state, in which their body temperature drops close to that of their surroundings. • Except for a few accidental records of the Rufous Hummingbird, the Ruby-throat is the only hummingbird commonly found in Manitoba.

ID: moth- or butterfly-sized; long bill; iridescent green back; light underparts; dark tail. *Male:* iridescent ruby red throat (appears black in poor light); forked tail. *Female and Immature:* fine, dark throat streaking; tail is blunt with white spots.
Size: *L* 7.5–9.5 cm.
Status: uncommon; mid-May to early September.
Habitat: open deciduous or mixed woodlands, orchards, parks and flower gardens.
Nesting: on a horizontal tree limb; bottlecap-sized cup nest of lichens, moss and plant fibres is bound with spider silk; female incubates 2 white, pea-sized eggs for 13–16 days; often

has 2 or 3 broods per year.
Feeding: drinks nectar from blooming flowers and sugar-sweetened water from special feeders; also eats small insects and spiders and feeds at sapsucker wells.
Voice: soft buzzing of the wings in flight; loud *chick* and other high squeaks when in courtship or territorial battles.
Similar Species: *Rufous Hummingbird:* male has a rufous-coloured back and flanks; female has rufous patches on the tail; accidental in Manitoba.
Best Sites: Whiteshell PP; Delta Marsh; Spruce Woods PP; Turtle Mountain PP; Riding Mountain NP; backyard feeders throughout southern Manitoba.

BELTED KINGFISHER

Ceryle alcyon

The Belted Kingfisher is never far from water, and it is commonly seen perched on a bare branch that extends over a productive pool of water. With a precise headfirst dive, the kingfisher can catch fish at depths of up to 60 cm, or snag a frog immersed in only a few centimetres of water. • Kingfishers are easily identified by their long, pointed bill, shaggy, blue crest, blue breast band, rusty abdominal belt (female) and boisterous, rattling call. Look for this 'king of the fishers' in summer near rivers and streams. • During the breeding season, a pair of kingfishers will typically take turns excavating the nest burrow. They use their bills to chip away at the soil and then kick loose material out of the tunnel with their small feet. Females have the traditional female reproductive role for birds, but, like phalaropes, they are more colourful than their mates. • Breeding bird surveys have revealed that kingfisher numbers are declining throughout North America.

ID: long, dagger-like bill; large, blue head with a shaggy crest; white collar; greyish-blue upperparts; blue breast band; white under-parts. *Female:* rust-coloured 'belt' (may be incomplete), sides and flanks. *Male:* lacks the rust-coloured belt, sides and flanks.
Size: *L* 27–36 cm.
Status: uncommon in central parts; fairly common elsewhere; mid-April to early October.
Habitat: rivers, large streams, lakes and marshes, especially near exposed soil banks. *Nesting:* in riverbanks and dirt cliffs.
Nesting: in a cavity at the end of an earth burrow, often up to 2–4 m deep, dug by the pair with their

bills and claws; nest cavity is lined with grass and leaves; pair incubates 6–8 white eggs.
Feeding: eats mostly small fish, frogs and tadpoles; may eat aquatic invertebrates, small rodents and birds; young are fed by regurgitation.
Voice: fast, repetitive cackling rattle, a little like a teacup shaking on a saucer.
Similar Species: *Blue Jay* (p. 103): brighter blue overall; much smaller bill; neatly crested head; behaves in a completely different fashion.
Best Sites: almost any fish-bearing water-body in Manitoba; Hecla/Grindstone PP; Spruce Woods PP; Riding Mountain NP; Duck Mountain PP.

RED-HEADED WOODPECKER

Melanerpes erythrocephalus

This woodpecker was once common throughout its range, but its numbers have declined dramatically over the past century. Red-headed Woodpeckers have been negatively affected by intensive agricultural practices and pesticide use, and since the introduction of the European Starling, they have been largely outcompeted for nesting cavities. Furthermore, the removal of dead standing trees in woodlots has been detrimental to their nesting success. As a nesting alternative, utility poles treated with creosote are sometimes used—with an often deadly outcome for young woodpeckers. Overall, Red-headed Woodpecker numbers are declining in Manitoba, and recent surveys across North America have revealed the same. • Red-headed Woodpeckers are opportunistic feeders; they eat a wide variety of food, including adult and larval invertebrates, seeds, nuts, fruit and even the odd mouse or bird egg. Although these woodpeckers are rarely found in our province over winter, birdfeeders that offer nuts, sunflower seeds, corn and suet will occasionally entice a few individuals to remain through the chilly weather.

ID: crimson-red head, chin, throat and bib; black back, wings and tail; white rump and underparts; large, white wing patches. *Juvenile:* brownish-grey head, breast, back, wings and tail; white rump and underparts; large, white wing patches.
Size: *L* 21–24 cm.
Status: rare to uncommon from mid-May to mid-September; a few may be present in winter.
Habitat: open deciduous woodlands (especially oak woodlands), urban parks, river edges and open areas with scattered trees.

Nesting: in a natural hole or cavity excavated in a dead tree or wooden pole; cavity is lined with wood chips; pair incubates 4–7 white eggs for about 14 days.
Feeding: omnivorous diet includes insects, worms, grubs, nuts, seeds and fruit; may eat mice, young birds and eggs.
Voice: loud series of *kweer* or *queer* notes; occasionally a chattering *kerr-r-ruck*.
Similar Species: adult is distinctive; juvenile is distinguished from other young woodpeckers by the white rump and the large, square wing patch near the speculum.
Best Sites: Assiniboine Park; Fort Whyte; Interlake area; Portage la Prairie to Delta Marsh; Pelican Lake; Riding Mountain NP.

YELLOW-BELLIED SAPSUCKER

Sphyrapicus varius

Lines of parallel 'wells' freshly drilled in tree bark are sure signs that a Yellow-bellied Sapsucker is in the neighbourhood. Throughout spring and summer, sapsuckers make routine visits to each of their well sites. As the wells fill with sweet, sticky sap, they attract insects, and the sapsuckers make their rounds eating both the trapped bugs and the pooled sap. Sapsuckers don't actually suck the sap; they lap it up with a tongue that resembles a paintbrush. Within their forest territory, a pair of sapsuckers might drill a number of sites. Other birds, including humming-birds, kinglets, some warblers and waxwings, are also attracted to sapsucker wells. • Yellow-bellied Sapsuckers are conspicuous in spring, when the males hammer out their Morse–code-like character-istic courtship and territorial rituals on hollowed trees.

ID: broad, black bib; red forecrown; black and white facial stripes; black overall with white barring on the back, wings and tail; large, white shoulder patch; yellow wash on the lower breast and belly. *Male:* red chin. *Female:* white chin. *Juvenile:* brownish overall; distinctive white shoulder patch.
Size: *L* 20–23 cm; *W* 35–40 cm.
Status: fairly common; early April to early October.
Habitat: deciduous and mixed forests, especially second-growth woodlands.
Nesting: in a cavity; usually in a live poplar or birch with heartrot; lines the cavity with wood chips; pair incubates 4–7 white eggs; nest trees are often reused.
Feeding: hammers trees for insects; drills 'wells' in live trees where it collects sap and trapped insects; also eats wild fruit and flycatches for insects.
Voice: a cat-like *meow* or a nasal squeal; territorial/courtship hammering has a Morse–code-like quality and rhythm; ham-mering is rapid then slows near the end.
Similar Species: *Red-headed Woodpecker* (p. 88): juvenile lacks the white patch on the wing. *Downy Woodpecker* (p. 90) and *Hairy Woodpecker:* lack the large, white wing patch and the red forecrown; red nape; white back patch. *Black-backed Woodpecker* (p. 91) and *Three-toed Woodpecker:* lack the white wing patch; yellow forecrown.
Best Sites: Whiteshell PP; Birds Hill PP; Hecla/Grindstone PP; Spruce Woods PP; Turtle Mountain PP; Riding Mountain NP.

DOWNY WOODPECKER

Picoides pubescens

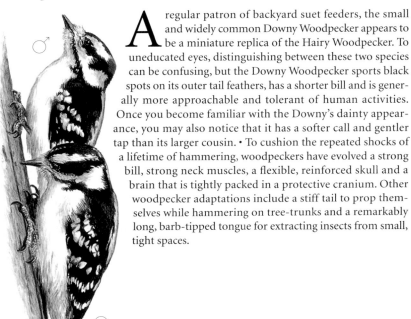

A regular patron of backyard suet feeders, the small and widely common Downy Woodpecker appears to be a miniature replica of the Hairy Woodpecker. To uneducated eyes, distinguishing between these two species can be confusing, but the Downy Woodpecker sports black spots on its outer tail feathers, has a shorter bill and is generally more approachable and tolerant of human activities. Once you become familiar with the Downy's dainty appearance, you may also notice that it has a softer call and gentler tap than its larger cousin. • To cushion the repeated shocks of a lifetime of hammering, woodpeckers have evolved a strong bill, strong neck muscles, a flexible, reinforced skull and a brain that is tightly packed in a protective cranium. Other woodpecker adaptations include a stiff tail to prop themselves while hammering on tree-trunks and a remarkably long, barb-tipped tongue for extracting insects from small, tight spaces.

ID: clean, white belly and back; black wings are faintly barred with white; black eye line, 'chin' stripe and crown; short, stubby bill; black tail; white outer tail feathers are spotted with black. *Male:* small, red nape patch. *Female:* no red nape patch.
Size: *L* 15–18 cm.
Status: fairly common to common; year-round.
Habitat: open deciduous or mixed forests, parks, orchards and riparian woodlots; avoids extensive forest.
Nesting: pair excavates a cavity in a dying or decaying trunk or limb; entrance hole is approximately 2.5 cm in diameter; cavity is lined with wood chips; pair incubates 3–6 white eggs.

Feeding: chips away at bark and probes trees for insect eggs, cocoons, larvae and adults; also eats nuts and seeds; attracted to sunflowers and suet feeders in winter.
Voice: long trill or a 'whinny' that descends in pitch; calls are a sharp *pik* (not as harsh as the *peek* of the Hairy), *ki-ki-ki* or whiny *queek queek.*
Similar Species: *Hairy Woodpecker:* larger overall; bill is as long as the head is wide; no spots on the white outer tail feathers. *Yellow-bellied Sapsucker* (p. 89): large, white shoulder patch; red forecrown; lacks the red nape and the clean, white back. *Black-backed Woodpecker* and *Three-toed Woodpecker:* yellow forecrown; black barring on the flanks.
Best Sites: Assiniboine Park; Birds Hill PP; Interlake area; Delta Marsh; Crescent Lake; Riding Mountain NP.

BLACK-BACKED WOODPECKER

Picoides arcticus

Even experienced naturalists can have difficulty locating the elusive, semi-nomadic Black-backed Woodpecker on its northern coniferous nesting grounds. This generally quiet woodpecker prefers a secretive life in remote, uninhabited tracts of boreal forest. Only during the brief courtship season does the male Black-backed Woodpecker advertise his presence by drumming on top of a broken, standing dead tree or snag (often referred to by biologists as 'wildlife trees'). The yellow-capped males are often so focused on this activity that they are easily approached. • This woodpecker is most active in recently burned forest patches where wood-boring beetles thrive under the charred bark of spruce, pine and fir trees. Like many woodpeckers, it has feathered nostrils to filter out the sawdust it produces when hammering. If you want to find a Black-backed Woodpecker, look for large flakes of bark missing from a dead coniferous tree—evidence that one of these birds has been in the area.

ID: glossy black back; white underparts; black barring on the sides; mostly black head; black 'moustache'; 3 toes; black tail with pure white outer tail feathers. *Male:* yellow crown. *Female:* black crown.
Size: *L* 23–25 cm.
Status: erratic and uncommon; localized in the south; year-round.
Habitat: coniferous forests, especially windfalls and burned-over sites with many standing dead trees and blackened stumps.
Nesting: usually in a burned-over area; excavates a cavity in a dead or dying conifer; pair incubates 3–6 white eggs.
Feeding: chisels away bark flakes to expose larval and adult wood-boring insects; may eat some nuts and fruits.
Voice: normally quiet; call is a sharp *kik*, sometimes rapidly repeated; drumming is a prolonged series of short bursts.
Similar Species: *Three-toed Woodpecker:* white back with black, horizontal barring; black spots on the white outer tail feathers. *Hairy Woodpecker:* clean white back; lacks the dark barring on the sides. *Yellow-bellied Sapsucker* (p. 89): black and whitish back; large, white wing patch; red forecrown; broad black bib; yellow-tinged underparts.
Best Sites: Whiteshell PP; Nopiming PP; Pinawa area; Spruce Woods PP; Riding Mountain NP.

NORTHERN FLICKER

Colaptes auratus

The Northern Flicker is the most widely distributed woodpecker in Manitoba, and it is also the most conspicuous. Northern Flickers have adapted well to human settlement, and they are as abundant in cities, towns and farmyards as they are in open woodlands. Unlike most woodpeckers, the Northern Flicker spends much of its time on the ground, feeding on ants and other land insects, appearing almost robin-like as it hops about on lawns, grassy meadows and along forest clearings. • There are two forms of the Northern Flicker in Manitoba: the 'Yellow-shafted Flicker' and the 'Red-shafted Flicker.' Prior to human settlement, only the 'Yellow-shafted' occurred in Manitoba, but modern-day forestry practices have since led to the arrival of the 'Red-shafted Flicker' from the West. Today, both forms intermingle and occasionally interbreed. • Flickers often bathe in dusty depressions, because dust particles absorb oil and bacteria that are harmful to the birds' feathers. To clean themselves more thoroughly, flickers squish ants and then preen themselves with the remains. Ants contain formic acid, which can kill small parasites on the skin and feathers.

'Yellow-shafted Flicker'

'Red-shafted Flicker'

ID: barred, brown back and wings; black spots on the buff underparts; black bib; white rump; long bill; brownish to buff face; grey crown; red nape crescent. *'Yellow-shafted' male:* yellow underwings and undertail; black 'moustache.' *'Red-shafted' male:* red underwings and undertail; red 'moustache'; rare in Manitoba. *Females:* no 'moustache.' *In flight:* white rump is obvious.
Size: *L* 30–36 cm; *W* 47–53 cm.
Status: rare to uncommon in the north; common elsewhere; early April to mid-October; a few may be present in winter.
Habitat: open deciduous, mixed and coniferous woodlands, forest edges, city parks and riparian woods.

Nesting: excavates a cavity in a dead or dying deciduous tree; may use a pole, nest box or usurp a nest tunnel in a dirt bank; nest may be reused; lines the cavity with wood chips; pair incubates 5–12 white eggs.
Feeding: gleans the ground and probes bark for ants; also eats worms, berries, nuts, beetles and other insects; may also flycatch; young are fed by regurgitation.
Voice: loud, laughing, rapid *kick-kick-kick-kick-kick-kick*; rapidly repeated *woika* or *flicker* call (softer than the Pileated Woodpecker's call) issued during courtship; also drums soft, muffled volleys.
Similar Species: none.
Best Sites: widespread in semi-open areas, towns, wooded parks and yards.

PILEATED WOODPECKER

Dryocopus pileatus

With its flaming red crest, swooping flight, maniacal call and resonant drumming habits, this large, deep-forest dweller is a most impressive and unforgettable bird. It's no surprise that the Pileated Woodpecker once inspired the creation of the famous cartoon character. • Using its powerful, dagger-shaped bill and stubborn determination, the Pileated Woodpecker chisels out distinctive oval-shaped cavities in its unending search for ants and grubs. With all the pecking it does on a daily basis, it is no surprise that its bill becomes shorter as the bird ages. • A pair of breeding Pileated Woodpeckers require more than 40 ha of mature forest to settle, so they are absent from many habitats, including agricultural areas and small woodlots. • As a primary excavator of large tree cavities, this woodpecker plays an important role in forest ecosystems. Other birds and even mammals depend on the activities of this woodpecker—Wood Ducks, Common Mergansers, Common Goldeneyes, American Kestrels, Eastern Screech-Owls and even flying squirrels all use abandoned Pileated cavities for nesting.

ID: black overall; flaming red crest; black and white striped head and neck; stout, dark bill. *Male:* red 'moustache'; red crest extends from the bill. *Female:* duller; black 'moustache'; red crest starts on the crown. *In flight:* white wing linings.
Size: *L* 40–50 cm; *W* 68–76 cm.
Status: uncommon in its preferred habitat; localized in the south; year-round.
Habitat: extensive tracts of mature deciduous forest or dense, mature deciduous stands; may also use extensive, heavily wooded river corridors in agricultural areas.
Nesting: excavates a cavity in a dead or dying tree; cavity is lined with wood chips; pair incubates 3–5 white eggs.
Feeding: often hammers at the base of a rotting tree; creates fist-sized or larger, oblong (or rectangular) holes; eats ants, wood-boring beetles, larvae, berries and nuts.

Voice: much louder flicker-like call; irregular *kik-kik-kikkik-kik-kik* or a fast, rolling *woika-woika-woika-woika;* also a long series of *kuk* notes and loud resonant drumming.
Similar Species: *Other woodpeckers:* much smaller; lack the crest. *American Crow* (p. 105) and *Common Raven* (p. 106): lack the white underwings and the flaming red crest.
Best Sites: Whiteshell PP; Nopiming PP; Hecla/Grindstone PP; Riding Mountain NP; Duck Mountain PP.

OLIVE-SIDED FLYCATCHER

Contopus cooperi

A morning hike through the lush conifers of Manitoba's boreal forest often reveals a most curious and incessant whistled call: *Quick, three-beers! Quick, three-beers!* This interpretation of the male Olive-sided Flycatcher's courtship song may seem silly, but it is surprisingly accurate. If alarmed, this flycatcher changes its tune to an equally enthusiastic, but less memorable *pip-pip-pip*. • Olive-sided Flycatchers nest high in the forest canopy far above the daily hubbub of the forest floor. Among the lofty spires of spruce, pine and fir, they have easy access to an abundance of flying insects that inhabit the sunny forest heights. These feisty birds are difficult to spot, so look for them perched at the tip of a dead conifer. • Most flycatchers are extremely territorial, and they will often chase other birds, including other flycatchers, from their territory.

ID: olive grey sides form a dark 'vest'; white underparts; olive-grey upperparts; 2 white rump tufts; relatively large head; dark upper mandible; dull orange lower mandible; inconspicuous eye ring.
Size: *L* 18–20 cm.
Status: fairly common in the north and in central parts; uncommon in the south; mid-May to early September.
Habitat: semi-open mixed and coniferous forests near water; burned areas and boggy sites with standing dead conifers.
Nesting: high in a conifer, usually on a horizontal branch; nest of twigs, moss, lichens and plant fibres is lined with grass and rootlets and bound with spider silk; female incubates 3 or 4 buff-white eggs for 14 days.

Feeding: flycatches insects from an elevated perch.
Voice: *Male:* chipper and lively *quick-three-beers*, with the 2nd note highest in pitch and the 3rd note sliding; descending *pip-pip-pip* when excited.
Similar Species: *Eastern Wood-Pewee* and *Western Wood-Pewee:* much smaller; lack the white rump tufts; grey breast; faint wing bars. *Eastern Phoebe* (p. 96): lacks the white rump tufts; all-dark bill; often wags its tail. *Eastern Kingbird* (p. 98): lacks the white rump tufts; back and tail are much darker; all-white underparts; white-tipped tail.
Best Sites: Nopiming PP; Mantagao Lake WMA; Riding Mountain NP; Duck Mountain PP; Grass River PP.

LEAST FLYCATCHER

Empidonax minimus

At first glance, the Least Flycatcher may appear sweet and innocent, but a closer look is sure to reveal this bird's bold and pugnacious character. Competitive males will not hesitate to chase other birds from their territory, and they have frequent run-ins with American Redstarts, because the two birds share similar habitat preferences. During the nesting season, males repeat their simple *che-bek* or *Quebec* calls throughout the day to ensure that their territorial boundaries are respected. • Other similar-looking members of the genus *Empidonax* that regularly occur in Manitoba include the Alder, Willow and Yellow-bellied flycatchers, all of which are best distinguished from the Least Flycatcher by their distinctive songs.

ID: olive grey upperparts; 2 white wing bars; bold, white eye ring; fairly long, narrow tail; dark upper mandible; yellow-orange lower mandible; white throat; whitish-grey breast; mostly white belly and undertail coverts; flicks its tail and wings. *Juvenile:* buff wing bars.

Size: *L* 13–15 cm.

Status: common in the north and in central parts; abundant in the south; mid-May to mid-September.

Habitat: open deciduous woodlands, forest openings and forest edges; often in second-growth poplar stands and occasionally near human habitation.

Nesting: on a horizontal limb or in the fork of a tree; small cup nest of grass, plant fibres and shredded bark is lined with fine grass, plant down and feathers; female incubates 3–6 creamy white eggs for about 15 days.

Feeding: flycatches, hovers and gleans ants, caterpillars and other insects; may eat some fruits and seeds.

Voice: constantly repeated, *che-bec che-bec* or *Quebec Quebec*; call note is a dry *whit*.

Similar Species: *Eastern Wood-Pewee* and *Western Wood-Pewee:* stouter head; lack the distinct eye ring and the conspicuous wing bars. *Alder Flycatcher:* faint eye ring; song is *free-beer*; mostly found near water. *Willow Flycatcher:* lacks the distinct eye ring; greener upperparts; yellower underparts; song is *fwitch-be-hear*. *Yellow-bellied Flycatcher:* yellowish eye ring; greener upperparts; yellower underparts; song is *je-bunk* or *per-wee*. *Ruby-crowned Kinglet* (p. 119): bold, broken eye ring; much daintier bill; shorter tail.

Best Sites: Assiniboine Park; Delta Marsh; Spruce Woods PP; Turtle Mountain PP; Riding Mountain NP.

EASTERN PHOEBE

Sayornis phoebe

Eastern Phoebes once nested on cliffs and fallen trees, but their mud nests are now found on buildings and under bridges. They are among the earliest flycatchers to return to our province in spring, and their nest-building activities are normally well underway by the time other songbirds make appearances here. With such an early start, phoebe pairs often raise two broods during the nesting season, and they often reuse the same nest. • Other birds pump their tails while perched, but few Manitoba species can match the zest and frequency of the Eastern Phoebe's tail pumping and fanning. • The Say's Phoebe is also found in Manitoba, but it is less common and occurs only in the southwestern part of the province in drier, more open habitat.

breeding

ID: grey-brown upperparts; all-black bill; white underparts with a grey wash on the breast and sides; no eye ring or conspicuous wing bars; dark legs; frequently pumps and spreads its tail. *Juveniles:* browner upperparts; yellowish underparts; faint buff wing bars.
Size: *L* 16–19 cm.
Status: fairly common; early April to mid-September.
Habitat: open deciduous woodlands, riparian woods and forest edges; usually near a source of water and often near bridges or buildings.
Nesting: under the ledge of a building, culvert, bridge or cliff; often in an abandoned Barn Swallow nest; bulky nest of moss, grass, rootlets, fur and feathers is often attached with mud to a ledge;

female incubates 4–8 white eggs for 16 days; has 2 broods per year.
Feeding: flycatches flying beetles, flies, wasps, grasshoppers, mayflies and other insects; may eat some frogs and tiny fish.
Voice: hearty, snappy *phoe-be* or *fee-bee* (2nd note alternates from higher to lower than the first); call is a sharp *chip*.
Similar Species: *Eastern Wood-Pewee* and *Western Wood-Pewee:* pale wing bars; bicoloured bill; do not wag their tail. *Olive-sided Flycatcher* (p. 94): dark sides form an open 'vest'; 2 white, fluffy rump patches. *Empidonax flycatchers* (p. 95): most have an eye ring and conspicuous wing bars. *Eastern Kingbird* (p. 98): white-tipped tail; blackish upperparts.
Best Sites: Whiteshell PP; Interlake area; Hecla/Grindstone PP; Riding Mountain NP; Duck Mountain PP.

WESTERN KINGBIRD

Tyrannus verticalis

When Ernest Thompson Seton wrote *Birds of Manitoba* in 1891, the Western Kingbird was not even mentioned, presumably because it was absent from the province. Today, the Western Kingbird is relatively common in Manitoba, especially among farm shelterbelts and in towns in southwestern parts of the province. • The Western Kingbird's bickering call and aggressive nature make it a difficult bird to miss. Once you have witnessed its brave attacks on much larger birds, such as crows and hawks, it is easy to understand why this brawler was awarded the name 'kingbird.' In some instances, Western Kingbirds will even dive-bomb housecats that approach too closely to their nest. • Western Kingbirds are adept at catching insects in mid-air, and they are commonly seen surveying for prey from fenceposts, powerlines and utility poles. • The tumbling aerial courtship display of the Western Kingbird is a good sign that this bird might be nesting nearby. Twisting and turning, the male rises up into the sky, stalls and then plummets back to earth.

ID: grey head and breast; dark grey eye line; thin, orange-red crown (rarely seen); white chin; black bill; yellow belly and undertail coverts; ashy grey upperparts; darker wings and tail; white outer tail feathers.
Size: *L* 20–23 cm.
Status: uncommon and local in central parts; common in the south; early May to early September.
Habitat: riparian woodlands, towns, farm shelterbelts and open scrubland areas with scattered patches of brush or hedgerows.
Nesting: in a deciduous tree near the trunk; often on a barn ledge, tower, utility pole or in a nest box; bulky cup nest of grass, weeds, wool and twigs is lined with fur, plant down and feathers; female incubates 3–7 whitish, heavily blotched eggs for 14 days.
Feeding: flycatches for aerial insects, including bees, wasps, butterflies, moths, grasshoppers and flies; occasionally eats berries.
Voice: chatty, bickering calls: *whit-ker-whit*, a short *kit* or extended *kit-kit-keetle-dot*.
Similar Species: *Eastern Kingbird* (p. 98): black upperparts; white underparts; white-tipped tail. *Great Crested Flycatcher:* slightly crested head; reddish-brown tail and wings; faint wing bars; lacks the white outer tail feathers.
Best Sites: Birds Hill PP; Interlake area; Delta Marsh; Lyleton; Poverty Plains; towns and farms throughout SW Manitoba.

97

EASTERN KINGBIRD

Tyrannus tyrannus

The Eastern Kingbird is sometimes referred to as the 'Jekyll and Hyde bird,' because it is a gregarious fruit eater while wintering in South America and an antisocial, aggressive insect-eater while nesting in Canada. Its tyrant nature is reflected in its scientific name, *Tyrannus tyrannus*, and it is the boldest of brawlers, often fearlessly attacking crows, hawks and even humans that pass through its nesting territory. Intruders may be vigorously pursued, pecked and plucked for some distance, until the kingbird is satisfied that there is no further threat. It is not uncommon to see an Eastern Kingbird chase a soaring hawk and pull feathers from its head! • The kingbird's fluttery courtship flight, which is characterized by short, quivering wingbeats belies the gentle side of this bird's personality. • In courtship displays, males tumble and hover, often revealing their red crown patch and white tail band.

ID: dark grey to blackish upperparts; white underparts; white-tipped tail; black bill; thin orange-red crown (rarely seen); no eye ring; black legs; quivering flight style.

Size: *L* 20–23 cm.

Status: occasional to rare in the north; fairly common in central parts; abundant in the south; early May to early September.

Habitat: rural fields with scattered shrubs, trees or hedgerows, forest fringes, clearings, shrubby roadsides, towns and farmyards.

Nesting: on a horizontal limb of an isolated tree; rarely in cavities, on stumps, artificial structures or fenceposts; cup nest of weeds, twigs, string, wool and grass is lined with soft materials; female incubates 3–5 darkly blotched, white to pinkish-white eggs for up to 14 days.

Feeding: flycatches aerial insects; infrequently eats berries.

Voice: call is a quick, loud, chattering *kit-kit-kitter-kitter*; also a buzzy *dzee-dzee-dzee*; also a nasal *dzeep*.

Similar Species: *Tree Swallow* (p. 109): iridescent dark blue or green back; lacks the white-tipped tail; smaller and more streamlined; smaller bill. *Olive-sided Flycatcher* (p. 94): lacks the white-tipped tail; dark sides form an open 'vest'; 2 white rump tufts. *Eastern Wood-Pewee* and *Western Wood-Pewee:* smaller; bicoloured bill; lack the white-tipped tail; underparts are not all white.

Best Sites: along powerlines and fencerows in rural areas and near farms and towns.

NORTHERN SHRIKE

Lanius excubitor

Each fall, Northern Shrikes retreat from their taiga nesting grounds in northern Manitoba to replace southbound Loggerhead Shrikes in southern parts of our province. The fact that the Northern Shrike is a winter species, while the Loggerhead Shrike is here in summer, makes distinguishing between these similar birds less onerous for the average birder. • The Northern Shrike looks like a raptor, but it is actually a songbird. Although it lacks powerful talons, it has a strong, hooked bill which it uses to catch insects, small birds and mammals. Males display their hunting competence to females by impaling their prey on thorns or barbed wire (this behaviour may also serve as a means of storing excess food). It is this habit that has earned the Northern Shrike the nickname 'butcher bird.' • Winter feeding stations tempt many a shrike to test its hunting skills. These birds are owed respect for their hunting prowess, but people with backyard winter feeders often get annoyed when the shrikes scare away neighbourhood birds.

ID: black tail with white outer feathers; black wings with white spots; bluish-grey upperparts; fine grey barring on the light underparts; black mask through the eyes; hooked bill. *In flight:* white wing patches; white-edged tail. *Immature:* faint brownish mask; pale brownish-grey upperparts; heavier, brownish barring on the underparts.
Size: *L* 25 cm.
Status: uncommon in the north; May to September; uncommon and erratic; mid-October to mid-April.
Habitat: *Nesting:* sparse mixed and coniferous woodlands, taiga, scrub and muskeg near treeline. *Non-nesting:* open country, farmyards, towns and roadsides.
Nesting: in a spruce tree or shrub; loose, bulky nest of twigs, shredded bark, grass and moss is lined with feathers and hair; female incubates 4–8 greyish eggs for about 16 days.

Feeding: swoops down on prey from a perch or chases prey through the air; eats small birds, shrews, rodents and large insects; may eat some snakes and frogs.
Voice: usually silent; song is an odd series of harsh *sheks* and musical notes; also a long, grating laugh: *raa-raa-raa-raa*. *Male:* high-pitched, hiccuppy *hee-toodle-toodle-toodle* during summer.
Similar Species: *Loggerhead Shrike:* adult's mask extends above the bill onto the forehead; adult lacks the barring on the underparts; juvenile has a finely barred crown, back and underparts; absent in winter. *Northern Mockingbird:* slim, unhooked bill; no mask; slimmer overall; paler wings and tail; rare in Manitoba.
Best Sites: *Nesting:* Wapusk NP; Cape Churchill PP; Seal River. *Non-nesting:* Birds Hill PP; Spruce Woods PP.

WARBLING VIREO

Vireo gilvus

The Warbling Vireo is a gifted singer named for its oscillating, warbled song. Beginning in May, its bubbly tune can be heard wherever there are open deciduous woodlands. Some male vireos are so persistent that they will continue to sing through the midday heat, and they may even repeat their melody while they perform their incubation duties. • Lacking any flashy field marks, this bird is difficult to spot as it moves through the dense upper foliage of trees and shrubs. Its hanging nest is even harder to find than the bird itself. In winter, however, nests are revealed as they swing precariously from bare deciduous branches. • This bird's song lacks the pauses that are distinctive in other vireos, and it prefers smaller woodlands than its relatives.

breeding

ID: partial greyish eye line bordering the white eyebrow; no wing bars; olive grey upperparts; pale yellowish-buff flanks; white underparts; brown eyes; grey crown. *Immature:* more yellow in the flanks.
Size: *L* 12.5–15.5 cm.
Status: fairly common in central parts; common to abundant in the south; mid-May to early September.
Habitat: open deciduous and riparian woodlands, urban parks and gardens, wooded coulees, shelterbelts and forest fragments.
Nesting: in a fork of a deciduous tree or shrub; nest is a hanging cup of grass, roots, plant down, spider silk and a few feathers; pair incubates 3–5 darkly specked white eggs for 12 days.

Feeding: gleans foliage for insects; occasionally hovers for invertebrates; eats some fruit.
Voice: oscillating, musical warble of slurred whistles (like the Purple Finch's song, but less spirited and always ending on a high note); call note is a querulous *twee*.
Similar Species: *Philadelphia Vireo:* yellow breast, sides and flanks; full, dark eye line bordering the white eyebrow. *Red-eyed Vireo* (p. 101): black eye line extends to the bill; blue-grey crown contrasts with the olive back; red eyes. *Tennessee Warbler* (p. 127): blue-grey cap contrasts against the olive green back; complete eye line; slimmer bill. *Blue-headed Vireo:* 2 wing bars; bold, white eye ring.
Best Sites: Assiniboine Park; Oak Hammock Marsh; Grand Beach PP; Delta Marsh; Spruce Woods PP; Turtle Mountain PP.

RED-EYED VIREO

Vireo olivaceus

The Red-eyed Vireo is Manitoba's undisputed champion of vocal endurance. In spring and early summer, males sing continuously through the day until long after most songbirds have curtailed their courtship melodies. One particularly vigorous Red-eyed Vireo, although not from Manitoba, holds the current world record for the most songs delivered by an individual bird in a single day: 22,197! • Red-eyed Vireos sound a lot like American Robins, and you might be surprised to discover this vireo hiding behind a 'familiar' song right in front of your eyes. When learning these birds' calls, you should remember that Red-eyed Vireos are not commonly heard in our province until mid-May (robins arrive here as early as mid-March). • Red-eyed vireos are common throughout much of Manitoba, but you might still have to search to find one. They are difficult to spot because they blend in well with their leafy background and move slowly among the upper forest canopy. If you are lucky enough to spot one, you will probably notice that, when perched, it is more hunched over than other songbirds (a little like a gargoyle), and it hops along branches with its body diagonal to its direction of travel.

breeding

ID: dark eye line; white eyebrow; black-bordered blue-grey crown; olive green back and wings; pale grey cheeks; white to pale grey underparts; may have a yellow wash on the sides, flanks and undertail coverts, especially in fall; no wing bars; adults have red eyes.
Size: *L* 14–16 cm.
Status: common to abundant; mid-May to early September.
Habitat: pure or mixed deciduous groves and forests, especially those of aspen poplar; well-treed yards and towns; prefers a semi-open canopy and shrubby understorey.
Nesting: in the fork of a tree or shrub; nest is a hanging, basket-like cup of grass, rootlets, shredded bark, spider silk and lichen; female incubates 3–5 dark-spotted, white eggs for 11–14 days.

Feeding: gleans foliage for insects, especially caterpillars; also hovers; rarely eats snails and berries.
Voice: song is a continuous, robin-like run of phrases, with pauses in-between: *Look-up way-up tree-top see-me here-I-am*; call note is a nasal, whining *chway*.
Similar Species: *Philadelphia Vireo:* yellow breast; lacks the black border to the blue-grey cap; song is very similar (slightly higher pitched). *Warbling Vireo* (p. 100): incomplete, faint eye line; lacks the contrast between the cap and the back. *Tennessee Warbler* (p. 127): blue-grey cap and nape; white eyebrow; olive green back; slimmer bill; dark eyes.
Best Sites: Whiteshell PP; Assiniboine Park; Hecla/Grindstone PP; Delta Marsh; Turtle Mountain PP; Riding Mountain NP.

GRAY JAY

Perisoreus canadensis

Few birds rival the mischievous Gray Jay for curiosity and boldness. Attracted by any foreign sound or potential feeding opportunity, small family groups glide gently and unexpectedly out of conifer woods. Campgrounds and picnic areas throughout Manitoba's northern shield country are the easiest places to find these curious birds. • In preparation for winter, Gray Jays often cache food. Their specialized salivary glands coat the food with a sticky mucous helping to preserve it. • Gray Jays nest earlier than any other Manitoba songbird. They lay their eggs in late February, and it is not unusual to see fledged young before the last of the winter snow has melted. • The Gray Jay has some interesting alternate names: 'Canada Jay,' 'Whiskey Jack' and 'Camp Robber.'

ID: fluffy, pale grey undersides; dark grey upperparts; white crown, forehead, cheek, throat and undertail coverts; dark grey nape; fairly long tail; dark bill. *Immature:* dark sooty grey overall; white whisker line is distinctive. *In flight:* flap-and-glide flyer.
Size: *L* 25–33 cm.
Status: uncommon in the north; common in central parts; rare and local in the south; year-round.
Habitat: coniferous and mixed forests, bogs, townsites, picnic sites and campgrounds.
Nesting: usually in a conifer; bulky, well-woven nest of plant fibres, roots, moss and twigs is lined with feathers, hair and fur;

female incubates 3–5 brown-spotted, pale green eggs for 17 days.
Feeding: diet includes insects, fruit, seeds, fungi, eggs, nestlings and carrion; stores food at scattered cache sites.
Voice: complex vocal repertoire includes a soft, whistled *quee-oo*, a chuckled *cla-cla-cla* and a *churr*; also imitates other birds.
Similar Species: *Northern Shrike* (p. 99) and *Loggerhead Shrike:* black mask; black and white wings and tail; hooked bill. *Northern Mockingbird:* white wing patch and outer tail feathers; longer, slimmer bill; rare in Manitoba.
Best Sites: Whiteshell PP; Hecla/Grindstone PP; Riding Mountain NP; Grass River PP; Duck Mountain PP; Churchill.

BLUE JAY
Cyanocitta cristata

The large coniferous trees and fruit-bearing shrubs of Manitoba's suburban neighbourhoods and rural communities seem particularly appealing to the remarkable Blue Jay. This adaptable bird is common wherever plants bear fruit and backyard feeding stations are maintained with a generous supply of sunflower seeds and peanuts. • Whether on its own or gathered in a mob, the Blue Jay will rarely hesitate to drive away smaller birds and squirrels from winter feeders. It seems there is no predator, not even the Great Horned Owl, that is too formidable for this bird to cajole or harass. Conversely, a pair of nesting Blue Jays are so quiet and secretive that they will go unnoticed by all but the most observant of birdwatchers. • The Blue Jay embodies all the admirable traits and aggressive qualities of the corvid family, which includes the magpie, crow and raven. Although it is beautiful and resourceful, its noisy vocalizations and bossy nature has resulted in a love-hate relationship between this bird and its human neighbours.

ID: blue crest; black 'necklace,' bill and eye line; white face; blue upperparts; white to dull grey underparts; white wing bar; white corners on the blue tail.
Size: *L* 28–32 cm.
Status: common; year-round; often transient in winter.
Habitat: open deciduous and mixed woodlands, scrubby fields, suburban and urban parks and backyards.
Nesting: usually in a conifer; bulky nest of twigs, bark, cloth and moss is lined with mud and fine rootlets; pair incubates 4–7 spotted, pale bluish-green eggs for 18 days.

Feeding: diet includes insects, nuts, seeds, berries, carrion, eggs and nestlings; frequents feeders for nuts, suet, sunflower seeds and table scraps.
Voice: noisy, screaming *jay-jay-jay* or *jeeah*; nasal *queedle queedle queedle-queedle* sounds a little like a muted trumpet; often imitates various sounds, including the call of some hawks.
Similar Species: *Belted Kingfisher* (p. 87): duller blue upperparts; much larger bill; tousled crest; completely different behaviour.
Best Sites: Whiteshell PP; Assiniboine Park; Birds Hill PP; Spruce Woods PP; Turtle Mountain PP; Riding Mountain NP.

BLACK-BILLED MAGPIE

Pica hudsonia

Black-billed Magpies are year-round residents throughout much of southern Manitoba, and it is hard to imagine our province without them. Magpies withdrew from Manitoba during the time of the great bison slaughters, but they soon returned to recolonize southern parts of the province, cleverly adapting to life in urban areas. By the 1930s, the magpie population had grown to the point where the birds were despised by humans—their incessant chatter, grating calls and penchant for robbing eggs and young hatchlings made them unpopular birds. Contests were held and bounties were offered to encourage their extermination. Fortunately, these adaptable birds persevered, and many people now recognize the valuable role they play in consuming large numbers of grasshoppers, grubs and other harmful insects. • The Black-billed Magpie is one of the most exceptional architects among our birds. Its elaborate, domed nest is constructed of sticks and held together with mud; the nest is so well built that abandoned sites remain in trees for years, often serving as nest sites for non-builders, such as Great Horned Owls.

ID: colourful iridescent wings and very long tail may appear black; black head, breast, back and undertail coverts; white belly; large, black bill. *In flight:* rounded, black and white wings.
Size: *L* 46–56 cm.
Status: fairly common to common; year-round.
Habitat: farmyards, hedgerows and open tree and shrub groves, often near human habitations.
Nesting: often colonial; in a tree or tall shrub; domed stick and twig nest, often with a mud or manure base, is lined with mud, grass, rootlets and hair; female incubates 5–13 spotted, greenish-grey eggs for up to 24 days.
Feeding: omnivorous; forages for insects, carrion, human food-waste, nuts, seeds and berries; picks insects and ticks off livestock and deer; occasionally takes the eggs and nestlings of other birds.
Voice: loud, nasal, frequently repeated *yeck-yeck-yeck* or *wah-wah-wah-wah*; also a nasal *maag* or *aag-aag*; many other vocalizations include a repertoire of 'soft talk.'
Similar Species: none.
Best Sites: Pinawa area; Interlake area; Crane River; Poverty Plains; Broomhill WMA.

AMERICAN CROW

Corvus brachyrhynchos

The American Crow is one of Manitoba's most common birds, and it is also among the most unpopular. It has developed a taste for agricultural crops, and it is maligned for its occasional habit of preying on the eggs and young of other birds. Its wary nature and intelligence, however, have enabled it to flourish in spite of considerable human efforts, over many generations, to reduce its numbers. Crows are generalists, and much of their strength lies in their ability to adapt to a variety of habitats, food types and changing environmental conditions. • In fall, most crows group together in flocks numbering in the hundreds or thousands. These thrilling aggregations, known as 'murders,' migrate southward to the U.S. for winter. On any given winter night, thousands of noisy crows may converge at a communal roosting site. • The American Crow's scientific name, *Corvus brachyrhynchos*, despite sounding cumbersome, is Latin for 'raven with the small nose.'

ID: all-black body may show a slight purplish iridescence; black bill and legs; fan-shaped tail; sleek head and throat. *In flight:* rarely glides.

Size: *L* 43–53 cm; *W* 94 cm.

Status: uncommon in the north; common in the central boreal forest; abundant in the south; early March to mid-October; a few may be present in winter.

Habitat: open woodlands, hedgerows and farm shelterbelts, riparian woodlands, urban parks and shrubby clumps in open areas.

Nesting: in a coniferous or deciduous tree or shrub; medium-sized stick nest is lined with bark,

rootlets, fur and soft plant materials; female incubates 4–9 brownish-blotched, blue-green eggs for about 18 days.

Feeding: very opportunistic; feeds on carrion, small rodents, reptiles, amphibians, berries, seeds, human food-waste, invertebrates and the eggs and nestlings of other birds.

Voice: distinctive, far-carrying *caw-caw-caw*.

Similar Species: *Common Raven* (p. 106): larger; wedge-shaped tail; shaggy throat; much heavier bill; often glides in flight.

Best Sites: Whiteshell PP; Assiniboine Park; Birds Hill PP; Spruce Woods PP; Turtle Mountain PP; Riding Mountain NP; Churchill.

COMMON RAVEN

Corvus corax

Whether stealing food from a flock of gulls, harassing a soaring hawk in mid-air, dining from a roadside carcass or strutting confidently around a campground, the raven is worthy of its reputation as a bold and clever bird. Glorified in native cultures across the Northern Hemisphere, the Common Raven does not by instinct alone. Whether it is performing complex vocalizations or playfully sliding down a snowbank, this bird exhibits behaviours that many people think of as exclusively human. • Breeding ravens form and maintain loyal, lifelong pair bonds, enduring everything from harsh weather and food scarcity to the raising of young. • When bison roamed the prairies, Common Ravens were year-round residents in southern Manitoba. Their numbers declined with the slaughter of the great bison herds, but there have been recent reports that these birds have recolonized parts of their former range. • Common Ravens have adapted well to urbanization, and they are frequent visitors to local garbage dumps.

ID: all-black plumage may show a slight purplish iridescence; heavy, black bill; shaggy throat; rounded wings. *In flight:* often glides; wedge-shaped tail.

Size: *L* 61 cm; *W* 1.3 m.

Status: fairly common to common; year-round; common in the south; November to April.

Habitat: coniferous and mixed forests and woodlands, tundra, townsites, campgrounds and landfills; often forages at dumps and along roadways.

Nesting: on steep cliffs, ledges, bluffs, tall coniferous trees and utility poles; large stick nest is lined with bark, grass, fur, hair and soft

plant materials; female incubates 4–7 brown-blotched, greenish eggs for about 21 days.

Feeding: very opportunistic; feeds on carrion, small mammals, reptiles and amphibians, the eggs and nestlings of other birds, berries, invertebrates and human food-waste.

Voice: deep, guttural, far-carrying, repetitive *craww-craww* or *quork quork*; also a croaking *cr-r-ruck* or *prruk* and a metallic *tok*; many other vocalizations.

Similar Species: *American Crow* (p. 105): smaller; fan-shaped tail; slim throat; slimmer bill; rarely glides in flight; call is higher pitched and less variable.

Best Sites: Nopiming PP; Hecla/Grindstone PP; Interlake area; Crane River; Riding Mountain NP; Duck Mountain PP; Churchill.

HORNED LARK

Eremophila alpestris

The tinkling sounds of Horned Larks flying overhead are a sure sign that spring has arrived. Small flocks make their appearances along roadsides in southwestern Manitoba as early as February, and many of the birds continue north toward the Arctic. • The Horned Lark is one of the first birds to usher in the new day, and it is one of the last songsters to be silenced by nightfall. • Horned Larks usually begin nesting before the spring melt and before farmers begin work in their fields. Zero-tillage practices are helping to increase nesting success for these and other ground-nesting birds. • During the nesting season, male larks spend a great deal of time circling above their territory and singing from great heights. The displaying males fly and glide in circles before plummeting to the ground in dramatic, high-speed dives. While on the ground, Horned Larks tend to walk rather than hop.

ID: small, black 'horns' (not always evident); black line extends from the eye to the cheek; light yellow to white face; black breast band; dull brown upperparts; dark tail with white outer tail feathers. *Female* and *Immature:* less distinctive head patterning; duller plumage overall. *In flight:* pale underparts; white outer tail features are obvious.
Size: *L* 18 cm.
Status: uncommon in the central boreal forest; common to abundant in the north and south; mid-February to mid-November; rare to locally common and erratic; October to April.
Habitat: open areas, including pastures, native prairie, cultivated or sparsely vegetated fields, golf courses, airfields and tundra.
Nesting: on the ground; in a shallow scrape among short, sparse vegetation, often beside a rock or dry cow dung; nest is lined with grass, plant fibres and fine roots; female incubates 3–5 pale grey to greenish eggs, blotched and spotted with brown, for about 12 days; often has 2 broods per year.
Feeding: gleans the ground for seeds and insects.
Voice: call note is a tinkling *tsee-titi* or *zoot*; flight song (sometimes given from the ground) is a long series of irregular, tinkling chimes *trick trick trick trick trick t-r-r-r-r-r-r-r.*
Similar Species: *Sparrows* (pp. 138–44), *Longspurs* (p. 146), *American Pipit* and *Sprague's Pipit:* all lack the 'horns,' the distinctive facial pattern and the solid black breast band.
Best Sites: Oak Hammock Marsh; Delta Marsh; Poverty Plains; Churchill; Wapusk NP.

PURPLE MARTIN

Progne subis

At scattered localities throughout parts of Manitoba, Purple Martins attempt to hold their ground against pushy European Starlings and House Sparrows. Purple Martins once nested in natural tree hollows and on cliff ledges, but nest-site usurpation and the loss of snags through logging has diminished their numbers. Today, most Purple Martins nest in modern apartment-style martin complexes or 'condos.' To be successful in attracting these large swallows to your backyard, martin condos should be placed high on a pole in a large, open area, preferably near water. The complexes must be designed with perfectly sized cavity openings, and they must be cleaned out each winter. Over winter, the cavity openings should also be covered to prevent House Sparrows or starlings from moving in.

ID: large, bluish-black swallow; glossy upperparts; slightly forked tail; pointed wings; small bill. *Male:* the only swallow with dark underparts. *Female:* sooty grey underparts. *In flight:* alternates quick flaps with swooping glides; often spreads its tail.

Size: *L* 18–20 cm.

Status: fairly common; late April to mid-September.

Habitat: attracted to martin condos in towns, farmyards and semi-open areas, often near water.

Nesting: colonial; usually in a human-made, apartment-style birdhouse; rarely in tree cavities or on cliff ledges; nest materials include feathers, grass, mud and vegetation; female incubates 4–8 unmarked, white eggs for 15–17 days.

Feeding: mostly while in flight; usually eats flies, ants, dragonflies, mosquitoes and other flying insects; may also walk on the ground, taking insects and rarely berries.

Voice: rich, fluty *pew-pew* or *tchew-wew*; gurgling song is often heard in flight.

Similar Species: *European Starling* (p. 125): longer bill (yellow in summer); lacks the forked tail. *Barn Swallow* (p. 111): deeply forked tail; buff underparts. *Tree Swallow* (p. 109): smaller; white underparts.

Best Sites: Whiteshell PP; Hecla/Grindstone PP; Interlake area; Turtle Mountain PP; Neepawa.

TREE SWALLOW

Tachycineta bicolor

Nesting pairs of Tree Swallows are often seen perched along rural fencelines adorned with bluebird nest boxes. Although these swallows are generally not the intended occupants of the bluebird nest boxes, they nevertheless prove to be delightful tenants. When conditions are favourable, these busy birds return to their nest site and feed their young up to 20 times an hour, which provides observers with plenty of opportunity to watch and photograph the birds in action. • Unlike other North American swallows, female Tree Swallows do not acquire their full adult plumage until their second or third year. • The scientific name *bicolour* is Latin for 'two colours,' in reference to the contrast between the bird's dark upperparts and light underparts. In fall, their upperparts often take on a greenish look.

ID: iridescent bluish-black upperparts; white underparts; small bill; long, pointed wings; shallowly forked tail. *Female:* slightly duller. *Fall adult:* iridescent green upperparts. *Immature:* dusky brown upperparts; white underparts (may show a pale brown wash on the breast).

Size: *L* 14 cm.

Status: uncommon in the north; common in the central boreal forest; abundant in the south; mid-April to mid-September.

Habitat: open areas, fencelines with bluebird nest boxes and fringes of open woodlands, especially near water.

Nesting: in a tree cavity or nest box lined with weeds, grass and feathers; female incubates 4–7 pale pink to white eggs for up to 19 days.

Feeding: catches flies, midges, mosquitoes, beetles and ants on the wing; also takes emergent flying insects over water; may eat some berries and seeds.

Voice: alarm call is a metallic, buzzy *klweet* or *chi-veet;* song is a liquid, chattering twitter: *weet, trit, weet.*

Similar Species: *Purple Martin* (p. 108): female has sooty grey underparts; male is dark overall. *Eastern Kingbird* (p. 98): larger; white-tipped tail; larger bill; dark grey to blackish upperparts. *Bank Swallow:* brown upperparts; brown breast band. *Northern Rough-winged Swallow:* brown upperparts; pale brown wash on the throat and upper breast. *Barn Swallow* (p. 111): buff underparts; deeply forked tail.

Best Sites: Birds Hill PP; Oak Hammock Marsh; Hecla/Grindstone PP; Turtle Mountain PP; Riding Mountain NP; Churchill.

CLIFF SWALLOW

Petrochelidon pyrrhonota

Cliff Swallows once nested on cliffs and riverbanks, but now they seem comfortable nesting under bridges and the eaves of buildings. If the Cliff Swallow were to be renamed in the 21st century, it would probably be called the 'Bridge Swallow,' because so many river bridges in North America have a colony of Cliff Swallows nesting under them. If you stop to inspect the underside of a bridge, you might see hundreds of gourd-shaped mud nests stuck to the pillars and structural beams. • Master mud masons, Cliff Swallows roll mud into balls with their bills and press the pellets together to form their characteristic nests. The nests may be reused, but colony sites are often alternated to avoid infestations of invertebrate nest parasites. • Cliff Swallows are occasional brood parasites—females often lay one or more eggs in the temporarily vacant nests of neighbouring birds. Upon returning to a parasitized nest, adults accept the foreign eggs and tend to them as though they were their own. • Cliff Swallows are easily recognized by their distinctive flight style: they twist and turn through the air, then plummet downward, ending the dive with an abrupt climb.

ID: buff rump patch and forehead; dark chestnut cheek and throat; blue-grey cap and shoulders; white belly. *In flight:* squarish tail; dark spots on the white undertail coverts. *Immature:* brown-buff head, throat and breast.

Size: *L* 14 cm.

Status: common to locally abundant; mid-April to early September.

Habitat: steep riverbanks, cliffs, bridges, buildings, culverts, tunnels, dams and steep road cuts; almost always near water.

Nesting: usually colonial; nests under bridges, on cliffs, buildings and other artificial structures; gourd-shaped mud nest, with a small opening on the side, is lined with grass and feathers; pair incubates 3–6 brown-spotted, white to pinkish eggs for up to 16 days.

Feeding: drinks and catches flying insects on the wing; may eat some berries.

Voice: twittering chatter *churrr-churrr* or *zayrp*; also a *nyew* or *keer* alarm call.

Similar Species: *Barn Swallow* (p. 111): deeply forked tail; dark rump; rust-coloured underparts and forehead. *Tree* (p. 109), *Bank* and *Northern Rough-winged swallows:* all lack the buff forehead and the rump patch.

Best Sites: widespread near bridges; Whiteshell PP; Assiniboine Park; Hecla/Grindstone PP; Delta Marsh; Souris River Bend WMA.

BARN SWALLOW

Hirundo rustica

In the late 19th century when Ernest Thompson Seton wrote *Birds of Manitoba*, the Barn Swallow was listed as a very rare bird in our province. It has since found tremendous success here, and in other parts of North America, through an affiliation with human beings. These birds were once cliff nesters, but their cup-shaped mud nests are now found in the ceiling rafters of abandoned buildings and barns. These sites provide protection from predators and shelter from rainfall, which could easily wash away a swallow's mud nest. Barn Swallows have even been known to nest on ferries and farm machinery. Unfortunately, not everyone appreciates nesting Barn Swallows. The young can be very messy, and the nests are often scraped off buildings just as the nesting season has begun. However, these graceful birds are pest controllers, and by tearing down a swallow nest, humans miss the opportunity to observe the normally secretive reproductive cycle of birds.

ID: long, deeply forked tail; dark chestnut throat and forehead; buff-coloured underparts; bluish-black upperparts. *Female* and *Immature:* duller underparts; tail is less forked.
Size: *L* 18 cm.
Status: rare in the north; common in central parts; abundant in the south; late April to early October.
Habitat: farmyards and townsites, especially where buildings are found near water.
Nesting: singly or in loose colonies; on a building under an overhang, under a bridge or in a culvert; often in an abandoned building; half-cup nest is made of mud and is lined with grass and feathers; pair incubates 4–7 spotted, white eggs for 12–17 days; has 2 or more broods per year.
Feeding: catches flying insects on the wing; rarely eats berries; often drinks and bathes on the wing.
Voice: continuous twittering chatter: *zip-zip-zip*; also *kvick-kvick*.
Similar Species: *Cliff Swallow* (p. 110): squared tail; buff rump and forehead; light-coloured underparts. *Purple Martin* (p. 108): shallowly forked tail; male is blue-black overall; female has sooty grey underparts. *Tree Swallow* (p. 109): clean white underparts; notched tail.
Best Sites: Birds Hill PP; Oak Hammock Marsh; Hecla/Grindstone PP; Lake Francis; Turtle Mountain PP; Riding Mountain NP.

BLACK-CAPPED CHICKADEE
Poecile atricapillus

This chickadee's cheerful call and curious disposition make it a favourite guest at any backyard birdfeeder and welcome company during a brisk morning walk. During winter, Black-capped Chickadees frequent well-stocked seed and suet feeders and can occasionally be enticed to land on an outstretched hand to grab a sunflower seed. • In winter, chickadees must work almost constantly to keep their metabolic fires stoked. It is estimated that on a −40° day, a chickadee spends about 20 times longer feeding than on a typical summer day. • If you want to attract small wintering birds to your backyard feeder, you must feed them through winter and early spring; the birds that depend on your offerings could starve during cold weather if food is suddenly unavailable. • In late summer and early fall, family groups of chickadees often join the company of foraging mixed-species flocks that consist of warblers, vireos, kinglets, nuthatches, creepers and small woodpeckers. • Manitoba is also home to the Boreal Chickadee, a less common relative of the Black-capped Chickadee that resides in the northern boreal forest. It has a grey-brown cap and calls a soft, nasal, whistled *sick-a day day.*

ID: black cap and bib; white cheek; grey back; dark grey wing feathers are edged with white; white underparts; buff sides.
Size: *L* 13–15 cm.
Status: common; year-round.
Habitat: deciduous and mixed forests, riparian woodlands, wooded urban parks and wooded backyards with birdfeeders.
Nesting: in a natural cavity, abandoned woodpecker nest or nest box; may also excavate its own cavity; nest is lined with fur, feathers, moss and fine grass; female incubates 6–8 finely dotted, white eggs for up to 13 days.
Feeding: gleans vegetation, branches and the ground for small insects, spiders, seeds and berries; frequents seed and suet feeders in winter; also eats conifer seeds and invertebrate larvae and eggs.
Voice: call is a chipper, whistled *chick-a-dee-dee-dee*; song is a simple, whistled *swee-tee* or *fee-bee-ee*; as spring approaches its song may change to *'spring-is-here.'*
Similar Species: *Boreal Chickadee:* grey-brown cap and back; dusky cheeks; rich brown flanks; wing feathers lack the white edgings. *Blackpoll Warbler:* breeding male has a streaked back, 2 white wing bars and dark streaking on the flanks.
Best Sites: Whiteshell PP; Assiniboine Park; Birds Hill PP; Hecla/Grindstone PP; Delta Marsh; Turtle Mountain PP; Riding Mountain NP.

RED-BREASTED NUTHATCH

Sitta canadensis

Darting out from the cover of a coniferous tree, a Red-breasted Nuthatch makes a precise landing within reach of the neighbourhood birdfeeder. Rifling through the empty shells, the nuthatch selects the seed it wants, pivots 180° in a single, fluid motion, then retreats to eat the seed in private or stash it for later consumption. • In winter, nuthatches often forage with chickadees, creepers and woodpeckers; during migration, they often join bird waves that include warblers, vireos and kinglets. Within these flocks, the Red-breasted Nuthatch is set apart by its striped head, unusual body form, loud, nasal calls and habit of foraging headfirst down tree-trunks. • Red-breasted Nuthatches typically excavate their nests in conifer trees, and they have a tendency to smear the entrance of their nesting cavity with resin.

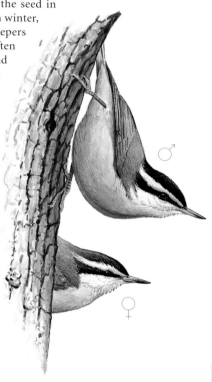

ID: rusty underparts; grey-blue upperparts; white eyebrow; black eye line; black cap; straight bill; short tail. *Female:* light rusty wash on the underparts; dark grey cap.

Size: *L* 11 cm.

Status: fairly common in the north and in central parts; April to October; uncommon to fairly common in the south; year-round; uncommon in the south; October to April.

Habitat: *Nesting:* coniferous forests and plantations and coniferous stands in mixed forests (prefers mature forest stands). *Non-nesting:* generally near coniferous stands, especially those with nearby birdfeeders.

Nesting: excavates a cavity in the trunk or branch of a rotting tree or shrub; rarely in an abandoned woodpecker cavity; cavity is lined with bark shreds, fine grass, fur and moss; female incubates 5–7 white eggs, spotted with reddish-brown, for up to 14 days.

Feeding: forages down tree-trunks; probes crevices and under loose bark for larval and adult invertebrates; eats pine and spruce seeds during winter; frequents seed and suet feeders.

Voice: sounds like the original toy tin horn; higher, slower and more nasal than the White-breasted Nuthatch's calls: *yank-yank-yank* or *rah-rah-rah-rah*; also a short *tsip*.

Similar Species: *White-breasted Nuthatch* (p. 114): larger; lacks the black eye line; white face and breast.

Best Sites: Whiteshell PP; Nopiming PP; Mars Hill WMA; Interlake area; Riding Mountain NP; Duck Mountain PP.

113

WHITE-BREASTED NUTHATCH

Sitta carolinensis

Nuthatches make their gravity-defying struts down tree-trunks look incredibly easy. Unlike woodpeckers and creepers, nuthatches do not use their tails to brace themselves against tree-trunks—they grasp the tree using foot power alone. • Nuthatches are regular visitors to winter feeders, and they are especially fond of beef suet, a delicacy that can be purchased at your local butcher shop. • Nuthatches have been known to use a sliver of wood as a tool to search for insects under loose bark. • Unlike its red-breasted relative, which regularly inhabits conifer woodlands, the White-breasted Nuthatch prefers mature deciduous stands. • According to recent breeding bird surveys, nuthatch numbers are on the rise throughout Canada and the U.S. • The scientific name *carolinensis* means 'of Carolina'—the first scientific specimen was collected in the Carolina Mountains of the eastern U.S.

ID: greyish-blue back; white face and underparts; rusty undertail coverts; short tail; straight bill; beady, black eyes. *Male:* black cap. *Female:* grey cap.

Size: *L* 15 cm.

Status: uncommon in central parts; fairly common in the south; year-round.

Habitat: mature deciduous woods, deciduous stands in mixed forests, riparian woods, open woodlots and backyards.

Nesting: in a natural cavity or an abandoned woodpecker nest; may use a nest box; cavity is lined with bark, grass, fur and feathers;

female incubates 5–10 white eggs, spotted with reddish-brown, for up to 14 days.

Feeding: forages down tree-trunks; probes crevices and loose bark for larval and adult invertebrates; also eats nuts and seeds; regularly visits seed and suet feeders.

Voice: song is a rapid series of similar notes *wer wer wer wer wer* or *whi whi whi whi*; calls include *ha-ha-ha ha-ha-ha, ank ank* and *ip*.

Similar Species: *Red-breasted Nuthatch* (p. 113): black eye line; rusty underparts; calls are higher and more nasal. *Black-capped Chickadee* (p. 112): black bib.

Best Sites: Whiteshell PP; Assiniboine Park; Delta Marsh; Turtle Mountain PP.

BROWN CREEPER

Certhia americana

The Brown Creeper is one Manitoba's most inconspicuous birds. Embracing old-growth forests during much of the year, it often goes unnoticed because it blends perfectly with the tree-trunks and tree limbs that it forages on. If a creeper is frightened, it will freeze or flatten itself against a tree-trunk, making it even tougher to see. The creeper is only detected until a flake of bark suddenly takes the shape of a bird. • In contrast to nuthatches, which forage down tree-trunks, the Brown Creeper works its way up. Its long, stiff tail feathers prop it up against vertical tree-trunks as it hitches its way skyward. When it reaches the upper branches, the creeper floats down to the base of a neighbouring tree to begin another foraging ascent. • Like nuthatches and chickadees, groups of creepers occasionally roost together in tree cavities—an activity that effectively reduces heat loss. • The creeper's call is similar to the high-pitched whistle of the Golden-crowned Kinglet, except that the creeper's *tseee* is typically issued as a single note. To further the confusion, the creeper's song often takes on the boisterous warbling quality of a wood-warbler song.

ID: brown back and cap are heavily streaked; white eyebrow stripe; long, downcurved bill; white underparts; long, pointed, rust-coloured tail feathers; rusty rump.

Size: *L* 13 cm.

Status: uncommon in the central boreal forest; year-round; rare to fairly common in the south; December to late March.

Habitat: *Nesting:* mature coniferous and mixed forests; favours wet areas and bogs with large, dead trees, especially pine. *Non-nesting:* may appear in deciduous stands, especially mature cottonwoods.

Nesting: under loose bark; hammock-like cup-nest of twigs, shredded bark, moss, fine grass and conifer needles is woven together with spider silk; female incubates 5–8 whitish eggs, with reddish-brown dots, for 15–17 days.

Feeding: spirals up tree-trunks to probe under loose bark for adult and larval invertebrates; eats some acorns and nuts.

Voice: song is a faint, high-pitched *trees-trees-trees see the trees*; call is a single, high *tseee* note (similar to the Golden-crowned Kinglet's call).

Similar Species: *Nuthatches* (pp. 113–14): grey-blue back; straight or slightly upturned bill. *Woodpeckers* (pp. 88–93): all are much larger, lack the brown back streaking and have a straight, heavy bill.

Best Sites: Whiteshell PP; Hecla/Grindstone PP; Riding Mountain NP; Duck Mountain PP.

HOUSE WREN

Troglodytes aedon

The House Wren's bubbly song and spirited disposition make it a welcome addition to any Manitoba neighbourhood. Its courtship rituals are a treat to watch—it sings its delightful tunes with its tail raised and wings quivering. • A small cavity in a standing dead tree or a custom-made nest box is usually all it takes to attract this joyful bird to most backyards. The cavity entrance is tiny, and the wren often finds it challenging to fit bulky twigs and grass through the small opening. Persistent males will often struggle for extended periods of time to place a desirable twig inside a nest. Don't despair if a nest box in your backyard is packed full of sticks and left abandoned without any nesting birds in sight. Wrens often build numerous nests, and a nesting pair might return to your backyard to raise a second brood later in the season. • House Wrens are extremely territorial, and they will often destroy the eggs of other wrens or songbirds nesting nearby.

ID: brown upperparts; fine, dark barring on the wings; 'cocked' tail is finely barred with black; sharp, slightly decurved bill; faint eyebrow stripe; pale eye ring; whitish throat; whitish to buff underparts; faintly barred flanks.
Size: L 12 cm.
Status: fairly common in central parts; common in the south; early May to mid-September.
Habitat: open thickets and shrubby edges of deciduous or mixed woodlands; often in shrubs and thickets near towns and farmyards.
Nesting: in a natural or artificial cavity; commonly uses wren or bluebird nest boxes; nest of twigs and grass is lined with feathers, fur and soft materials; female incubates 6–12 white eggs with heavy reddish-brown dotting, for up to 19 days; has 2 or 3 broods per year.
Feeding: gleans the ground and vegetation for insects, especially beetles, caterpillars, grasshoppers and spiders.
Voice: bubbly song lasts about 2–3 seconds, rising in a musical burst and falling at the end: *tsi-tsi-tsi-tsi oodle-oodle-oodle-oodle.*
Similar Species: *Winter Wren:* smaller; much darker overall; shorter, stubby tail; prominent dark barring on the flanks. *Sedge Wren:* heavily streaked on the crown and back; short tail. *Marsh Wren* (p. 117): bold, white eyebrow; black back with white streaks.
Best Sites: Pinawa area; St. Malo WMA; Assiniboine Park; Oak Hammock Marsh; Interlake area; Delta Marsh; Spruce Woods PP.

MARSH WREN

Cistothorus palustris

Fueled by newly emerged aquatic insects, the Marsh Wren zips about in short bursts through tall stands of cattails and bulrushes. This expert hunter catches flying insects with lightning speed, but don't expect to see this bird in action—the Marsh Wren is difficult to spot among its dense marshland habitat. Marsh Wrens are compulsive vocalists, however, and they typically sing atop conspicuous perches. • Marsh Wrens build numerous globe-shaped nests within their territory, but they will only choose one as an actual nesting site. The remaining decoy or 'dummy' nests are not wasted: they serve to divert predators from the real nest and as dormitories for later in the season. • Marsh Wrens occasionally destroy the nests and eggs of other Marsh Wrens and other marsh-nesting songbirds, such as the Red-winged Blackbird. The Red-winged Blackbird, however, is often prevented from doing the same, because the wren's globed nest keeps the wren eggs well hidden, and the 'dummy' nests divert the bird from the real nest.

ID: white underparts; dusky flanks; brown upperparts; unstreaked, dark crown; distinctive black triangle on the upper back and shoulder is streaked with white; bold, white eyebrow; long, thin, downcurved bill.
Size: *L* 13 cm.
Status: fairly common in central parts; common in the south; mid-May to mid-October.
Habitat: large cattail and bulrush marshes interspersed with open water; may use tall grass or sedge marshes.
Nesting: among tall emergent vegetation, usually up to 1 m above water; globe-like nest, woven with marsh reeds and grass, is lined with cattail down and feathers; female incubates 4–10 heavily dotted, pale brown eggs for 12–16 days; occasionally polygamous; usually has 2 broods per year.
Feeding: gleans vegetation and flycatches for adult aquatic invertebrates, especially dragonflies and damselflies.
Voice: rapid, rattling, warbled *cut-cut-turrrrrrr-ur* like an old sewing machine or rapid gunfire; call is a harsh *chek* or *tsuck*.
Similar Species: *Sedge Wren:* smaller; streaked crown; buff undertail; song is sweeter and subtler. *House Wren* (p. 116): faint eyebrow; lacks the white streaking and the black triangle on the back.
Best Sites: Oak Hammock Marsh; Hecla/Grindstone PP; Delta Marsh; Turtle Mountain PP; Oak/Plum lakes; Minnedosa pothole region.

GOLDEN-CROWNED KINGLET
Regulus satrapa

The Golden-crowned Kinglet is not much larger than a hummingbird, so it can be difficult to spot as it flutters among the upper canopy of mature conifers. The kinglet is the smallest songbird in North America, and because of its size and flitty behaviour, it was mistaken for a wren in the early days of ornithological study. • Like other small birds, kinglets spend an inordinate amount of time engaging in refueling exercises. As they forage, they use tree branches as swings and trapezes, occasionally flashing their regal crowns and constantly flicking their tiny wings. Kinglets also forage near ground level, often making headfirst descents down tree-trunks. • Their extremely high-pitched *tzee-tzee-tzee* calls are often muffled by neighbouring spruce boughs, but kinglets are continually on the move, so once they are heard, they can be spotted darting across open areas in the canopy. Kinglets have acquired a reputation of friendliness and approachability, and, on occasion, they have been known to allow themselves to be petted or even picked up by humans.

ID: olive back; dark wings and tail; light grey underparts; 2 white wing bars; black eye line; white eyebrow; brightly coloured crown is bordered with black; tiny bill; short tail. *Male:* reddish-orange crown bordered by yellow. *Female:* yellow crown.
Size: *L* 10 cm.
Status: fairly common in the central boreal forest; early April to mid-November; rare to fairly common in the south; late September to April.
Habitat: mixed and pure, mature coniferous forests, especially open stands dominated by spruce.
Nesting: usually high in a conifer; hanging nest of moss, lichens, spider silk and leaves is lined with hair and feathers; female incubates 5–11 variably spotted, white eggs for about 15 days; usually has 2 broods per year.
Feeding: gleans and hovers for insects, berries, seeds and occasionally sap.
Voice: song is a faint, high-pitched, accelerating *tsee-tsee-tsee-tsee, why do you shilly-shally?*; call is a very high-pitched *tsee tsee tsee.*
Similar Species: *Ruby-crowned Kinglet* (p. 119): bold, broken, white eye ring; lacks the black eye line and the black border to the crown. *Chickadees* (p. 112): lack the colourful crown and the olive-green coloration.
Best Sites: Nopiming PP; Atikaki PP; Riding Mountain NP; Duck Mountain PP; Grass River PP.

RUBY-CROWNED KINGLET

Regulus calendula

The boisterous, rolling song of the Ruby-crowned Kinglet is a familiar tune that resounds through Manitoba's boreal forest in May and June. At this time of year, the male kinglet displays his brilliant red crown to impress onlooking females. Throughout most of the year, however, his crown remains hidden among dull feathers and is impossible to see even through binoculars. • While in migration, Ruby-crowned Kinglets are regularly seen flitting about treetops, intermingling with a colourful assortment of warblers and vireos. They stop only briefly, however, moving quickly to their boreal nesting grounds or wintering grounds in the southern U.S., Central America or South America. • This bird might be mistaken for a Least Flycatcher, but the kinglet's frequent hovering techniques and energetic wing-flicking behaviour set it apart from look-alikes.

ID: bold, broken eye ring; 2 bold, white wing bars; dark patch below the lower wingbar; olive green upperparts; dark wings and tail; whitish to yellowish underparts; short tail; flicks its wings. *Male:* small, red crown (usually not seen). *Female:* lacks the red crown.
Size: *L* 10 cm.
Status: rare in the north; fairly common to common in central parts and in the south; early April to mid-October.
Habitat: mixed woodlands and pure coniferous forests, especially those dominated by spruce; often near forest openings and edges.
Nesting: usually in a conifer; hanging, globular nest of moss, lichens, twigs and leaves is lined with feathers, hair and plant down; female incubates 5–11 variably spotted, white eggs for up to 16 days.
Feeding: gleans and hovers for insects and spiders; rarely eats seeds and berries.
Voice: 3-part song is an accelerating and rising *tea-tea-tea tew-tew-tew look-at-Me, look-at-Me, look-at-Me;* call note is a husky *ji-dit.*
Similar Species: *Golden-crowned Kinglet* (p. 118): dark eye line; black border to the crown; male has an orange crown bordered by yellow; female has a yellow crown. *Orange-crowned Warbler:* olive yellow overall; no eye ring or wing bars. *Empidonax flycatchers* (p. 95): complete eye ring or no eye ring at all; larger bill; longer tail; lack the red crown.
Best Sites: Whiteshell PP; Hecla/Grindstone PP; Mantagao Lake WMA; Riding Mountain NP; Duck Mountain PP; Grass River PP.

119

EASTERN BLUEBIRD

Sialia sialis

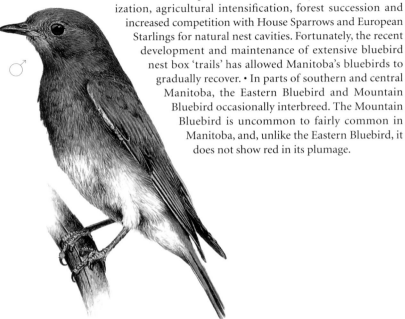

Perhaps no other bird is as cherished and admired in Manitoba's countrysides as the lovely Eastern Bluebird. Bluebirds were once more common in Manitoba, but their numbers declined in the latter part of the 20th century because of urbanization, agricultural intensification, forest succession and increased competition with House Sparrows and European Starlings for natural nest cavities. Fortunately, the recent development and maintenance of extensive bluebird nest box 'trails' has allowed Manitoba's bluebirds to gradually recover. • In parts of southern and central Manitoba, the Eastern Bluebird and Mountain Bluebird occasionally interbreed. The Mountain Bluebird is uncommon to fairly common in Manitoba, and, unlike the Eastern Bluebird, it does not show red in its plumage.

ID: rusty red throat, breast and sides; white belly and undertail coverts; dark bill and legs. *Male:* deep blue upperparts. *Female:* thin, white eye ring; greyish head and back are tinged with blue; bluish-grey wings and tail; paler rust colour on the underparts. *Immature:* greyish overall; hints of blue in the tail and wings; speckled breast.
Size: *L* 18 cm.
Status: uncommon; mid-April to mid-October.
Habitat: open country with scattered trees, fencelines, forest clearings and fringes, golf courses and cemeteries; often near bluebird nest boxes.

Nesting: in an abandoned woodpecker cavity, natural cavity or nest box; nest of grass, stems and twigs is lined with feathers and hair; female incubates 3–7 pale blue to white eggs for 12–16 days; usually has 2 broods per year.
Feeding: swoops from a perch and pursues flying insects; also forages on the ground for worms, snails, other invertebrates and berries.
Voice: song is gurgling *turr, turr-lee, turr-lee;* call is a chittering *pew.*
Similar Species: *Mountain Bluebird:* lacks the rusty red underparts; female has a pronounced eye ring.
Best Sites: rural areas with fenceline nest box 'trails'; Interlake area; Spruce Woods PP; Riding Mountain NP.

SWAINSON'S THRUSH

Catharus ustulatus

With every rising note, the flute-like, spiraling song of the Swainson's Thrush lifts the soul of each listener. This thrush is an integral part of the morning chorus, and its song is also heard at dusk—the Swainson's Thrush is routinely one the last of the forest songsters to be silenced by nightfall. • Although it is often found nesting in the same habitat as the similar-looking Hermit Thrush, the Swainson's Thrush is less dependent on coniferous forests and is more common along forest margins than in deep woods. • In migration, this bird skulks low on the ground under shrubs and tangles, occasionally finding itself in backyards and neighbourhood parks. Most thrushes feed on the ground, but the Swainson's Thrush is also adept at gleaning food from the airy heights of trees, sometimes hover-gleaning like a warbler or vireo. • The Veery, Gray-cheeked Thrush and Hermit Thrush are similar-looking, spot-breasted birds that can be seen in various parts of Manitoba throughout most of the year. • This thrush is named after William Swainson, an English zoologist and illustrator.

ID: grey-brown upperparts; noticeable buff eye ring; buff wash on the cheek and upper breast; triangular spots arranged in streaks on the throat and breast; white belly and undertail coverts; brownish-grey flanks.
Size: *L* 18 cm.
Status: occasional in the north; common in central parts and in the south; early May to late September.
Habitat: *Nesting:* dense understorey in coniferous and mixed boreal forest; prefers moist areas with spruce and fir. *In migration:* moist riparian areas and shrubby parks and gardens.
Nesting: usually a shrub or small tree; cup nest of weeds, grass, leaves, roots and lichens is lined with fur and soft fibres; female incubates 3–5 spotted, pale blue eggs for 12 or 13 days.
Feeding: gleans vegetation and forages on the ground for invertebrates; may hover-glean; also eats berries.
Voice: song is a slow, rolling, rising spiral: *Oh, Aurelia will-ya, will-ya will-yeee;* call is a sharp *wick*.
Similar Species: *Gray-cheeked Thrush:* lacks the conspicuous eye ring; greyish cheeks; less or no buff wash on the breast. *Hermit Thrush:* reddish tail and rump contrast against the greyish-brown back; darker breast spotting on a whiter breast. *Veery:* lacks the bold eye ring; more reddish upperparts; faint breast streaking.
Best Sites: Whiteshell PP; Nopiming PP; Hecla/Grindstone PP; Riding Mountain NP; Duck Mountain PP; Grass River PP.

AMERICAN ROBIN

Turdus migratorius

American Robins are fairly abundant in many of Manitoba's natural habitats, but they are familiar to most of us because they commonly inhabit residential lawns, gardens and parks. Of the birds most well-adapted to urban life, the American Robin is among the most well known. They are widely recognized as harbingers of spring, and when March rolls around Manitobans look forward to the arrival of the robins. • When hunting, robins appears as though they are listening for prey beneath a lawn, but they are actually looking for movements in the soil—they tilt their heads because their eyes face to the side. • Robins usually raise two broods per year. While the male cares for the fledged young from the first brood, the female incubates the second clutch. Young robins are easily distinguished from their parents by their dishevelled appearance and heavily spotted undersides. • Concerns in the 1950s regarding the effects of DDT were sparked by the negative effects this chemical had on the American Robin. According to recent breeding bird surveys, American Robin numbers are increasing significantly throughout North America.

ID: grey-brown back; dark head, tail and wings; white throat is streaked with black; white undertail coverts; incomplete, white eye ring; yellow, black-tipped bill. *Male:* deep brick red breast; darker head. *Female:* dark grey head; light brick red breast. *Juvenile:* heavily spotted, rusty breast.

Size: *L* 25 cm.

Status: fairly common in the north; common in the central boreal forest; abundant in the south; mid-March to mid-November; a few may be present in winter.

Habitat: *Nesting:* residential lawns, gardens, urban parks, woodlot edges and openings, burned areas, clear-cuts, bogs and fens. *Non-nesting:* near fruit-bearing trees.

Nesting: often in a coniferous tree or shrub; sometimes on a protected building ledge; well-built cup nest of grass, moss and loose bark is cemented with mud and grass; female incubates 4 light blue eggs for 11–16 days; usually has 2 broods per year.

Feeding: forages on the ground for larval and adult insects, earthworms, other invertebrates and berries.

Voice: song is a prolonged series of rising and falling phrases: *cheerily cheer-up cheerio;* call is a rapid *tut-tut-tut* or *tyeep.*

Similar Species: *Varied Thrush:* orange eye stripe and wing bars; dark breast band; accidental in Manitoba.

Best Sites: extremely widespread among residential lawns, gardens, city parks and woodlands.

GRAY CATBIRD

Dumetella carolinensis

True to its name, the Gray Catbird has a call that sounds much like the mewing of a house cat. These birds are often far easier to hear than to see—throughout their time in Manitoba, they typically remain hidden among dense deciduous shrubs, thorny fenceline thickets and streamside brambles. Catbirds are typically shy birds, but their curiosity occasionally brings them close to a patient, motionless observer. • Catbirds vigorously defend their nesting territories, and their defence tactics are so effective that the nesting success of neighbouring warblers and sparrows may increase as a result of the catbird's constant vigilance. • The Gray Catbird's song is similar to the Brown Thrasher's, but the catbird's song phrase is repeated. • By preserving brushy tangles in your backyard, you could attract catbirds and a variety of other songbirds. • The scientific name, *Dumetella*, means 'small thicket' in Latin.

ID: dark grey overall; black cap; long tail may be dark grey to black; chestnut undertail coverts; black eyes, bill and legs.

Size: *L* 20–23.5 cm.

Status: fairly common in central parts; fairly common to common in the south; early May to late September.

Habitat: dense thickets, brambles, shrubby or brushy areas and hedgerows, often near water; also along forest edges, but not in deep forest.

Nesting: low in a dense shrub; bulky cup nest of twigs, leaves and grass is lined with fine materials; female incubates 2–6 greenish-blue eggs for up to 15 days; often has 2 broods per year.

Feeding: gleans the ground and vegetation for ants, beetles, grasshoppers, caterpillars, moths and spiders; also eats berries and visits feeders.

Voice: calls include a cat-like *meoow* and a harsh *check-check;* song is a variety of warbles, squeaks and mimicked phrases issued only once and often interspersed with a *mew* call.

Similar Species: *Gray Jay* (p. 102) and *Northern Mockingbird:* lack the black cap and the chestnut undertail coverts.

Best Sites: Oak Hammock Marsh; Beaudry PP; Delta Marsh; Assiniboine River Trail (Brandon); Turtle Mountain PP.

BROWN THRASHER

Toxostoma rufum

Brown Thrashers have the most extensive vocal repertoire of any North American bird—it is estimated that a male thrasher is capable of producing up to 3000 distinctive song phrases. The male adds new phrases to his repertoire by reproducing sounds made by other male thrashers and neighbouring birds. This thrasher's complex song of repeated phrases distinguishes it from the similar-sounding Gray Catbird, which rarely repeats each phrase, and the Northern Mockingbird, which tends to issue each phrase three times. • The Brown Thrasher frequently feeds in the open, but it is rarely found far from cover. At the slightest sign of danger, it scurries for safety—a typical thrasher sighting consists of nothing more than a flash of rufous as the bird zips beneath a shrubby tangle. • Because they nest close to the ground, their eggs and nestlings are particularly vulnerable to predation by snakes, weasels, skunks and other animals. Brown Thrashers are aggressive nest-defenders, however, and desperate pairs have been known to attack nest robbers to the point of drawing blood. • Placing fences around thick patches of shrubs and wooded areas bordering wetlands, rivers and streams can prevent cattle from devastating thrasher habitat.

ID: reddish-brown upperparts; light-coloured underparts with heavy, brown spotting and streaking; long, downcurved bill; orange-yellow eyes; long, rufous tail; 2 white wing bars.
Size: *L* 27–30 cm.
Status: uncommon in central parts; fairly common to common in the south; early May to late September; a few may be present in winter.
Habitat: dense shrubs and thickets, overgrown pastures (especially those with hawthorns), woodland edges and brushy areas; rarely close to human habitation.
Nesting: low in a shrub; rarely on the ground; cup nest of grass, twigs, leaves and bark is lined with rootlets and fine vegetation;

pair incubates 3–6 reddish-brown dotted, pale blue eggs for up to 14 days; often has 2 broods per year.
Feeding: gleans the ground and digs among debris for larval and adult invertebrates; also eats seeds and berries.
Voice: sings a variety of phrases similar to the catbird's song, but each phrase is usually repeated: *dig-it dig-it, hoe-it hoe-it, pull-it-up, pull-it-up;* calls include a harsh *shuck,* a soft *churr* or a whistled 3-note *pit-cher-ee.*
Similar Species: *Hermit Thrush:* shorter tail; grey-brown back and crown; dark brown eyes; much shorter bill; lacks the wing bars.
Best Sites: St. Malo PP; Beaudry PP; Grand Beach PP; Delta Marsh; Spruce Woods PP; Broomhill WMA.

EUROPEAN STARLING

Sturnus vulgaris

The European Starling was brought to North America in 1890 and 1891, when about 60 of the birds were released in New York City's Central Park as part of a local Acclimatization Society's plan to introduce all the birds mentioned in Shakespeare's writings. The starling then spread to almost every corner of the continent, usurping nesting sites from native cavity-nesting birds. Despite concerted efforts to control or even eradicate the European Starling, the species continues to thrive. Its rapid spread across North America and its effect on native birds is a classic example of the hazards of introducing exotic species into an environment we are still learning about.

breeding

ID: short, squared tail; dark eyes. *Breeding:* blackish, iridescent plumage; yellow bill. *Fall adult:* dark plumage is heavily speckled with white on the head, neck and underparts; dark bill. *In flight:* pointed, triangular wings; swift flight. *Juvenile:* grey-brown plumage; dark bill.
Size: *L* 22 cm.
Status: uncommon and local in the north; April to October; fairly common in central parts; common to locally abundant in the south; year-round; less common in all regions over winter.
Habitat: *Nesting:* cities, towns, residential areas, farmyards, woodland fringes and clearings. *Non-nesting:* near feedlots and livestock pastures.
Nesting: in a natural or artificial cavity; nest is made of grass, twigs, feathers and straw; mostly the female incubates 4–6 bluish to greenish eggs for 12–14 days; has 2 or 3 broods per year.
Feeding: very diverse diet includes invertebrates, berries, seeds and human food-waste.
Voice: variety of whistles, squeaks and gurgles, including a harsh *tseeeer* and a whistled *whooee;* often imitates other birds, including Killdeers, hawks and jays.
Similar Species: *Rusty Blackbird:* longer tail; black bill; lacks the spotting; yellow eyes; rust-tinged upperparts in fall. *Brewer's Blackbird* (p. 153): longer tail; black bill; lacks the spotting; male has yellow eyes; female is brown overall. *Brown-headed Cowbird* (p. 155): lacks the spotting; dark, stout bill; longer tail; adult male has a brown head; juvenile has streaked underparts.
Best Sites: widespread in most urban areas and farmyards.

CEDAR WAXWING

Bombycilla cedrorum

Waxwings have a remarkable ability to digest a wide variety of berries, some of which are inedible or even poisonous to humans. Waxwings will gorge on berries for hours, and they appear to have insatiable appetites. If the fruits have fermented, the waxwings may show signs of tipsiness. • Waxwings are among Manitoba's most attractive birds. They get their name from the colourful spots on their wing tips. • Cedar Waxwings have adapted well to urban life, and they are common in cities, towns and farms throughout most parts of the province. Recent breeding bird surveys indicate an increase in local waxwing numbers as well as a significant increase throughout North America. • Unlike Bohemian Waxwings, which nest in remote coniferous forests of northern Manitoba, Cedar Waxwings are familiar summer residents. They are late nesters, ensuring that the berry crops will be ripe when nestlings are ready to be fed.

ID: brown crest, back, neck and breast; grey wings and tail; black mask; yellow wash on the belly; white undertail coverts; yellow terminal tail band; small, waxy, red 'drops' on the wings. *Juvenile:* streaked underparts; grey-brown body.

Size: *L* 18 cm.

Status: common; mid-May to mid-October; a few may be present in winter.

Habitat: forest edges, second-growth, riparian and open deciduous woodlands, farm shelterbelts and wooded residential parks and gardens, especially near fruit trees and water.

Nesting: often in a coniferous tree; cup nest made of twigs, grass, moss and lichens is often lined with fine grass and seed fluff; female incubates 3–5 spotted, pale bluish-grey eggs for 12–16 days.

Feeding: catches flying insects on the wing; also eats large amounts of berries and wild fruit.

Voice: faint, high-pitched, trilled whistle: *tseee-tseee-tseee*.

Similar Species: *Bohemian Waxwing:* chestnut undertail coverts; small white, red and yellow markings on the wings; often abundant in southern Manitoba in winter.

Best Sites: Nopiming PP; Assiniboine Park; Mantagao Lake WMA; Delta Marsh; Turtle Mountain PP; Duck Mountain NP.

TENNESSEE WARBLER

Vermivora peregrina

Tennessee Warblers lack the bold, brilliant colours of other Manitoba warblers. Even so, they are difficult birds to miss, because they have a loud and distinctive three-part song, and they are relatively common in our province. • Migrating Tennessee Warblers usually sing their tunes and forage for insects in the high upper canopy of trees where they are difficult to see. However, inclement weather and the need to rest after a long flight often force these birds to lower levels where they are more readily seen. • Females build their nests on the ground, and, unlike the males, they usually remain close the forest floor when feeding. • Spruce budworm outbreaks are welcomed by Tennessee Warblers, which generally produce larger clutches with higher survival rates during such events.

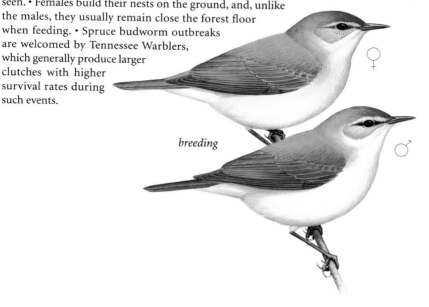

breeding

ID: *Breeding male:* grey cap; olive green back, wings and tail; white eyebrow stripe; grey to black eye line; clean white underparts; thin bill. *Breeding female:* yellow wash on the breast and eyebrow; olive grey upperparts (including the cap). *Fall adult:* olive yellow upperparts; yellow eyebrow; yellow underparts, except for the white undertail coverts; males may have a white belly.
Size: *L* 12 cm.
Status: uncommon in the north; common to abundant in central parts and in the south; mid-May to late September.
Habitat: mature deciduous or mixedwood forests and forest edges; may also use spruce bogs and swamps.
Nesting: on the ground; often on a raised hummock in a swampy area; small cup nest of grass, moss and rootlets is lined with hair; female incubates 4–7 white eggs, marked with brown or purple, for 12 days.
Feeding: gleans foliage and buds for small insects, caterpillars and other invertebrates; may also eat berries.
Voice: *Male:* accelerating, loud, 3-part song: *ticka ticka ticka ticka swit-swit-swit chew-chew-chew-chew-chew;* call is a sweet *chip.*
Similar Species: *Warbling Vireo* (p. 100): stouter overall; thicker bill; greyer upperparts. *Philadelphia Vireo:* stouter; thicker bill; yellow breast and sides. *Orange-crowned Warbler:* lacks the white eyebrow and the blue-grey head.
Best Sites: Whiteshell PP; Nopiming PP; Hecla/Grindstone PP; Mantagao Lake WMA; Riding Mountain NP; Paint Lake PP.

127

YELLOW WARBLER

Dendroica petechia

The Yellow Warbler is one of Manitoba's most common wood-warblers; as a result, it is often the first warbler that birdwatchers learn to identify. It is often called a 'wild canary' because of its bright yellow plumage, but an observant eye and a discriminating ear will quickly reveal the unique character of this bird. • Yellow Warblers routinely nest in human-influenced habitats, such as hedgerows, farm shelterbelts and urban parks and gardens, and they are among the most frequent victims of cowbird parasitism. Unlike many bird species of the forest interior, however, Yellow Warblers can recognize the foreign cowbird eggs and many will abandon their nests or build another overtop the old eggs. • Different species of warblers can coexist in a limited environment because they partition their food supplies by foraging exclusively in certain areas. Yellow Warblers also partition among each other (intraspecies partitioning): males tend to forage in treetops, while females forage closer to ground level. In the forest heights, males can take advantage of the exposed singing perches, and the females remain in the dense under-storey foliage where their nests are concealed.

breeding

ID: bright yellow underparts; black bill and eyes; grey to olive yellow upperparts with bright yellow highlights. *Breeding male:* red streaks on the breast, sides and flanks. *Breeding female:* red streaks are faint or absent; olive yellow upperparts.
Size: *L* 13 cm.
Status: common in the north and in central parts; abundant in the south; mid-May to early September.
Habitat: habitat generalist; moist, open woodlands, dense scrub, shrubby meadows, second-growth woodlands, riparian woods and urban parks and gardens.
Nesting: in the fork of a deciduous tree or shrub; compact cup nest of grass, weeds and shredded bark is lined with fine grass, seed fluff and hair; female incubates 4–6 speckled greenish-white eggs for 11 or 12 days.
Feeding: gleans foliage and vegetation for caterpillars, inchworms, beetles, aphids and cankerworms; will also hover.
Voice: song is a fast, frequently repeated, but variable *sweet-sweet-sweet summer sweet*.
Similar Species: *Orange-crowned Warbler:* duller yellow underparts (undertail coverts are brightest); lacks the reddish breast streaks; darker olive upperparts; dark eye line. *American Goldfinch* (p. 162): black wings and tail. *Wilson's Warbler:* bright yellow eyebrow; male has a black cap; female has a darker crown. *Common Yellowthroat* (p. 136): darker face; whitish belly and undertail; female lacks the bright yellow wing highlights.
Best Sites: Nopiming PP; Assiniboine PP; Birds Hill PP; Interlake area; Delta Marsh; Turtle Mountain PP.

MAGNOLIA WARBLER

Dendroica magnolia

The male Magnolia Warbler is striking as its bright colours flash among green forest foliage. It has white patches on its tail and wings and a white eye stripe, which distinguishes it from the somewhat similar-looking Canada Warbler. • Magnolia Warblers—sometimes referred to as the Black-and-yellow Warbler—typically nest in open coniferous stands, where they are often seen feeding and singing at eye level. When they migrate with large, mixed-species flocks, Magnolia Warblers are often seen foraging away from the pack, usually along the lower branches of trees and shrubs. • Magnolia Warblers travel long distances between their nesting grounds, which are mostly in Canada, and their wintering grounds in Central America and the West Indies. • Magnolia Warblers and many other songbirds migrate primarily at night. Unfortunately, many night-flying birds are killed each year when they collide with buildings, radio towers and tall smokestacks.

breeding

ID: *Breeding male:* yellow underparts with bold, black streaks; black mask; white eyebrow stripe; blue-grey crown; dark upperparts; white wing bars often blend into a larger patch. *Breeding female* and *Fall male:* duller overall; 2 distinct white wing bars; streaked, olive back. *In flight:* yellow rump; dark uppertail has 2 white patches.
Size: *L* 12–13 cm.
Status: occasional in the north; common in central parts; uncommon to fairly common in the south; mid-May to late September.
Habitat: open coniferous and mixed forests, mostly in natural openings and along edges, often near water; young balsam fir and white spruce stands are favoured.
Nesting: on a horizontal limb in a conifer; loose cup nest of grass, twigs and weeds is lined with

rootlets; female incubates 3–5 white eggs, marked with brown and grey, for 11–13 days.
Feeding: gleans vegetation and buds and also flycatches for beetles, flies, wasps, caterpillars and other insects; may also eat some berries.
Voice: song is weak and variable, but always ends with a 2-note phrase that rises at the end: *pretty pretty lady, swee swee swee witsy* or *wheata wheata wheet-zu; clank* call.
Similar Species: *Yellow-rumped Warbler* (p. 130): mostly white underparts; yellow patches on the rump, cap and shoulders. *Cape May Warbler:* olive green upperparts; chestnut cheek patch; lacks the white tail patches. *Canada Warbler:* lacks the yellow rump and the white patches on the wing and tail.
Best Sites: Whiteshell PP; Nopiming PP; Hecla/Grindstone PP; Riding Mountain NP; Duck Mountain PP.

YELLOW-RUMPED WARBLER

Dendroica coronata

Each spring, Yellow-rumped Warblers arrive in our province in mixed-species flocks that include vireos and other warblers. Most Yellow-rumps are headed for Manitoba's northern boreal forest but a few will remain to nest in areas of southern Manitoba. • Yellow-rumped Warblers coexist with other wood-warblers through a partitioning of foraging and nesting 'niches' and feeding strategies. By foraging and nesting on different parts of the same trees and by employing different feeding styles and nesting at slightly different times, competition for food sources is reduced and the exhaustion of particular resources is avoided. • Both races of the Yellow-rumped Warbler, which were once considered separate species, occur in Manitoba: the 'Myrtle Warbler' has a white throat; the 'Audubon's Warbler' has a yellow throat and is rare in Manitoba.

'Myrtle Warbler'
breeding

ID: yellow crown, foreshoulder patches and rump; white underparts; dark cheek; faint white wing bars; thin, white eyebrow stripe. *Male:* blue-grey upperparts with black streaking; black cheek; black breast patches; black streaking along the sides and flanks. *Female:* grey-brown cheek and upperparts; dark streaking on the breast, sides and flanks. *Immature:* like the female, but with faint streaking on the breast and sides.

Size: *L* 13–15 cm.

Status: uncommon in the north; uncommon to abundant in central parts and in the south; late April to early October.

Habitat: open coniferous and mixed forests; rarely in pure deciduous woodlands.

Nesting: on a horizontal limb or in a crotch of a conifer; compact cup nest of twigs, grass, bark strips,

moss, lichens and spider silk is lined with hair and feathers; female incubates 4 or 5 white eggs, splotched with brown and grey, for up to 13 days; often has 2 broods per year.

Feeding: hawks, hovers or gleans vegetation for beetles, flies, wasps, caterpillars, moths and other insects; may also eat some berries.

Voice: song is 6–8 repetitions of the same note followed by a rising or falling trill: *seet-seet-seet-seet trrrrrr*; call is a distinctive *chip*.

Similar Species: *Magnolia Warbler* (p. 129): yellow underparts, including the throat; lacks the yellow crown and shoulder patches; white tail patches. *Cape May Warbler:* lacks the yellow crown and shoulder patches; bold, white wing patches; yellow underparts with heavy dark streaks.

Best Sites: Whiteshell PP; Birds Hill PP; Hecla/Grindstone PP; Riding Mountain NP; Duck Mountain PP; Grass River PP.

PALM WARBLER

Dendroica palmarum

Contrary to its common name, the Palm Warbler has little to do with palm trees. This bird's summer range lies exclusively in Canada, and it could just as easily have been named the 'Bog Warbler' because of its preference for northern bogs of sphagnum moss and black spruce. • In spring, the Palm Warbler is among the earliest arrivals to our province. It often travels with large flocks of Yellow-rumped Warblers, and it is easily recognized by its incessant tail-wagging—its tail pumps whether the bird is hopping on the ground or perched momentarily on an elevated limb. Even during fall migration, when its distinctive chestnut crown has faded to olive brown, its incessant tail wagging is its most prominent field mark. • In most years, the Palm Warbler is a common migrant in southern parts of the province; in summer, it is rare or absent south of the boreal forest.

breeding

ID: *Breeding:* chestnut cap; yellowish eyebrow; yellow throat, breast and undertail coverts; dark streaking on the breast and sides; unstreaked, white belly; olive brown upperparts; yellowish-green rump; 2 faint wing bars; frequently bobs its tail. *Immature* and *Fall adult:* greyish-brown cap and upperparts; buff underparts; buff line over each eye; faint streaking and a hint of yellow on the throat, breast and sides.
Size: *L* 11–14 cm.
Status: occasional in the north; fairly common in central parts; rare to common in the south; early May to early October.
Habitat: *Nesting:* mature sphagnum bogs with scattered black spruce; also in cutline openings in spruce-tamarack forests and young jack pine stands. *In migration:* riparian woodlands, woodland edges and shrubby field margins.

Nesting: on the ground, in a low shrub or on a stunted spruce; cup nest of grass, weeds and bark is lined with feathers; mostly the female incubates 4 or 5 brown-marked, creamy white eggs for 12 days.
Feeding: insects are gleaned from the ground and vegetation; also hover gleans and flycatches; eats some berries and seeds.
Voice: weak notes repeated 6 or 7 times: *zhe-zhe-zhe-zhe-zhe-zhe*; call is a sharp *sup* or *check*.
Similar Species: *Yellow-rumped Warbler* (p. 130): female has a bright yellow rump, crown patch and shoulder patches; white wing bars, throat and undertail coverts. *Chipping Sparrow* (p. 139) and *American Tree Sparrow:* stouter bills and bodies; lack the yellow plumage. *Pine Warbler:* lacks the chestnut cap; whitish wing bars and undertail coverts.
Best Sites: *Nesting:* Whiteshell PP; Hecla/Grindstone PP; Grass River PP. *In migration:* Birds Hill PP; Assiniboine Park; Delta Marsh.

BLACK-AND-WHITE WARBLER

Mniotilta varia

In a general sense, this is a normal-looking warbler, but its foraging behaviour stands in sharp contrast to most of its kin. Rather than dancing or flitting quickly from perch to perch, Black-and-white Warblers behave like creepers and nuthatches. Birders who have developed frayed nerves, tired eyes and sore necks from trying to locate other flitty warblers will be refreshed by the sight of this bird as it creeps methodically up and down tree-trunks. A keen ear also helps to identify this forest-dweller. Although the male's high-pitched call does not carry far, it is quite distinctive—it sounds somewhat like a wheel in need of greasing. • According to recent breeding bird surveys, Black-and-White Warbler numbers are increasing over many parts of their range. • The Black-and-White Warbler is Manitoba's only representative of the genus *Mniotilta*.

breeding

ID: black and white striped crown, back and sides; 2 white wing bars; black legs. *Breeding male:* black cheek and throat; heavier streaking on the back and sides. *Breeding female:* grey cheek; white throat. *Immature:* resembles the female, but has a brown-tinged back and flanks.
Size: *L* 11–14 cm.
Status: fairly common to common; mid-May to mid-September.
Habitat: deciduous or mixed forests; often on hillsides or in ravines near water.
Nesting: on or near the ground; cup nest of grass, leaves, bark

strips and rootlets is lined with fur and fine grass; female incubates 4 or 5 darkly flecked, creamy white eggs for 10 days.
Feeding: insect eggs, larval insects, beetles, spiders and other invertebrates.
Voice: song is a thin, high-pitched *wee-see wee-see wee-see wee-see wee-see wee-see* like a squeaky wheel; calls are a sharp *pit* and a soft, high *seat*.
Similar Species: *Blackpoll Warbler:* male has orangy legs, a solid black cap and a clean white cheek and undertail coverts.
Best Sites: Whiteshell PP; Assiniboine Park; Hecla/Grindstone PP; Turtle Mountain PP; Riding Mountain PP; Duck Mountain PP.

AMERICAN REDSTART

Setophaga ruticilla

Behaving more like a butterfly than a bird, the American Redstart flits from branch to branch in dizzying pursuit of prey. Even when perched, its tail flicks open and closed, revealing colourful orange (male) and yellow (female) tail patches. The American Redstart is consistently listed as a favourite among birdwatchers for its contrasting plumage, approachability and amusing behaviour. Perhaps that is why it is affectionately known as *candelita* (the little candle) in parts of its Central American wintering grounds. • The American Redstart is equipped with flycatcher-like bristles around its mouth, which help it to catch flying insects. Its genus name *Setophaga* comes from the Greek for 'insect-eater.' • In parts of their range, redstarts compete with male Least Flycatchers for food and nesting sites. In some cases, an aerial chase will result, usually with the flycatcher in pursuit. • You may be surprised to hear a female redstart singing, but the bird is most likely a second-year male that has not yet acquired his striking black and orange adult plumage.

ID: *Male:* black overall; bright orange shoulder, wing and tail patches; white belly and undertail coverts. *Female:* olive brown upperparts; olive grey head; yellow shoulder, wing and tail patches; clean white underparts. *Immature male:* resembles a female, but has dark breast streaks.

Size: *L* 13 cm.

Status: common; mid-May to mid-September.

Habitat: shrubby woodland edges, second-growth woodlands and open or semi-open deciduous or mixed forests, often with a dense deciduous understorey; often near water.

Nesting: in the fork of a shrub or sapling; rarely on the ground; open cup nest of plant fibres, bark shreds, grass and rootlets is lined with hair and feathers; female incubates 3–5 brown-marked, white eggs for 12 days.

Feeding: actively gleans foliage and hovers or hawks for insects and spiders; rarely eats seeds and berries.

Voice: *Male:* highly variable series of high notes, including *tsee tsee tsee tsee tsee-o* (with the last note dropping), *zee zee zee zee zwee* (with a high last note) and *teetsa-teetsa-teetsa-teet;* call is a sharp, sweet *chip.*

Similar Species: *Red-winged Blackbird* (p. 150): male is much larger, black overall, lacks the orange in the tail, has a much heavier bill and red on the shoulder.

Best Sites: Nopiming PP; St. Malo WMA; Hecla/Grindstone PP; Spruce Woods PP; Turtle Mountain PP; Duck Mountain PP.

OVENBIRD

Seiurus aurocapillus

The Ovenbird's loud and joyous ode to 'teachers' is a common song that echoes through Manitoba's deciduous and mixed forests in spring. Unfortunately, pinpointing the exact location of this resonating call is not always easy. An Ovenbird will rarely expose itself to the open forest, and it usually stops calling as soon as an intruder enters its territory. • The name 'Ovenbird' refers to this bird's unusual, oven-shaped ground nest. An incubating female nestled within her woven dome is usually confident enough in her nest that, unless closely approached, she will choose to sit tight rather than flee approaching danger. In years when food is plentiful, such as during spruce budworm outbreaks, Ovenbirds usually lay more eggs, are successful in raising most of their young and are able to produce at least two broods in a single summer.

ID: olive brown upperparts; heavy dark streaking on the white breast, sides and flanks; white eye ring; orange crown bordered by black; pink legs.

Size: *L* 15 cm.

Status: common; mid-May to mid-September.

Habitat: *Nesting:* undisturbed mature deciduous forest or poplar stands in mixed forest; usually under a closed canopy with little understorey. *In migration:* dense riparian shrubs and thickets.

Nesting: on the ground; domed nest of grass, bark, twigs and dead leaves is lined with rootlets and hair; female incubates 4–6 darkly spotted, white eggs for 11–13 days.

Feeding: gleans the ground and leaf litter for worms, snails and insects; also eats some seeds.

Voice: loud, distinctive *tea-cher tea-cher Tea-CHER Tea-CHER* or *teach teach Teach Teach TEACH TEACH*, repeated up to 12 times, increasing in speed and volume; night song is an elaborate series of bubbly, warbled notes, often ending in *teacher-teacher*; call is a brisk *chip, cheep* or *chock*.

Similar Species: *Northern Waterthrush:* bold, yellowish or white eyebrow stripe; lacks the rufous crown. *Thrushes* (pp. 120–22): all are larger and lack the rufous crown bordered by black.

Best Sites: Whiteshell PP; Birds Hill PP; Hecla/Grindstone PP; Spruce Woods PP; Turtle Mountain PP; Duck Mountain PP.

MOURNING WARBLER

Oporornis philadelphia

The Mourning Warbler enjoys a slightly wider distribution in Manitoba than the similar-looking Connecticut Warbler, but it tends to share its counterpart's elusiveness. This warbler seldom leaves the protection of its often impenetrable habitat, which is typically dense, shrubby thickets, raspberry brambles and nettle patches. Although Mourning Warblers can be quite common in some areas, they are seen less frequently than we might expect. They tend to sing only on their nesting territory, and even then the males rarely sing from exposed perches. • This warbler is named for its dark hood, which reminded early naturalists of someone in mourning. Some birders like to remember this bird's name by thinking that it is mourning the loss of its eye ring.

breeding

ID: grey hood; yellow underparts; olive green upperparts; short tail; pinkish legs. *Male:* no eye ring; black upper breast patch. *Female:* hood is light grey; may show a thin eye ring. *Immature:* pale grey to yellow chin and throat; buffy breast; thin, incomplete eye ring.
Size: *L* 13–14 cm.
Status: fairly common to common; mid-May to early September.
Habitat: dense shrubs in open deciduous woods or along the edges of bogs and marshes; also found in deciduous second growth.
Nesting: on or near the ground, often at the base of a shrub; bulky nest of leaves, weeds and grass is lined with fur and fine grass; female

incubates 3–5 brown-spotted or blotched, creamy white eggs for about 12 days.
Feeding: forages in dense, low shrubs for caterpillars, beetles, spiders and other invertebrates.
Voice: husky, 2-part song is variable, but often descends at the end: *blee blee blee blee-blee choochoo*; call is a loud, low *check*.
Similar Species: *Connecticut Warbler:* bold, complete eye ring; lacks the black breast patch; long undertail coverts make the tail look very short; immature has a light grey throat. *Nashville Warbler:* bright yellow throat; dark legs.
Best Sites: Whiteshell PP; Assiniboine Park; Hecla/Grindstone PP; Turtle Mountain PP; Riding Mountain NP; Duck Mountain PP.

135

COMMON YELLOWTHROAT

Geothlypis trichas

Despite its bright colours and abundance in wetland areas of Manitoba, the Common Yellowthroat can be surprisingly difficult to find. It favours cattails, bulrushes and shrubby shoreline tangles, shunning the forest habitat preferred by most wood-warblers. In May and June, male yellowthroats issue their distinctive songs while perched atop tall cattails or shrubs. An extended look at the male in action will reveal the location of his favourite singing perches, which he visits in rotation. These strategic outposts mark the boundary of his territory, and they are fiercely guarded from the intrusions of other males. • Common Yellowthroats maintain their plumage by 'bathing'—they immerse themselves or roll in water and shake off the excess water by flicking or flapping their wings. Other birds with limited access to water will bathe themselves in dust. • In Ernest Thompson Seton's *Birds of Manitoba*, the author noted that: 'Like the Mourning Warbler, the Common Yellowthroat seems to take a mischievous delight in playing Jack o'Lantern…for it will lead one for hours through a maze of dank alders and water-willows, pausing now and then to encourage its distressed, mud-splashed, bramble-scratched follower, by calling loudly and plainly *what a pity, what a pity, what a pity, pit.*'

ID: yellow throat and breast; white belly; olive green upperparts. *Breeding male:* broad, black mask with a white upper border. *Female* and *Immature:* no mask; may show a faint white eye ring; tan-coloured sides. *Immature:* similar to the female; males may show a hint of a mask.
Size: *L* 11–14 cm.
Status: rare in the north; common in central parts and in the south; mid-May to mid-September.
Habitat: open marshes with scattered shrubs, riparian willow and alder clumps, sedge wetlands, bogs and damp, overgrown meadows or fields.
Nesting: on or near the ground; in aquatic vegetation or in a shrub; bulky, open cup nest of grass, sedges and shredded bark is lined with hair and soft plant fibres; female

incubates 3–6 brown-specked, creamy white eggs for 12 days; usually has 2 broods per year.
Feeding: hovers and gleans vegetation for insects and beetles; may eat some seeds.
Voice: clear, oscillating song: *witchety witchety witchety-witch*; call is a sharp *tcheck* or *tchet*.
Similar Species: male is distinctive. *Yellow Warbler* (p. 128): yellow highlights in the wings; all-yellow underparts. *Wilson's Warbler:* yellow forehead, eyebrow and cheek; all-yellow underparts; male has a dark cap. *Orange-crowned Warbler:* dull greenish-yellow underparts (undertail coverts are the brightest); faint, dark grey breast streaks.
Best Sites: Nopiming PP; Oak Hammock Marsh; Hecla/Grindstone PP; Delta Marsh; Turtle Mountain PP; Minnedosa pothole region.

SCARLET TANAGER

Piranga olivacea

Scarlet Tanagers are uncommon and found only locally in Manitoba, so it is a treat to catch a glimpse of one. Males sport brilliant red plumage and jet black wings, but despite their showy colours, they can be difficult to spot as they move among the forest canopy. Like most tanagers, the male Scarlet Tanager does not acquire full breeding plumage until its second year; a male in first-summer plumage is dull red to orange overall with brownish-black wings. • The Scarlet Tanager is the only tanager that routinely nests in Manitoba. In Central and South America there are over 200 species of tanager, representing every colour of the rainbow.

breeding

ID: *Breeding male:* bright scarlet red overall; black wings and tail. *Female, Fall male* and *Immature:* uniformly olive green upperparts; dull yellow underparts (moulting male may have patches of red); greyish-brown (female) or dark (male) wings. *2nd-year male:* orange to dull red overall; brownish-black wings.
Size: *L* 16–19 cm.
Status: uncommon; mid-May to late August; a few may remain as late as November.
Habitat: fairly extensive, mature, upland deciduous and mixed forests.
Nesting: well away from the trunk of a high horizontal branch; flimsy cup nest of grass, weeds and twigs is lined with fine grass and rootlets;

female incubates 2–5 speckled, pale green eggs for about 14 days.
Feeding: gleans and hover-gleans insects from vegetation; also hawks insects; may eat some berries.
Voice: series of 4 or 5 short, hoarse, robin-like phrases; call is a *chip-burrr* or *chip-churrr*.
Similar Species: *Northern Cardinal:* red bill, wings and tail; prominent head crest; male has a black mask and bib; very rare in Manitoba. *Western Tanager:* obvious wing bars; very rare in Manitoba. *Baltimore Oriole* (p. 156) and *Orchard Oriole:* females have wing bars and sharper bills.
Best Sites: Moose Lake/Birch Point PP; Whiteshell PP; Assiniboine Park; Beaudry PP; Spruce Woods PP.

EASTERN TOWHEE

Pipilo erythrophthalmus

Distinctive *drink your teeeee* or *cheweee* calls are usually the first hint that an Eastern Towhee is nearby. It may take some time to locate this wary singer, but the effort is usually rewarded with a peak at the bird's bright plumage. Towhees are cheeky birds that typically rustle about in dense undergrowth, craftily scraping back layers of dry leaves to expose the seeds, berries, earthworms and insects hidden beneath. • Although you wouldn't guess it, this colourful bird is a member of the American Sparrow family—a group that is usually drab in colour. • The Eastern Towhee and its western relative, the Spotted Towhee, were once grouped together as a single species known as the Rufous-sided Towhee. • According to recent surveys, Eastern Towhee numbers are declining throughout eastern North America.

ID: dark hood, wings and upperparts; rufous sides and flanks; white outer tail corners; white lower breast and belly; buff undertail coverts; red eyes; dark bill. *Male:* black hood and upperparts. *Female:* dusky brown hood and upperparts. *Immature:* dusky brown upperparts; heavily streaked white-buff underparts; white tail corners.
Size: *L* 18–21 cm.
Status: rare and local in the central boreal forest; uncommon in the south; early May to late September; occasional in winter.
Habitat: dense shrubs with leaf litter, woodland openings and edges and shrubby abandoned fields.
Nesting: on the ground or in a

dense, low shrub; cup nest is made of twigs, bark strips, grass, weeds, rootlets and animal hair; mostly the male incubates 3–6 spotted, creamy white to pale grey eggs for 10–12 days; usually has 2 broods per year.
Feeding: scratches at leaf litter for insects, seeds and berries.
Voice: song is 2 high, musical whistled notes followed by a trill: *drink your teeeee*; call is a scratchy, slurred *cheweee!* or *chewink!*
Similar Species: *Spotted Towhee:* white spots on the back and wings. *Dark-eyed Junco* (p. 145): much smaller; pale bill; black eyes; outer tail feathers are completely white.
Best Sites: Birds Hill PP; Spruce Woods PP; Brandon Hills; Pelican Lake; Turtle Mountain PP.

138

CHIPPING SPARROW

Spizella passerina

The Chipping Sparrow and the Dark-eyed Junco do not share the same tailor, but they must have attended the same voice lessons, because their songs are remarkably similar. The rapid trill of the Chipping Sparrow is slightly faster, drier and less musical, and even experienced birders can have difficulty identifying this singer. • Chipping Sparrows are widespread throughout most of Manitoba. In southern parts of the province, they are generally restricted to cities, towns and farmsteads, especially where conifers have been planted. They are summer birds here, so watch for them from late April to late September. • The Chipping Sparrow was once known as the 'hairbird,' owing to its preference for hair as lining material for its nest. • Approximately five percent of male Chipping Sparrows are polygynous. A polygynous male will nest with a second female while his first mate incubates his first brood.

breeding

ID: *Breeding adult:* prominent rufous cap; white eyebrow; black eye line; grey cheek; light grey underparts; mottled brown upperparts, except for the grey rump; dark bill; 2 faint wing bars; light-coloured legs. *Female:* generally duller; may have dark streaks through the crown. *Non-breeding:* pale brown crown with dark streaks; brown eye line; tan grey cheek; grey rump; pale lower mandible. *Juvenile:* brown-grey overall with dark brown streaking through the crown, back, breast and sides; grey rump; pale lower mandible.
Size: *L* 13–15 cm.
Status: rare in the north; common to abundant in central parts and in the south; late April to late September.
Habitat: open coniferous or mixed forests and woodland fringes; often in yards and gardens with tree and shrub borders.
Nesting: at mid-level in a small

tree or shrub (often coniferous); compact cup nest is woven with grass and rootlets and lined with hair or fur; female incubates 3–5 pale blue eggs, lightly spotted with brown, for 11–14 days; usually has 2 broods per year.
Feeding: gleans the ground and vegetation for small seeds and invertebrates; may also visit feeding stations.
Voice: a chipping rattle, given at a constant pitch (faster and less metallic than the Dark-eyed Junco's call); call note is a high-pitched *chip*.
Similar Species: *American Tree Sparrow:* dark central breast spot; lacks the bold, white eyebrow; red eye line. *Swamp Sparrow:* lacks the white eyebrow, black eye line and white wing bars. *Clay-colored Sparrow:* immature has a brownish rump.
Best Sites: Whiteshell PP; Birds Hill PP; Hecla/Grindstone PP; Spruce Woods PP; Turtle Mountain PP; Duck Mountain PP.

139

CLAY-COLORED SPARROW

Spizella pallida

With a buzzing call that sounds more like an insect than a bird, the Clay-colored Sparrow can often go unnoticed by humans. Keen ears, however, will quickly lead you to shrubby woodland clearings, forest edges or brushy pastures where these sparrows are common inhabitants. Clay-colored Sparrows are particularly partial to patches of silverberry, and they favour snowberry shrubs as nesting sites. • Clay-colored Sparrows are common hosts of cowbird eggs. They often recognize the foreign eggs and many will either abandon their nest or build another in a new territory. • Clay-colored Sparrows benefited from the forest-clearing practices of the late 1800s and early 1900s, flourishing along the margins of agricultural fields and wherever brushy patches grew in forest clearcuts. Recently, breeding bird surveys have revealed that their numbers are in significant decline throughout North America.

breeding

ID: unstreaked, white underparts; buff breast and flanks; grey nape; light brown rump; sharply outlined pale brown ear patch; brown crown with dark streaks and a pale central stripe; buff-white eyebrow; white jaw stripe bordered by brown; white throat; largely pale bill. *Juvenile:* buffier breast, sides and flanks.
Size: *L* 13–14 cm.
Status: occasional in the north; fairly common in central parts; common in the south; early May to mid-September.
Habitat: brushy open areas, woodland edges and openings, abandoned fields and riparian thickets.
Nesting: low in a grass tuft or shrub; open cup nest of twigs, grass and weeds is lined with rootlets, fine grass and fur; pair incubates

3–5 pale blue eggs, speckled with brown, for 10–12 days; often has 2 broods per year.
Feeding: forages on the ground and in low vegetation for seeds and insects.
Voice: song is generally 3 or 4 unmusical, insect-like buzzes; call is a soft *chip*.
Similar Species: *Chipping Sparrow* (p. 139): prominent rufous cap; grey cheek; greyish-white underparts; 2 faint white wing bars; all-dark bill; juvenile has a grey rump and lacks the grey nape and buff sides. *Le Conte's Sparrow:* buff-orange face; buff breast and sides with some fine, dark streaks. *Grasshopper Sparrow:* top of the head is flattened; buff cheek; lacks the grey nape.
Best Sites: Birds Hill PP; Oak Hammock Marsh; Hecla/Grindstone PP; Lake Francis; Spruce Woods PP; Poverty Plains.

VESPER SPARROW

Pooecetes gramineus

The sweet melody of the Vesper Sparrow, issued from atop an elevated perch, is a common summer sound in the southern half of our province. It is this lovely song, reminiscent of vesper worship services given at dusk, that gave the Vesper Sparrow its name. • When the business of nesting begins, Vesper Sparrows scour their neighbourhood for a potential nesting site. More often than not, the nest ends up nestled in a grassy hollow at the base of a clump of weeds or small shrub. • An early Manitoba naturalist once noted this bird's habit of 'flitting along a trail or pathway in front of an advancing wagon or person, alighting every few yards…it seems probable that this proceeding is a relic of a habit acquired by the bird of flitting before the buffalo along the paths made by these animals.' • Recent surveys has revealed that Vesper Sparrow numbers are declining throughout North America.

ID: streaky brown upperparts; chestnut shoulder patch (often hidden); white outer tail feathers; weak breast and flank streaking; white eye ring; dark ear patch bordered by a white 'moustache.'

Size: *L* 14–17 cm.

Status: fairly common in central parts; common in the south; mid-April to mid-September.

Habitat: open fields and grasslands bordered by or interspersed with shrubs, shrubby woodland fringes and clearings.

Nesting: in a scrape on the ground, often under a canopy of grass or at the base of a shrub; loosely woven grass cup nest is lined with rootlets, fine grass and hair; mostly the female incubates 3–6 whitish eggs, speckled with brown, for 11–13 days; has 2 broods per year.

Feeding: gleans the ground for grasshoppers, beetles, cutworms, other invertebrates and small seeds.

Voice: 2 pairs of preliminary notes, with the 2nd pair higher in pitch: *here-here there-there*, followed by a bubbly trill.

Similar Species: *Other Sparrows:* lack the white outer tail feathers and the chestnut shoulder patch. *Lark Sparrow:* white-tipped tail; striking facial pattern. *American Pipit* and *Sprague's Pipit:* thinner bills; lack the chestnut shoulder patch; bob their tails when feeding. *Lapland Longspur* (p. 146): non-breeding plumage shows a broad, pale eyebrow, reddish edgings on the wing feathers and a buff wash on the upper breast.

Best Sites: Birds Hill PP; Mantagao Lake WMA; Delta Marsh; Spruce Woods PP; Poverty Plains.

141

SAVANNAH SPARROW

Passerculus sandwichensis

Through spring and summer, the male Savannah Sparrow belts out his distinctive, buzzy tunes, usually while perched atop a prominent shrub, blade of grass or strategic fencepost. The Savannah Sparrow is one of Manitoba's most common open-country birds, and most of us have probably seen or heard one at one time or another. It typically inhabits the weedy margins of sloughs, dugouts, wet ditches and other wetlands and tends to avoid short-grass habitats. • Like most sparrows, the Savannah Sparrow prefers to stay out of sight. It takes flight only as a last resort, fluttering only a short distance before it touches ground again. Much of the time it scurries along the ground like a mouse, remaining out of sight under the cover of concealing grass. • Most beginner birdwatchers have a tough time distinguishing between the many different sparrows in our province and simply call them all 'LBJs' (Little Brown Jobs). One of the best ways to identify a sparrow is to first learn its distinctive song.

ID: brown streaking on the breast, sides and flanks; mottled brown upperparts; whitish underparts; pale stripe through the crown; prominent yellowish or whitish eyebrow stripe; short, notched tail. *Immature:* buffier upperparts and underparts.
Size: *L* 11–16 cm.
Status: uncommon to abundant in the north; common in central parts; abundant in the south; mid-April to mid-October.
Habitat: agricultural fields (especially hay and alfalfa), weedy fields, marsh edges, pastures, tundra, bogs, roadside ditches and overgrown fencelines.
Nesting: on the ground; shallow scrape is well concealed by overhanging vegetation; open, grassy cup nest is lined with fine grass and hair; mostly the female incubates 3–6 greenish-blue eggs,

speckled with brown, for 12 or 13 days.
Feeding: gleans the ground for insects and small seeds.
Voice: song is a buzzy *tsip-tsip-tsip-tsooreeeeeeyoo* or *tea tea tea teeeeea* today (rising on the 2nd-last note and dropping at the end); call is a high tsit.
Similar Species: *Vesper Sparrow* (p. 141): white outer tail feathers; chestnut shoulder patches. *Lincoln's Sparrow:* buff jaw line; buff wash across the breast; broad grey eyebrow. *Baird's Sparrow:* face and crown stripe are washed with buff-orange; lacks the yellow lores. *Grasshopper Sparrow:* unstreaked breast. *Song Sparrow* (p. 143): lacks the yellow eyebrow stripe; bold 'moustache' stripes.
Best Sites: Oak Hammock Marsh; Interlake area; Delta Marsh; Spruce Woods PP; Poverty Plains; Churchill.

SONG SPARROW

Melospiza melodia

Song Sparrows are found throughout most of Manitoba, spreading their cheerful song across the landscape wherever shrubs and thickets are found near water. • Song Sparrows (and many other songbirds) learn to sing by listening to their fathers or rival males. By the time a young male is a few months old, he will have formed the basis of his own courtship tune. He will test his song the following spring but will most likely fail to attract a mate or secure a territory. • The Song Sparrow is one of North America's most variable songbirds, with 31 recognized subspecies. With the Yellow Warbler, it also shares the distinction of being the most common host of cowbird eggs.

ID: whitish underparts with heavy brown streaking that converges into a central breast spot; greyish face; brown eye line; white jaw line is bordered by a dark whisker and 'moustache' stripes; dark crown with a pale central stripe; mottled brown upperparts; rounded tail tip; often pumps its tail in flight. *Immature:* buffier and less grey.

Size: *L* 14–18 cm.

Status: rare to uncommon in the north; fairly common in central parts; common in the south; early April to late September; a few may be present in winter.

Habitat: shrubby areas, usually near water, including willow shrublands, riparian thickets, forest openings, fencelines and lakeshores; also brushy edges of gardens, fields and roads.

Nesting: on the ground or low in a shrub; open cup nest of grass, weeds, leaves and bark is lined with fine materials; female incubates 3–6 pale bluish-green eggs, blotched with brown, for 12–14 days; has 2 or 3 broods per year.

Feeding: gleans and scratches in ground litter for seeds, cutworms, beetles, ants and other invertebrates.

Voice: musical, buzzy melody usually starts with 3 or 4 introductory notes: *Hip Hip Hip Hooray Boys, the spring is here again* or *Sweet, Sweet, Sweet Tea in your tea kettle kettle tea;* calls include a short *tsip* and a nasal *tchep.*

Similar Species: *Fox Sparrow:* larger; much heavier spots and streaks on the underparts; head is mostly dark; dark, unstreaked upperparts. *Lincoln's Sparrow:* lightly streaked breast with a buff breast band; buff jaw line. *Savannah Sparrow* (p. 142): yellow eyebrow; lacks the dark 'moustache'; notched tail. *Vesper Sparrow* (p. 141): white outer tail feathers; chestnut shoulder patch.

Best Sites: Birds Hill PP; Hecla/Grindstone PP; Assiniboine River Trail; Turtle Mountain PP; Duck Mountain PP.

WHITE-THROATED SPARROW

Zonotrichia albicollis

This patriot of Canada's northern forests arrives in our province each spring singing its glorious, familiar tribute: *dear sweet Canada Canada Canada*. While many weekend cottagers and campers might not know this bird, they probably remember its song—the White-throated Sparrow is one of the last birds to be silenced by nightfall. If you are an early riser, you might be treated to the sight of a White-throated Sparrow scratching at patches of leaf litter in search of seeds, insects and grubs. • During the nesting season, the White-throated Sparrow shuns large tracts of forest in favour of second-growth woodlands and forest clearings. During migration, it commonly inhabits small shrubs or thickets, and it often intermingles with other sparrows. • This handsome sparrow is easily identified by its bold, white throat and striped crown. Two colour morphs are common throughout Manitoba: one has black and white stripes on its head; the other has brown and tan stripes. • Like many 'snowbirds,' most White-throated Sparrows move to warmer climates in fall and early winter.

ID: black and white (or brown and tan) striped head; well-defined white throat; grey cheek; yellow lores; grey, unstreaked breast; lighter belly; rusty upperparts with black streaks; greyish bill. *Immature:* brown and greyish buff head stripes; breast has dusky streaks.

Size: *L* 17–18 cm.

Status: rare in the north; common to abundant in the central boreal forest; fairly common to common in the south; mid-April to late October; rare in winter.

Habitat: *Nesting:* semi-open deciduous, coniferous and mixed forests, regenerating clearings and shrubby forest edges. *Non-nesting:* brushy edges of gardens, fields and roads, often near feeders.

Nesting: on or near the ground; open cup nest of moss, grass, twigs and conifer needles is lined with rootlets, fine grass and hair; female incubates 4–6 speckled, bluish-white eggs for 11–14 days.

Feeding: scratches the ground for invertebrates, seeds and berries; gleans insects from vegetation and while in flight.

Voice: variable song is a clear and distinct whistled *dear sweet Canada Canada Canada*; call is a sharp *chink* or slurred *tseet*.

Similar Species: *White-crowned Sparrow:* lacks the well-defined white throat and the yellow lores; upperparts are not as rusty; pinkish bill; grey collar.

Best Sites: Mars Hill WMA; Hecla/Grindstone PP; Riding Mountain NP; Grass River PP; Paint Lake PP; Churchill.

DARK-EYED JUNCO

Junco hyemalis

Dark-eyed Juncos migrate through cities, towns and farmsteads in southern Manitoba in such abundance that few people could say they have not encountered one. During spring snowstorms, large numbers of juncos often linger around human dwellings, their slate-grey colours contrasting boldly against an all-white background. • Juncos spend most of their time on the ground, and they are readily flushed from wooded trails and backyard feeders. They are trusting by nature, sometimes picking up grain and seeds at the feet of a silent observer. • Juncos rarely perch at feeders, preferring to snatch up seeds that are knocked to the ground by other birds. • North America boasts a great diversity of junco subspecies. Our province is typically home to the subspecies known as the 'Slate-colored Junco,' and occasionally the 'Oregon Junco' subspecies wanders here from the West. These birds frequently interbreed, producing many confusing junco variations.

'Slate-colored Junco'

ID: white outer tail feathers are obvious in flight; pinkish bill. *Male:* dark slate grey overall, except for the white lower breast, belly and undertail coverts. *Female:* brownish-grey rather than dark grey. *Juvenile:* like the female, but streaked with darker brown.
Size: *L* 14–17 cm.
Status: rare to uncommon in the north; common to abundant in central parts; uncommon in the south, except abundant in migration; late March to mid-November; rare to uncommon in winter.
Habitat: *Nesting:* open coniferous and mixed forests, bogs, burned-over areas and shrubby regenerating clearings. *Non-nesting:* near granaries, spilled grain or feeders.
Nesting: on the ground, often against a vertical bank; rarely in a tree, shrub or building; cup nest of twigs, bark shreds, grass and moss is lined with fine grass, moss and hair; female incubates 3–6 speckled, pale bluish eggs for 12 or 13 days; usually has 2 broods per year.
Feeding: scratches the ground for invertebrates; also eats berries and seeds.
Voice: song is a long, dry trill very similar to, but slower and more musical than, the Chipping Sparrow's song; distinctive 'smacking' alarm note can be imitated by smacking the tongue from the roof of the mouth.
Similar Species: *Eastern Towhee* (p. 138) and *Spotted Towhee:* much larger; black bill; red eyes; only the outer tail corners are white.
Best Sites: Pinawa area; Riding Mountain NP; Duck Mountain PP; Clearwater Lake PP; Churchill.

LAPLAND LONGSPUR

Calcarius lapponicus

In late fall and early spring, huge flocks of Lapland Longspurs and other arctic-nesting songbirds pass through southern Manitoba, making brief stop-overs in fallow fields. The flocks can be surprisingly inconspicuous until they are closely approached—anyone attempting a closer look will be awed by the sight of the birds suddenly erupting into the skies, flashing their white outer tail feathers. • In fall, these birds arrive from their breeding grounds looking like mottled, brownish sparrows, and they retain their drab plumage throughout the winter months. When the farmers work their fields in spring, Lapland Longspurs have already moulted into their bold breeding plumage, which they will wear through summer. • Like the Chestnut-collared Longspur of southwestern Manitoba, the male Lapland Longspur's courtship displays include a conspicuous flight song issued as the male rises into the air and then glides downward with outstretched wings and a spread tail.

non-breeding

ID: white outer tail feathers; pale yellowish bill. *Breeding male:* black crown, face and bib outlined with white; chestnut collar. *Breeding female* and *Non-breeding male:* rusty nape; often has rufous in the wings; mottled brown and black upperparts; finely streaked breast and sides on otherwise light underparts. *Non-breeding female:* mottled brown with black streaks on the upperparts; narrow, lightly streaked buff breast band. *Immature:* greyish nape; broader buff-brown breast band.
Size: *L* 16 cm.
Status: common to abundant in most parts; mid-March to mid-May and early September to mid-November; fairly common in the north; May to September; rare in winter.
Habitat: *Nesting:* wet meadows and scrub on coastal tundra. *Non-nesting:* open areas, pastures, meadows, roads and weedy fields.
Nesting: on a dry tundra hummock, often concealed by dwarf shrubs; cup nest of grass and sedges is lined with fine grass, hair and feathers; female incubates 4–7 pale olive-buff eggs, marked with brown or black, for 12 or 13 days.
Feeding: gleans the ground for insects and some small seeds; eats mostly seeds and waste grain in winter.
Voice: flight song is a rapid, slurred warble; various musical calls; flight calls include *tickt-tick-tew* and a descending *teew*.
Similar Species: *Snow Bunting* (p. 147): winter adults have an unstreaked tan head and mostly white wings with black tips. *Smith's Longspur:* completely buff to buff-orange underparts. *Chestnut-collared Longspur:* nesting male has all-black underparts (except the throat and lower belly), a black crown, black eye line and rusty nape. *Vesper Sparrow* (p. 141): bold, white eye ring; chestnut shoulder patch.
Best Sites: *Nesting:* Churchill; Wapusk NP. *Non-nesting:* widespread in open country in southern Manitoba.

SNOW BUNTING

Plectrophenax nivalis

In early winter, huge flocks of Snow Buntings descend on fields and roadsides in open areas of southern Manitoba, their startling black and white plumage flashing in contrast with the snow-covered backdrop. It may seem strange that Snow Buntings are whiter in summer than in winter, but the darker winter plumage may help these birds absorb heat on the coldest, clear winter days. • Most Snow Buntings spend their summers north of our province, but small numbers have been known to nest in Manitoba along the Hudson Bay coast. Snow Buntings have beautiful, clear courtship songs, but most Manitobans will only hear the twittering of huge flocks as they sweep across the province in winter or during migration.

non-breeding

ID: black and white wings and tail; white underparts. *Breeding male:* black back; all-white head and rump; black bill. *Breeding female:* unstreaked, tan head; streaked, brown back; white rump; dark bill. *Non-breeding:* yellowish bill; unstreaked, golden-brown crown and rump.
Size: *L* 15–18 cm.
Status: common to irregularly abundant in central parts and in the south; early October to early May; fairly common in the north; May to September.
Habitat: *Nesting:* rough, rocky terrain or rock outcroppings on coastal tundra. *Non-nesting:* cultivated or stubble fields, on pastures, grassy meadows, lake-shores, roadsides and railways.

Nesting: on the ground among rocks or natural debris; bulky cup nest of grass and moss is lined with feathers, hair, fine grass and rootlets; female incubates 3–9 brown-blotched, bluish-white eggs for 10–16 days.
Feeding: gleans the ground and vegetation for insects and small seeds; seeds and waste grain are taken during winter and migration.
Voice: song is a musical, high-pitched *chi-chi-churee*; call is a whistled *teer* or *tew;* also a rough purring *brrrt.*
Similar Species: *Lapland Longspur* (p. 146): lacks the black and white wing pattern; streaked head pattern in winter plumage.
Best Sites: *Nesting:* Churchill; Wapusk NP. *Non-nesting:* widespread but erratic in open country in southern Manitoba.

147

ROSE-BREASTED GROSBEAK

Pheucticus ludovicianus

The vibrant, spirited song and distinctive sharp *tick* call note of the Rose-breasted Grosbeak are common sounds heard among Manitoba's mixed woodlands in spring and summer. Its song is quite similar to that of the robin, but this grosbeak runs its song phrases together without pausing to take a breath. Although the female lacks the magnificent colours of the male, she shares his talent for beautiful song. • Grosbeaks often raise two broods per year. When this is the case, the male will care for the fledged young from the first brood while the female builds the second nest. • The decline of the Rose-breasted Grosbeak and other forest songbirds has been blamed largely on the loss of tropical rainforests. Perhaps more significant is the loss of valuable habitat in eastern North America.

breeding

ID: pale, stout bill; dark wings with large, white wing bars and bold, white patches (obvious in flight); dark tail. *Male:* black head, throat and back; red breast and underwings; white rump and belly. *1st-spring male:* may show brown instead of black. *1st-fall male:* like the female, but with a streaked orangish breast and sides; reddish wing linings. *Female:* bold, whitish eyebrow and thin crown stripe; brown upperparts; light buff underparts with dark brown streaking; yellow underwings.
Size: *L* 18–21 cm.
Status: common; mid-May to mid-September.
Habitat: riparian woodlands, wooded urban parks, woodlots and deciduous and mixed boreal forest with tall, sparse undergrowth.

Nesting: fairly low in a tree or shrub, often near water; flimsy cup nest of twigs, bark strips, grass and leaves is lined with rootlets and hair; pair incubates 3–5 spotted, pale bluish-green eggs for 9–12 days.
Feeding: gleans tree foliage for insects, seeds, buds, blossoms, berries and some fruit; may visit feeding stations.
Voice: song is a long, melodious series of whistled notes, much like a fast and more varied version of a robin's song; call is a distinctive metallic *kik*.
Similar Species: male is distinctive. *Purple Finch* (p. 158): female is much smaller, has a darker bill, heavier streaking on the underparts and lacks the yellow underwings.
Best Sites: Whiteshell PP; Birds Hill PP; Delta Marsh; Spruce Woods PP; Turtle Mountain PP; Riding Mountain NP.

BOBOLINK

Dolichonyx oryzivorus

During the nesting season, male and female Bobolinks rarely interact with one another. For the most part, the males perform aerial displays and sing their bubbly, tinkling songs from exposed grassy perches while the females carry out the nesting duties. The male's unique song, which attracts females and keeps other males at bay, has earned it the nickname 'Bubbling Bob, the Bobolink.' • Once the young have hatched, the males become scarce, spending much of their time on the ground foraging for insects to feed their young. Like many ground-nesting birds, a wary female will run several feet from the nest before taking flight so as not to draw attention to her nest. • Bobolinks once benefited from agricultural activity in Manitoba (particularly from the cultivation of hay), but modern practices, such as harvesting hay early in the season, have had negative effects on their reproductive success.

breeding

ID: *Male:* black bill, head, wings, tail and underparts; buff-yellow nape; white rump and wing patch. *Female* and *Fall male:* yellowish bill; brownish upperparts; buff face and underparts; streaked back, sides, flank and rump; dark eye line; buff central crown stripe bordered by dark stripes; whitish throat.
Size: *L* 15–20 cm.
Status: fairly common in central parts; common in the south; early May to early September.
Habitat: grassy meadows, ditches, native prairie, hayfields and some croplands (especially standing rye fields).
Nesting: on the ground; well-concealed nest, made of grass and forbs, is placed in a shallow depression and lined with fine grass; female incubates 4–7 heavily marked, greyish to light reddish-brown eggs for 10–13 days.
Feeding: gleans the ground and low vegetation for adult and larval invertebrates; also eats various seeds.

Voice: bubbly song rollicks upward: *bobolink bobolink spink spank spink*; issues a *pink* warning call.
Similar Species: *Lark Bunting:* thicker, conical bill; male lacks the yellow nape and the white rump; females have a white wing patch. *Red-winged Blackbird* (p. 150): female has a longer bill, heavily streaked underparts and lacks the pale crown stripe. *Savannah Sparrow* (p. 142): darker breast streaking; whitish underparts; yellow lores. *Vesper Sparrow* (p. 141): streaked breast; white outer tail feathers; no central crown stripe. *Grasshopper Sparrow:* white belly; unstreaked sides and flanks.
Best Sites: Birds Hill PP; Oak Hammock Marsh; Hecla/Grindstone PP; Delta Marsh; Poverty Plains.

RED-WINGED BLACKBIRD
Agelaius phoeniceus

Male Red-winged Blackbirds get an early start on the spring season, arriving in Manitoba's marshes and wetlands a week or so before the females. In the females' absence, the males stake out territories through song and visual displays. A male's bright red shoulder patches, or 'epaulettes,' and raspy song are his most important tools in the often intricate strategy he employs to defend his territory from rivals. In field experiments, males whose red shoulders were painted black soon lost their territories to rivals they had previously defeated. Since it takes a male a couple of years to acquire his full adult plumage, the paler younger males stand little chance of attracting females. On the other hand, the female's cryptic coloration enables her to blend perfectly with her surroundings and sit inconspicuously upon her nest. • In fall, Red-winged Blackbirds roost and feed together in flocks. In time, these groups become mixed-species flocks that include female Red-winged Blackbirds, grackles, Rusty Blackbirds, starlings and cowbirds.

ID: *Male:* all black, except for the large, red shoulder patch edged in yellow (occasionally concealed). *Female:* heavily streaked underparts; mottled brown upperparts; may have a pinkish tinge on the throat; light eyebrow stripe. *Immature male:* mottled blackish-brown plumage; faint red shoulder patch.
Size: *L* 18–24 cm.
Status: rare in the north; common in central parts; abundant in the south; late March to mid-November; rare in winter.
Habitat: cattail marshes, wet meadows and ditches, shoreline shrubbery and upland shrubs; ranges widely to feed in croplands and in open country.
Nesting: colonial and polygynous; in emergent vegetation near or over water; rarely in shoreline shrubs; bulky open cup nest of dried cattail leaves, grass, reeds and rootlets is lined with fine grass; female

incubates 3–6 bluish-white eggs, marked with purple and black, for 10–12 days; has 2 or 3 broods per year.
Feeding: gleans the ground or vegetation for seeds, insects, other invertebrates, grain and berries; also catches insects in flight; attracted to some crops in migration and to feeders or spilled grain in winter.
Voice: song is a loud, raspy *konk-a-ree* or *ogle-reeeee*; calls include a harsh *check* and a high *tseert*; female may give a loud *che-che-che chee chee chee.*
Similar Species: male is distinctive (when the shoulder patch shows). *Brewer's Blackbird* (p. 153) and *Rusty Blackbird:* females have unstreaked underparts. *Brown-headed Cowbird* (p. 155): juvenile is smaller and has a stubbier bill.
Best Sites: Oak Hammock Marsh; Netley-Libau Marsh; Hecla/Grindstone PP; Delta Marsh; Turtle Mountain PP; Minnedosa pothole region.

WESTERN MEADOWLARK

Sturnella neglecta

The Western Meadowlark is a bird of the open-country, and it is common in southern parts of our province. It typically inhabits agricultural areas, and it can be seen perched on fenceposts and powerlines wherever grassy meadows and pastures are found. Many people think of it as the true harbinger of spring, because it arrives early in the season, usually in late March. Its rich and varied song (males have up to 12 song types) is recognized as one of the most beautiful voices of the prairies. • The meadowlark has distinguishing features that include a black, V-shaped 'necklace,' bright yellow underparts and a short tail with white outer feathers, which are often flicked open and closed. It is shaped much like a starling, and it flies in a similar style, alternating several quick wingbeats with a short glide. • The Western Meadowlark has adapted fairly well to human settlement on the prairies, nesting in considerable abundance in healthy grasslands, haylands and grassy ditches.

breeding

ID: *Male:* yellow underparts, including the throat; dark streaks on white sides; broad, black breast band; mottled brown upperparts; short tail with white outer tail feathers; long, pinkish legs; yellow lores; brown eye line; light median crown stripe; long, sharp bill. *Female:* slightly smaller; paler yellow; black V on the breast is less defined.
Size: *L* 23–24 cm.
Status: occasional in the north; fairly common in central parts; abundant in the south; late March to mid-October; a few may be present in winter.
Habitat: grassy meadows, native prairie, pastures, hayfields and grassy road allowances.
Nesting: in a depression or scrape on the ground; domed grass nest, with a side entrance, is woven into and concealed by surrounding vegetation; female incubates 3–7 white eggs, spotted with brown and purple, for 13–15 days; usually has 2 broods per year.
Feeding: gleans the ground for grasshoppers, crickets, beetles, other insects and spiders; also eats some seeds and digs up grubs and worms.
Voice: song is a melodic series of fluty notes; calls include a low, loud *chuck* or *chup*, a rattling flight call or a few clear whistled notes: *who-who are you?*
Similar Species: *Dickcissel:* much smaller; solid dark crown; white throat; lacks the brown streaking on the light sides; accidental in Manitoba.
Best Sites: Oak Hammock Marsh; Delta Marsh; Spruce Woods PP; Poverty Plains.

YELLOW-HEADED BLACKBIRD

Xanthocephalus xanthocephalus

Y ou might expect a bird as handsome as the Yellow-headed Blackbird to have a song to match its splendid gold and black plumage. Unfortunately, a trip to a nearby marsh will quickly reveal the shocking truth: when the male arches his golden head backward, he struggles to produce a painful, discordant, grinding noise. In fact, this song is regarded by many birdwatchers as the worst in North America. • Where Yellow-headed Blackbirds occur with Red-winged Blackbirds, the larger Yellow-heads dominate, commandeering the centre of the wetland and pushing the red-winged competitors to the periphery. • Yellow-headed Black-birds routinely leave their marsh habitat to forage for seeds and insects in upland fields and pastures. Unlike other blackbirds, however, their nests are only ever found in areas of deep water away from the shoreline. • According to surveys, Yellow-headed Blackbird numbers are increasing across North America.

ID: *Male:* yellow head and breast; black body; white wing patches; black lores and bill. *Female:* dusky-brown overall; yellow wash on the breast, throat, eyebrow; partially yellow in the face; white lower breast.
Size: *L* 20–28 cm.
Status: occasional in the north; uncommon in central parts; common in the south; mid-April to mid-October; a few may be present in winter.
Habitat: permanent marshes and sloughs and river impoundments where cattails or dense stands of emergent vegetation dominate; will forage on upland fields, pastures and grasslands.

Nesting: in loose colonies; bulky, deep basket nest made of wet aquatic vegetation is lashed to emergent vegetation over water and lined with dry grass; female incubates 3–5 brown-blotched, greenish-white eggs for 11–13 days.
Feeding: gleans the ground and vegetation for seeds, beetles, snails, waterbugs and dragonflies; young are fed by regurgitation.
Voice: low, hoarse, grating song; call is a deep *kack* or *kruck*.
Similar Species: male is distinctive. *Other female blackbirds:* lack the yellow throat and face.
Best Sites: Oak Hammock Marsh; Grand Beach PP; Pinkerton Lakes; Alexander/ Griswold Marsh; Oak/Plum lakes; Minnedosa pothole region.

BREWER'S BLACKBIRD

Euphagus cyanocephalus

The Brewer's Blackbird is a summer inhabitant of southern Manitoba's agricultural belt, where it is commonly seen along roadsides searching for road-killed insects and squabbling with Rock Doves and European Starlings. • This blackbird is commonly mistaken for a Common Grackle because both birds jerk their head back and forth while walking, and when observed under the bright sunshine, their iridescent feathers reflect various hues of blue, purple or green. • The Brewer's Blackbird is highly gregarious throughout the year. Unlike the more solitary Rusty Blackbird of northern bogs and wetlands, the Brewer's Blackbird almost always nests in colonies. As fall approaches, the colonies join with other family groups to form large, migrating flocks.

ID: *Male:* pale yellow eyes; iridescent green body and purplish head often look black; fall males may show faint rusty feather edgings. *Female:* brownish-grey plumage; darker back, wings and tail; dark eyes.
Size: *L* 20–25 cm.
Status: uncommon to fairly common in central parts; common in the south; early April to early October; a few may be present in winter.
Habitat: *Nesting:* open country with scattered brush, field edges, shelterbelts and roadsides. *Non-nesting:* may overwinter in feedlots.
Nesting: in loose colonies; on the ground or low in a shrub or tree, often near water; bulky open nest of twigs, grass, mud and forbs is lined with rootlets, fine grass and hair; female incubates 3–7 brown-spotted, pale grey eggs for 12–14 days.

Feeding: gleans the ground for invertebrates and seeds while walking along shorelines and open areas; may eat some fruit and berries.
Voice: song a creaking *k-shee*; call is a metallic *chick* or *check*.
Similar Species: *Rusty Blackbird:* more slender bill; rusty wash overall in non-breeding plumage; breeding male has subtler green and blue gloss in the plumage; female has yellow eyes. *Common Grackle* (p. 154): much longer, keeled tail; larger body and bill. *Brown-headed Cowbird* (p. 155): shorter tail; stubbier, thicker bill; male has dark eyes and a brown head; female has paler streaked underparts and a pale throat. *European Starling* (p. 125): bill is yellow in summer; speckled appearance; dark eyes.
Best Sites: Whiteshell PP; Birds Hill PP; Oak Hammock Marsh; Interlake area; Delta Marsh; Poverty Plains.

COMMON GRACKLE

Quiscalus quiscula

Some people feel disdain for the Common Grackle because of its raucous call, habit of robbing other bird's nests and overall cheekiness. In the U.S., grain crop damage by large, post-breeding flocks of grackles has led some communities to support grackle population control programs. On the other hand, some people appreciate the grackle's boldness and its habit of ridding our lawns and gardens of pesky insects. • The Common Grackle is easily distinguished from other glossy blackbirds by its relatively large size, its heavy bill and long, 'keeled' or wedge-shaped tail. In flight, the grackle's tail trails behind it like a hatchet blade. • Grackles nest in isolated pairs in forested regions of the province, and in southern Manitoba they nest in colonies in cities, towns and farmsteads. In late fall and early winter, most grackles migrate to the U.S., but each year a few remain in our province, finding shelter among livestock in feedlots. • Grackles are widespread in North America, but their numbers are in decline.

ID: *Male:* iridescent plumage (purplish-blue head and breast, bronze back and sides and purple wings and tail) often looks black; long, keeled tail; yellow eyes; long, heavy bill. *Female:* smaller, duller and less iridescent. *Juvenile:* dull brown overall; dark eyes.
Size: *L* 28–34 cm.
Status: rare in the north; fairly common in central parts; uncommon to common in the south; early April to late October; a few may be present in winter.
Habitat: hedgerows, open forests, riparian woodlands, shrubby urban and suburban parks and gardens, partly open areas with scattered trees and along the edges of coniferous forests.
Nesting: in dense tree or shrub branches or emergent vegetation, often near water; sometimes in a conifer; bulky cup nest of twigs,

grass and mud is lined with fine grass or feathers; female incubates 3–6 brown-blotched, pale blue eggs for 12–14 days.
Feeding: gleans the ground for insects, earthworms, seeds, grain, aquatic invertebrates and fruit; may eat some bird eggs and nestlings.
Voice: song is a split rasping *tssh-schleek* or *gri-de-leeek*; call is a loud *graack* or *swaaaack*.
Similar Species: *Rusty Blackbird* and *Brewer's Blackbird* (p. 153): smaller overall; lack the heavy bill and the keeled tail. *Red-winged Blackbird* (p. 150): shorter, unkeeled tail; male has a red shoulder patch and dark eyes. *European Starling* (p. 123): very short tail; long, thin bill (yellow in summer); speckled overall; dark eyes.
Best Sites: widespread, often in open parks, townsites and yards with some conifers.

BROWN-HEADED COWBIRD

Molothrus ater

The Brown-headed Cowbird's song, a bubbling, liquidy *glug-ahl-whee*, might translate to other birds as 'here comes trouble!' Historically, Brown-headed Cowbirds followed bison herds across the plains and prairies—they now follow cattle—and their nomadic lifestyle made it impossible for them to construct and tend a nest. Instead, cowbirds engage in 'brood parasitism,' laying their eggs in the nests of other songbirds. Many of the songbirds do not recognize the cowbird eggs and raise the cowbirds as their own. Cowbird chicks typically hatch first and develop much more quickly than their nestmates, which are pushed out of the nest or out-competed for food. • The expansion of ranching, the fragmentation of forests and the extensive network of transportation corridors in North America has significantly increased the cowbird's range. It now parasitizes more than 140 bird species in North America, including species that probably had no contact with it prior to widespread human settlement.

ID: short, stubby bill; squared tail; dark eyes. *Male:* blackish body may show slight blue iridescence; brown head. *Female:* grey-brown overall; paler underparts with faint streaking; pale throat. *Immature:* paler buff-grey with soft breast streaking.
Size: *L* 15–20 cm.
Status: rare in the north; fairly common to common in central parts and in the south; late April to early August.
Habitat: woodland fringes, forest openings, shrubby grasslands and areas near cattle (pastures, feedlots and stockyards); also landfills, campgrounds and picnic areas.
Nesting: does not build a nest; females lay up to 40 eggs a year in the nests of other birds (usually 1 egg per nest); whitish eggs, marked with grey and brown, hatch after 10–13 days.

Feeding: gleans the ground for seeds, waste grain and invertebrates, especially grasshoppers, beetles and true bugs.
Voice: song is a high, liquidy gurgle *glug-ahl-whee* or *glug-glug-gleee*; call is a whistled *seep* or *weee-titi*, often given in flight; also a fast, chipping *ch-ch-ch-ch-ch-ch*.
Similar Species: *Blackbirds:* larger; lack the contrasting brown head and darker body; slimmer, longer bills; longer tails; all have yellow eyes except for the female Brewer's Blackbird. *Common Grackle* (p. 154): much larger overall; longer, heavier bill; longer, keeled tail. *European Starling* (p. 125): immature has a longer bill and a shorter tail.
Best Sites: widespread, especially among cattle pastures, stockyards, feedlots, fencelines and roadsides.

BALTIMORE ORIOLE

Icterus galbula

Baltimore Orioles are fairly common in central and southern parts of our province, but they are often difficult to find because they inhabit the forest heights. The striking males are visible when they sing from perches, but the females typically remain near their nest, which is hidden in the upper canopy of a large shade tree. • Baltimore Orioles prefer open stands of deciduous trees over extensive forest, and they are particularly partial to small patches of shade trees in cities, towns and farmyards. They are some of the last birds to move into our province each spring, arriving when the trees have leaves and the insects have hatched. • Like many songbirds that nest in Manitoba, the Baltimore Oriole is really only a visitor to our province: it spends at least half of each year in the tropical forests of Central and South America.

ID: *Male:* black head, throat, back, wings and central tail feathers; bright orange underparts, shoulder stripe, rump and outer tail feathers; white wing bar and flight feather edgings. *Female:* olive-brown upperparts (darkest on the head); dull yellowish-orange underparts and rump; 2 white wing bars. *Immature:* resembles an adult female, but the juvenile male has brighter underparts and the juvenile female has duller upperparts.
Size: *L* 18–20 cm.
Status: fairly common in central parts; common in the south; mid-May to early September.
Habitat: parkland and open, mixed coniferous forests, mature riparian woodlands, forest fringes and openings, orchards and yards with scattered shade trees.
Nesting: high in a deciduous tree; deep hanging pouch nest of grass, shredded bark, string, hair and plant fibres is lined with fine grass, rootlets and fur; female incubates 4–6 greyish-white eggs, marked

with black, for 12–14 days.
Feeding: gleans canopy vegetation and shrubs for caterpillars, beetles, wasps and other invertebrates; eats some fruit and nectar; may visit hummingbird feeders.
Voice: 2- or 3-note phrases are strung together into a delightfully robust song: *peter peter here here peter*; other calls include a 2-note *tea-too*, a rapid chatter *ch-ch-ch-ch-ch* and a low, whistled *hewli* note.
Similar Species: *Bullock's Oriole:* male has a large white wing patch, black throat patch and an orange face with a black eye line; female has a greyer back and white belly; accidental in Manitoba. *Orchard Oriole:* smaller; male has darker chestnut plumage; female and immature are olive and yellow and lack the orange overtones. *Scarlet Tanager* (p. 137): females have a thicker, paler bill and lack the wing bars and orange underparts.
Best Sites: Whiteshell PP; Birds Hill PP; Interlake area; Delta Marsh; Spruce Woods PP; Turtle Mountain PP.

PINE GROSBEAK

Pinicola enucleator

Pine Grosbeaks are colourful nomads of the boreal forest. Much of their survival depends on the availability of conifer seeds, particularly from pine and spruce trees, so they are always in search of a good crop. They are erratic winter visitors to southern Manitoba, and it is a great moment in a typical winter when the Pine Grosbeaks emerge from the wilds to settle on your backyard feeder. These winter visits thrill southern Manitoba naturalists—the birds' bright colours and exciting flock behaviour are certainly a welcome sight. The invasions are not completely understood, but is thought that widespread cone crop failures or even changes to forest ecology caused by logging, forest fires or climatic factors may force these hungry 'finches' southward in search of food. • During the nesting season, adult grosbeaks develop pouches in their mouth for transporting seeds to their young.

ID: stubby, dark bill; 2 white wing bars; black wings and tail. *Male:* crimson-red head, rump and breast; streaked back; grey sides, flanks, belly and undertail coverts. *Female* and *Immature:* grey overall; males have yellow or orangy-crimson wash on the head and rump. *In flight:* deeply undulating flight style.
Size: *L* 20–25 cm.
Status: rare in the north; uncommon in the central boreal forest; March to October; highly erratic and rare in the north; common in central parts; fairly common in the south; mid-October to mid-March.
Habitat: *Nesting:* open spruce-fir coniferous forests and forest fringes. *Non-nesting:* conifer plantations and urban and rural yards with feeders and fruiting mountain ash and crabapple trees.
Nesting: in a conifer or tall shrub; bulky cup nest, loosely made of twigs, grass, forbs and rootlets, is lined with lichens, rootlets and fine grass; female incubates 3–5 speckled, pale greenish-blue eggs for 13–15 days.
Feeding: gleans buds, berries and seeds from coniferous and deciduous trees; may use feeders in winter.
Voice: typical flight call is a whistled *tew-tew-tew*; alarm call is a musical *chee-vli*.
Similar Species: *White-winged Crossbill* (p. 159): much smaller; lacks the stubby bill; larger white wing bars. *Red Crossbill:* much smaller; lacks the stubby bill and the white wing bars. *Evening Grosbeak* (p. 163): female has a yellow bill, tan underparts and bold, white wing patches.
Best Sites: *Nesting:* Paint Lake PP; Churchill. *Non-nesting:* Assiniboine Park; Victoria Beach; Sandilands Provincial Forest.

PURPLE FINCH

Carpodacus purpureus

The Purple Finch's gentle nature, rich song and lovely plumage make it a welcome guest in any backyard. Its presence near an ornamental shrub or feeder is certain to brighten a drab winter's day. • Purple Finches prefer to nest in shrubs and coniferous trees, and in migration and during winter they feed in deciduous trees and from feeders. • The courtship of Purple Finches is a gentle and appealing ritual. Upon the arrival of an interested female, the colourful male dances lightly around her, vocalizing and beating his wings until he lifts softly into the air. • It has been difficult to study Purple Finch population trends in the boreal forest because of a lack of breeding bird survey routes. Studies in other regions of North America have revealed declines in Purple Finch numbers.

ID: *Male:* crimson-red head, throat, breast and rump; brownish-red cheek patch, sides and streaked back; dark, notched tail; light, unstreaked belly and undertail. *Female* and *Immature:* dark brown cheek and jaw line; white eyebrow and lower cheek stripes; dark brown upperparts; heavily streaked underparts; lighter, unstreaked belly and undertail.
Size: *L* 13–15 cm.
Status: uncommon to fairly common; late March to mid-October; a few may be present in winter.
Habitat: *Nesting:* open coniferous and mixed forests, forest fringes and conifers in cities and towns. *In migration:* open coniferous, mixed or parkland forests. *Winter:* feeders or fruit trees.
Nesting: on a conifer branch; cup nest, woven with twigs, grass and

rootlets, is lined with fine grass, moss and hair; female incubates 3–6 pale greenish-blue eggs, marked with black and brown, for 13 days.
Feeding: gleans the ground and vegetation for seeds, buds, blossoms, berries and insects; also visits table-style feeders.
Voice: song is a fast, lively warble similar to the Warbling Vireo song but richer and more sustained; call is a metallic *tick* or *weet*.
Similar Species: *House Finch:* male has a distinct brown cap and cheek patch; female lacks the white eyebrow and the dark chin stripes. *Red Crossbill:* bill has crossed tips; male is a richer red overall and has darker wings.
Best Sites: *Nesting:* Whiteshell PP; Nopiming PP; Riding Mountain NP. *Non-nesting:* Assiniboine Park; Sandilands Provincial Forest.

WHITE-WINGED CROSSBILL

Loxia leucoptera

Crossbills are the gypsies of the bird world, wandering far and wide in search of ripe conifer cones. There is no telling when or where they will find the next bumper crop, and they might breed regardless of the season. White-winged Crossbills favour spruce and tamarack seeds, and their oddly shaped bills are an adaptation for prying open cones. Crossbills are so efficient at extracting seeds that a foraging flock high in a spruce tree can create an unforgettable shower of conifer cone scales. • When not foraging in spruce spires, White-winged Crossbills often drop to ground level, where they drink water from shallow forest pools or lick salt from winter roads. Unfortunately, the habit of licking salt from roadsides often results in crossbill fatalities. • Manitoba is also home to the Red Crossbill. They are nomadic birds, but they wander through our forests in search of pine, not spruce seeds.

ID: bill has crossed tips; 2 bold, white wing bars; dark wings and tail. *Male:* pinkish-red overall. *Female:* streaked olive-yellow upperparts; dusky yellow underparts, slightly streaked with brown. *Juvenile:* streaky olive-brown overall.
Size: *L* 15–17 cm.
Status: occasional in the north; highly irruptive and uncommon to locally common in the central and southern boreal forest; year-round; highly irruptive and uncommon to locally common in the south; October to March.
Habitat: coniferous forests (primarily spruce, fir and tamarack); may appear in conifers in townsites and parkland forests; may also forage in poplars in mixed stands or in sunflower fields.
Nesting: on an outer branch of a conifer; open cup nest of twigs, grass, bark shreds and forbs is lined with moss, lichens, rootlets,

hair, feathers and plant down; female incubates 2–5 pale bluish-green eggs, spotted with brown and lavender, for 12–14 days.
Feeding: prefers spruce and tamarack seeds; also eats deciduous tree seeds, buds, berries and some insects; often licks salt and minerals from roads; young are fed by regurgitation.
Voice: song is a mingling of warbles, trills and pure clear notes; call note is a liquid *cheat* and a dry *chif-chif*, often given in flight.
Similar Species: *Red Crossbill:* lacks the white wing bars; male is deeper red. *Pine Siskin* (p. 161): similar to the juvenile, but lacks the crossed bill, is smaller, has lighter coloured underparts and yellow highlights in the wing. *Pine Grosbeak* (p. 157): much larger, stubby bill; thinner wing bars; female is greyer. *Purple Finch* (p. 158) and *House Finch:* stubby bills; less red overall; lack the wing bars.
Best Sites: *Nesting:* Whiteshell PP; Nopiming PP; Atikaki PP; Grass River PP. *Non-nesting:* Assiniboine Park.

COMMON REDPOLL

Carduelis flammea

Common Redpolls are renowned for their effective winter adaptations, but they have a very small surface area relative to their internal volume, so they are in constant danger of running out of fuel and dying from hypothermia. Hence, redpolls must eat almost constantly during winter, and most of their time is spent gleaning waste grain from fields or stocking up on seed at winter feeders. Because of their focus on food, wintering redpolls are remarkably fearless of humans, provided the observer moves slowly and quietly. • Common Redpolls and Hoary Redpolls can be confusing to differentiate because they look alike, share similar ranges and have similar calls. The Hoary Redpoll is almost always seen with flocks of Common Redpolls, and it is generally paler and less streaked. Both redpolls are remote northern nesters and 'predictably unpredictable' winter visitors to our province— like many finches, they can be abundant one year and nearly absent the next.

non-breeding

ID: red forecrown; black chin patch; yellowish bill; streaky brown upperparts; lightly streaked rump, sides, flanks and undertail coverts; notched tail. *Male:* pinkish-red breast is brightest in breeding plumage. *Female:* whitish to pale grey breast.
Size: *L* 13 cm.
Status: fairly common to common, but irruptive in the north; year-round; common, but irruptive in central parts and in the south; mid-October to mid-April.
Habitat: *Nesting:* scattered shrubs within coastal tundra and boreal taiga. *Non-nesting:* weedy fields (especially sunflower fields), roadsides, railways, farmyards with spilled grain and backyards with feeders.
Nesting: in a low shrub, dwarf spruce or crevice among rocks; open cup nest of fine twigs, grass, plant stems, lichens and moss is lined with feathers, hair and seed

fluff; female incubates 4–7 blue eggs, spotted with purple, for 10 or 11 days.
Feeding: gleans the ground and weed patches in large flocks for seeds in winter; often visits feeding stations; may also eat suet; small seeds and insects are taken in summer.
Voice: song is a high-pitched melody, usually followed by rattling *chit* notes; twitters constantly in flight, interspersed by long 2-note *sssssss-eeeet* calls.
Similar Species: *Hoary Redpoll:* shorter bill; unstreaked or lightly streaked rump; usually has faint streaking or no streaking on the sides, flanks and undertail; generally paler and more plump overall.
Pine Siskin (p. 161): heavily streaked overall; yellow highlights in the wings and tail; lacks the red cap.
Best Sites: *Year-round:* Churchill; Wapusk NP. *Non-nesting:* throughout Manitoba in weedy patches, unthrashed flax, canola or sunflower fields and at backyard feeders.

PINE SISKIN

Carduelis pinus

Birdwatchers in pursuit of Pine Siskins are often met with frustration, aching feet and a sore, crimped neck. The smartest way to meet these birds is to set up a finch feeder filled with black niger seed in your backyard and wait for them to appear. Pine Siskins will visit feeders at just about any time of year, but they will disappear just as suddenly as they appeared. • Siskin flocks twitter incessantly and deliver frequent rising *zzzreeeee* calls. They are highly gregarious birds, and they are rarely found in small numbers, often feeding in mixed-species flocks that include gold-finches, juncos and crossbills. • Siskins are typically associated with pines and other conifers. Like most finches, they are highly nomadic and rarely occupy the same nesting territories in successive years.

ID: heavily streaked underparts; yellow highlights at the base of the tail feathers and in the wings (easily seen in flight); dull wing bars; darker brown, heavily streaked upperparts; deeply forked tail; striped facial pattern; pointed bill. *Immature:* dull white in the wings and tail.
Size: *L* 11–13 cm.
Status: irruptive; occasional in the north; common in central parts; uncommon to fairly common in the south (more common in migration); April to October; uncommon in central parts and in the south; October to March.
Habitat: *Nesting:* coniferous and mixed forests, urban parks, rural ornamental trees and shade trees. *Non-nesting:* often near feeders, weedy areas and sunflower fields.
Nesting: usually in loose colonies; on the outer branch of a conifer; loose cup nest of twigs, grass and rootlets is lined with feathers, hair, rootlets and seed fluff; female

incubates 3–6 lightly spotted, pale blue eggs for 13 days.
Feeding: coniferous and deciduous tree seeds, thistle seeds, buds, sap and some insects; attracted to road salts and birdfeeders.
Voice: song is similar to the American Goldfinch's but is coarser and wheezy, sometimes resembling a jerky laugh; call is a buzzy, rising *zzzreeeee*; also *tit-i-tit* and a loud *chlee-ip*.
Similar Species: *Common Redpoll* (p. 160) and *Hoary Redpoll:* red forecrown; much shorter bill; lack the yellow in the wings and tail; underparts are not streaked throughout. *Purple Finch* (p. 158) and *House Finch:* no yellow in the wings or tail; darker head and upperparts; females have a thicker bill. *Sparrows* (pp. 139–44): all lack yellow in the wings and tail; underparts are not streaked throughout.
Best Sites: Whiteshell PP; Nopiming PP; Birds Hill PP; Lake Francis; Spruce Woods PP; Duck Mountain PP.

AMERICAN GOLDFINCH
Carduelis tristis

The American Goldfinch is a bright, cheery songbird that is commonly seen in weedy fields, along roadsides and among backyard shrubs. It seems to delight in perching upon late-summer thistle heads as it searches for seeds, and in winter it eats niger seed at finch feeders or millet from hanging tassels. • Their territorial and flight songs are varied, but listen for their distinctive *po-ta-to-chip* or *per-chick-or-ree* call. Goldfinches are also readily identified by their undulating flight style and bright yellow plumage. • The male's black cap and wings distinguish him from the other yellow birds that are also mistakenly called 'wild canaries.' • In Manitoba, goldfinches nest in loose colonies among hawthorn shrubs, saskatoon shrubs and maple saplings. They are among the province's latest nesters, usually delaying their reproductive duties until late June to ensure there is a dependable source of thistles and dandelion seeds to feed their young.

breeding

ID: *Breeding male:* black cap (extends onto the forehead), wings and tail; bright yellow body; white wing bars and undertail; orange bill and legs. *Breeding female:* dull yellow-green upperparts; black wings with 2 bold, white wing bars; dark tail. *Winter adult:* similar to the summer female but is greyish-brown overall; some yellow on the throat, face and wings; pale rump.
Size: *L* 11–14 cm.
Status: fairly common in central parts; common in the south; mid-May to early October; rare to uncommon in winter.
Habitat: weedy fields, meadows and gardens, deciduous woodland fringes, shrubby riparian areas and open parks.
Nesting: in a deciduous shrub or tree; compact cup nest, woven with plant fibres, grass and spider silk, is lined with seed fluff and hair; female incubates 4–7 pale blue eggs for 10–12 days.
Feeding: primarily eats insects, berries and thistle, birch and alder seeds; commonly visits feeding stations; young are fed by regurgitation.
Voice: song is a canary-like series of trills, twitters and warbles; calls include *po-ta-to-chip* or *per-chic-or-ee* (often delivered in flight) and a whistled *dear-me, see-me*.
Similar Species: *Evening Grosbeak* (p. 163): much larger; massive bill; lacks the black forehead. *Wilson's Warbler:* olive upperparts; greenish wings without wing bars; thin, dark bill; black cap does not extend onto the forehead.
Best Sites: Assiniboine Park; Oak Hammock Marsh; Spruce Woods PP; Turtle Mountain PP; Riding Mountain NP.

EVENING GROSBEAK

Coccothraustes vespertinus

Unannounced, a large flock of Evening Grosbeaks descends upon a backyard feeder in southern Manitoba. These stunning gold and black birds are enjoyable to watch, but the proprietor of the feeder may soon come to realize that the grosbeaks are both an aesthetic blessing and a financial curse. The birds return day after day in large numbers, rapidly exhausting the supplies of expensive birdseed. Like most finches, Evening Grosbeaks are highly irruptive, meaning that large numbers are generally encountered every two to three years. However, dependable supplies of seed at backyard feeders has caused these birds to be less irruptive than they have been in the past. As April approaches, grosbeak numbers dwindle in southern parts of the province as the birds depart for their boreal nesting sites. • It was once thought that the Evening Grosbeak sang only in the evening, a fact that is reflected in both its common name and scientific names (*vespertinus* is Latin for 'of the evening').

ID: massive, light-coloured bill; black wings and tail; broad, white wing patches. *Male:* dark crown; bright yellow eyebrow and forehead band; dark brown head gradually fades into the golden-yellow belly and lower back. *Female:* grey head and upper back; yellow-tinged underparts; white undertail coverts.
Size: *L* 18–22 cm.
Status: common in the central boreal forest; year-round; uncommon and local in the south; April to October; fairly common in the south; November to March.
Habitat: *Nesting:* coniferous and mixed forests; also in second-growth woodlands and parks. *Non-nesting:* parks, towns and farms and coniferous, mixed and deciduous forests.

Nesting: on the outer limb of a conifer; flimsy cup nest of twigs and roots is lined with rootlets, fine grass, plant fibres, moss and pine needles; female incubates 3–5 pale greenish-blue eggs, speckled with brown and grey, for 11–14 days.
Feeding: eats tree and shrub seeds, buds and berries; also eats insects and licks mineral-rich soil; favours feeders with sunflower seeds.
Voice: song is a wandering, halting warble; call is a loud, sharp *clee-ip* or a clear *thew.*
Similar Species: *American Goldfinch* (p. 162): much smaller; small bill; smaller wing bars; male has a black cap. *Pine Grosbeak* (p. 157): female has a black bill, smaller wing bars and is grey overall.
Best Sites: *Nesting:* Whiteshell PP, Nopiming PP; Grass River PP. *Non-nesting:* Whiteshell PP; Birds Hill PP; Hecla/Grindstone PP.

HOUSE SPARROW

Passer domesticus

House Sparrows were introduced into North America in the 1850s near New York City as part of a plan to control the numbers of insects that were damaging grain and cereal crops. But the House Sparrow is largely vegetarian, so its impact on crop pests proved to be minimal. Since then, this Eurasian sparrow has managed to colonize most human-altered environments on the continent, and it has benefited greatly from a close association with humans. • House Sparrows were released in eastern Canada during the mid-1800s, and they were first noted in our province in 1892. In the early 1900s they were probably the most common bird in North America, but their populations declined somewhat when horses were replaced by automobiles. Recent 'clean' farming practices and better handling of human garbage have resulted in further declines. • House Sparrows are not closely related to other North American sparrows; they belong to the Weaver Finch family and are native to Eurasia and North Africa. • People who prefer to have Purple Martins, Tree Swallows or bluebirds rather than House Sparrows in their backyard nest boxes should plug the entrances in the fall and open them just before the birds return in the spring.

breeding

ID: *Breeding male:* grey crown, cheek; black lores; chestnut-brown eyebrows wrap around to the nape; white neck; black bib and bill; white wing bar; brown and mottled upperparts; grey rump and underparts.
Non-breeding male: smaller black bib; light-coloured bill. *Female:* brown upperparts; rusty brown, streaked wings and shoulders; greyish-brown underparts; buff eyebrow; lighter bill.
Size: *L* 14–17 cm.
Status: uncommon and local in the north; fairly common in central parts; abundant in the south; year-round.
Habitat: townsites, urban and suburban areas, farmyards, agricultural areas and other developed sites.

Nesting: often communal; in buildings, nest boxes, trees (especially conifers), shrubs or natural cavities; large, dome-shaped nest of grass, plant fibres and litter is lined with feathers; mostly female incubates 4–7 thickly speckled, dull white eggs for 10–13 days.
Feeding: seeds, insects and fruit; frequently visits feeding stations for seeds.
Voice: song is a plain, monotone *cheap-cheap-cheap-cheap*; call is a short *chill-up*.
Similar Species: *Harris's Sparrow:* grey face; black cap; pink-orange bill. *White-crowned Sparrow:* immature is similar to the female House Sparrow, but has a pink bill and a stripe through the crown.
Best Site: near farms and in urban areas.

GLOSSARY

accipiter: a forest hawk (genus Accipiter); characterized by a long tail and short, rounded wings; feeds mostly on birds.

brood: *n.* a family of young from one hatching; *v.* sit on eggs so as to hatch them.

covey: a brood or flock of partridges, quails or grouse.

creche: a 'daycare' for the young of colonially nesting birds.

crop: an enlargement of the esophagus; serves as a storage structure and (in pigeons) has glands that produce secretions.

dabbling: a foraging technique used by ducks, where the head and neck are submerged but the body and tail remain on the water's surface; dabbling ducks can usually walk easily on land, can take off without running and have brightly coloured speculums.

dimorphism: the existence of two distinct forms of a species, such as between the sexes.

eclipse: the dull, female-like plumage that male ducks briefly acquire after moulting from their breeding plumage.

fledgling: a young bird that has left the nest but is dependent upon its parents.

flycatching: a feeding behaviour where the bird leaves a perch, snatches an insect in mid-air and returns to the same perch; also known as 'hawking' or 'sallying.'

flushing: a behaviour where frightened birds explode into flight in response to a disturbance.

hawking: attempting to capture insects through aerial pursuit.

irruption: a sporadic mass migration of birds into a non-breeding area.

leading edge: the front edge of the wing as viewed from below.

lore: the small patch between the eye and the bill.

mantle: feathers of the back and upperside of folded wings.

moulting: the periodic replacement of worn out feathers (often twice a year).

nape: the back of the neck.

niche: an ecological role filled by a species.

parasitism: a relationship between two species where one benefits at the expense of the other.

plucking post: a perch habitually used by raptors to remove feathers or fur from prey.

polyandrous: having a mating strategy where one female breeds with several males.

polygynous: having a mating strategy where one male breeds with several females.

primaries: the outermost flight feathers.

raptor: a carnivorous (meat-eating) bird; includes eagles, hawks, falcons and owls.

rufous: rusty red in color.

scapulars: feathers of the shoulder, seeming to join the wing and back.

speculum: the patterned or colourful secondaries of ducks.

torpor: a state of lowered metabolism enabling a creature to endure conditions during which it cannot find sufficient food to sustain normal activity.

understorey: the shrub or thicket layer beneath a canopy of trees.

crown

eye line

eyebrow/supercilium

wing bars

lore

greater coverts

chin

rump

throat

tips of primary feathers

breast

tail feathers

flank

belly

undertail coverts

secondary feathers

SELECT REFERENCES

American Ornithologists' Union. 1998. *Check-list of North American Birds.* 7th ed. (and its supplements). American Ornithologists' Union, Washington, D.C.

Cadman, M.D., P.F.J. Eagles and F.M. Helleiner. 1987. *Atlas of the Breeding Birds of Ontario.* University of Waterloo Press, Waterloo.

Choate, E.A. 1985. *The Dictionary of American Bird Names.* Rev. ed. Harvard Common Press, Cambridge, Mass.

Cuthbert, C., J. Horton, M. McCowan, B. Robinson and N. Short. 1990. *Birder's Guide to Southwestern Manitoba.* Brandon Natural History Society, Brandon, Man.

Duncan, J.R. 1996. *Conservation Status Ranks of the Birds of Manitoba, MS Report 96–05.* Manitoba Conservation Centre, Winnipeg.

Ehrlich, P.R., D.S. Dobkin and D. Wheye. 1988. *The Birder's Handbook.* Fireside, New York.

Farrand, J., ed. 1983. *The Audubon Society Master Guide to Birding.* Vols. 1–3. Alfred A. Knopf, New York.

Godfrey, W.E. 1986. *The Birds of Canada.* Rev. ed. National Museum of Natural Sciences, Ottawa.

Hood, J., and D. Pisiak. 1998. *Birds–A Virtual Exhibition: The Birds of Manitoba Online.* Version 5.00. The Manitoba Museum of Man and Nature. <http://www.chin.gc.ca/Exhibitions/Birds/MMMN/English/>

Kaufman, K. 1996. *Lives of North American Birds.* Houghton Mifflin Co., Boston.

Manitoba Avian Research Committee. 1986. *Field Checklist of the Birds of Manitoba.* Manitoba Museum of Man and Nature and Manitoba Naturalists Society, Winnipeg.

National Geographic Society. 1999. *Field Guide to the Birds of North America.* 3rd ed. National Geographic Society, Washington, D.C.

Peterson, R.T. 1980. *A Field Guide to the Birds of Eastern and Central North America.* Houghton Mifflin Co., Boston.

Sauer, J.R., J.E. Hines, I. Thomas, J. Fallon and G. Gough. 1999. *The North American Breeding Bird Survey, Results and Analysis 1966–1998.* Version 98.1. USGS Patuxent Wildlife Research Center, Laurel, Md. <http://www.mbr-pwrc.usgs.gov/bbs/bbs.html>

Sauer, J.R., S. Schwartz and B. Hoover. 1996. *The Christmas Bird Count Home Page.* Version 95.1. USGS Patuxent Wildlife Research Center, Laurel, Md. <http://www.mbr-pwrc.usgs.gov/bbs/bbs.html>

Stokes, D.W., and L.Q. Stokes. 1996. *Stokes Field Guide to Birds: Eastern Region.* Little, Brown & Co., Toronto.

Stokes, D.W., and L.Q. Stokes. 1996. *Stokes Field Guide to Birds: Western Region.* Little, Brown & Co., Toronto.

Terres, J.K. 1995. *The Audubon Society Encyclopedia of North American Birds.* Wings Books, New York.

CHECKLIST

The following checklist contains 406 species of birds that have been officially recorded in Manitoba. Species are grouped by family and listed in taxonomic order in accordance with the A.O.U. *Check-list of North American Birds* (7th ed.) and its supplements.

Accidental species (species that do not regularly occur in Manitoba) are listed in italics. An (ep) identifies species that once occurred regularly in the province but are now unlikely to be seen. An asterisk (*) identifies species that nest or have nested in the province. A plus (+) identifies introduced species. An (e) identifies species that once occurred in the province but are now extinct.

Loons (Gaviidae)
- ❑ Red-throated Loon*
- ❑ Pacific Loon*
- ❑ Common Loon*
- ❑ *Yellow-billed Loon*

Grebes (Podicipedidae)
- ❑ Pied-billed Grebe*
- ❑ Horned Grebe*
- ❑ Red-necked Grebe*
- ❑ Eared Grebe*
- ❑ Western Grebe*
- ❑ Clark's Grebe*

Shearwaters & Petrels (Procellariidae)
- ❑ *Northern Fulmar*

Gannets (Sulidae)
- ❑ *Northern Gannet*

Pelicans (Pelecanidae)
- ❑ American White Pelican*

Cormorants (Phalacrocoracidae)
- ❑ Double-crested Cormorant*

Herons (Ardeidae)
- ❑ American Bittern*
- ❑ Least Bittern*
- ❑ Great Blue Heron*
- ❑ Great Egret*
- ❑ *Snowy Egret*
- ❑ *Little Blue Heron*
- ❑ *Tricolored Heron*
- ❑ Cattle Egret
- ❑ Green Heron*
- ❑ Black-crowned Night-Heron*
- ❑ *Yellow-crowned Night-Heron*

Ibises & Spoonbills (Threskiornithidae)
- ❑ *White Ibis*
- ❑ *Glossy Ibis*
- ❑ *White-faced Ibis*

Vultures (Cathartidae)
- ❑ Turkey Vulture*

Waterfowl (Anatidae)
- ❑ Greater White-fronted Goose
- ❑ Snow Goose*
- ❑ Ross' Goose*
- ❑ Canada Goose*
- ❑ Brant
- ❑ *Barnacle Goose*
- ❑ Mute Swan*+
- ❑ Trumpeter Swan (ep*)
- ❑ Tundra Swan*
- ❑ Wood Duck*
- ❑ Gadwall*
- ❑ *Eurasian Wigeon*
- ❑ American Wigeon*
- ❑ American Black Duck*
- ❑ Mallard*
- ❑ Blue-winged Teal*
- ❑ *Cinnamon Teal*
- ❑ Northern Shoveler*
- ❑ Northern Pintail*
- ❑ *Garganey*
- ❑ Green-winged Teal*
- ❑ Canvasback*
- ❑ Redhead*
- ❑ Ring-necked Duck*
- ❑ Greater Scaup*
- ❑ Lesser Scaup*
- ❑ *King Eider*
- ❑ Common Eider*
- ❑ *Harlequin Duck*
- ❑ Surf Scoter*
- ❑ White-winged Scoter*
- ❑ Black Scoter*
- ❑ Oldsquaw*
- ❑ Bufflehead*
- ❑ Common Goldeneye*
- ❑ *Barrow's Goldeneye*
- ❑ *Smew*
- ❑ Hooded Merganser*
- ❑ Common Merganser*
- ❑ Red-breasted Merganser*
- ❑ Ruddy Duck*

Kites, Hawks & Eagles (Accipitridae)
- ❑ Osprey*
- ❑ *Swallow-tailed Kite*
- ❑ *White-tailed Kite*
- ❑ Bald Eagle*
- ❑ Northern Harrier*
- ❑ Sharp-shinned Hawk*
- ❑ Cooper's Hawk*
- ❑ Northern Goshawk*
- ❑ *Red-shouldered Hawk*
- ❑ Broad-winged Hawk*
- ❑ Swainson's Hawk*
- ❑ Red-tailed Hawk*
- ❑ Ferruginous Hawk*
- ❑ Rough-legged Hawk*
- ❑ Golden Eagle*

Falcons & Caracaras (Falconidae)
❑ American Kestrel*
❑ Merlin*
❑ Gyrfalcon
❑ Peregrine Falcon*
❑ Prairie Falcon

Grouse & Allies (Phasianidae)
❑ Gray Partridge*+
❑ Ring-necked Pheasant*+
❑ Ruffed Grouse*
❑ *Sage Grouse*
❑ Spruce Grouse*
❑ Willow Ptarmigan*
❑ Rock Ptarmigan
❑ Sharp-tailed Grouse*
❑ Greater Prairie-Chicken (ep*)
❑ Wild Turkey*+

Rails & Coots (Rallidae)
❑ Yellow Rail*
❑ *Black Rail*
❑ *King Rail*
❑ Virginia Rail*
❑ Sora*
❑ *Common Moorhen*
❑ American Coot*

Cranes (Gruidae)
❑ Sandhill Crane*
❑ Whooping Crane (ep*)

Plovers (Charadriidae)
❑ Black-bellied Plover
❑ American Golden-Plover*
❑ Semipalmated Plover*
❑ Piping Plover*
❑ Killdeer*

Stilts & Avocets (Recurvirostridae)
❑ *Black-necked Stilt*
❑ American Avocet*

Sandpipers & Allies (Scolopacidae)
❑ Greater Yellowlegs*
❑ Lesser Yellowlegs*

❑ Solitary Sandpiper*
❑ Willet*
❑ *Wandering Tattler*
❑ Spotted Sandpiper*
❑ *Terek Sandpiper*
❑ Upland Sandpiper*
❑ Eskimo Curlew (ep)
❑ Whimbrel*
❑ Long-billed Curlew (ep*)
❑ Hudsonian Godwit*
❑ Marbled Godwit*
❑ Ruddy Turnstone*
❑ Red Knot
❑ Sanderling
❑ Semipalmated Sandpiper*
❑ *Western Sandpiper*
❑ Least Sandpiper*
❑ White-rumped Sandpiper
❑ Baird's Sandpiper*
❑ Pectoral Sandpiper*
❑ *Purple Sandpiper*
❑ Dunlin*
❑ *Curlew Sandpiper*
❑ Stilt Sandpiper*
❑ Buff-breasted Sandpiper
❑ *Ruff*
❑ Short-billed Dowitcher*
❑ Long-billed Dowitcher
❑ Common Snipe*
❑ American Woodcock*
❑ Wilson's Phalarope*
❑ Red-necked Phalarope*
❑ Red Phalarope

Gulls & Allies (Laridae)
❑ Pomarine Jaeger*
❑ Parasitic Jaeger*
❑ Long-tailed Jaeger*
❑ *Laughing Gull*
❑ Franklin's Gull*
❑ Little Gull*
❑ *Black-headed Gull*
❑ Bonaparte's Gull*
❑ *Black-tailed Gull*
❑ *Mew Gull*
❑ Ring-billed Gull*
❑ California Gull*
❑ Herring Gull*
❑ Thayer's Gull*
❑ *Iceland Gull*
❑ *Lesser Black-backed Gull*

❑ *Glaucous-winged Gull*
❑ Glaucous Gull
❑ *Great Black-backed Gull*
❑ Sabine's Gull*
❑ *Black-legged Kittiwake*
❑ Ross' Gull*
❑ *Ivory Gull*
❑ Caspian Tern*
❑ *Royal Tern*
❑ Common Tern*
❑ Arctic Tern*
❑ Forster's Tern*
❑ *Least Tern*
❑ *White-winged Tern*
❑ Black Tern*

Alcids (Alcidae)
❑ *Dovekie*
❑ *Thick-billed Murre*
❑ Black Guillemot*
❑ *Ancient Murrelet*

Pigeons & Doves (Columbidae)
❑ Rock Dove*
❑ *Band-tailed Pigeon*
❑ *White-winged Dove*
❑ Mourning Dove*
❑ Passenger Pigeon (e*)

Cuckoos (Cuculidae)
❑ Black-billed Cuckoo*
❑ *Yellow-billed Cuckoo*
❑ *Ani* (unidentified sp.)

Barn Owls (Tytonidae)
❑ *Barn Owl*

Owls (Strigidae)
❑ Eastern Screech-Owl*
❑ Great Horned Owl*
❑ Snowy Owl*
❑ Northern Hawk Owl*
❑ Burrowing Owl*
❑ Barred Owl*
❑ Great Gray Owl*
❑ Long-eared Owl*
❑ Short-eared Owl*
❑ Boreal Owl*
❑ Northern Saw-whet Owl*

Nightjars (Caprimulgidae)
- ❏ Common Nighthawk*
- ❏ *Common Poorwill*
- ❏ Whip-poor-will*

Swifts (Apodidae)
- ❏ Chimney Swift*

Hummingbirds (Trochilidae)
- ❏ Ruby-throated Hummingbird*
- ❏ *Rufous Hummingbird*

Kingfishers (Alcedinidae)
- ❏ Belted Kingfisher*

Woodpeckers (Picidae)
- ❏ *Lewis's Woodpecker*
- ❏ Red-headed Woodpecker*
- ❏ Red-bellied Woodpecker
- ❏ Yellow-bellied Sapsucker*
- ❏ *Red-breasted Sapsucker*
- ❏ Downy Woodpecker*
- ❏ Hairy Woodpecker*
- ❏ Three-toed Woodpecker*
- ❏ Black-backed Woodpecker*
- ❏ Northern Flicker*
- ❏ Pileated Woodpecker*

Flycatchers (Tyrannidae)
- ❏ Olive-sided Flycatcher*
- ❏ Western Wood-Pewee*
- ❏ Eastern Wood-Pewee*
- ❏ Yellow-bellied Flycatcher*
- ❏ *Acadian Flycatcher*
- ❏ Alder Flycatcher*
- ❏ Willow Flycatcher*
- ❏ Least Flycatcher*
- ❏ Eastern Phoebe*
- ❏ Say's Phoebe*
- ❏ Great Crested Flycatcher*
- ❏ Western Kingbird*
- ❏ Eastern Kingbird*
- ❏ *Scissor-tailed Flycatcher*

Shrikes (Laniidae)
- ❏ Loggerhead Shrike*
- ❏ Northern Shrike*

Vireos (Vireonidae)
- ❏ *White-eyed Vireo*
- ❏ *Bell's Vireo*
- ❏ Yellow-throated Vireo*
- ❏ Blue-headed Vireo*
- ❏ Warbling Vireo*
- ❏ Philadelphia Vireo*
- ❏ Red-eyed Vireo*

Crows, Jays & Magpies (Corvidae)
- ❏ Gray Jay*
- ❏ *Steller's Jay*
- ❏ Blue Jay*
- ❏ *Western Scrub-Jay*
- ❏ *Clark's Nutcracker*
- ❏ Black-billed Magpie*
- ❏ American Crow*
- ❏ Common Raven*

Larks (Alaudidae)
- ❏ Horned Lark*

Swallows (Hirundinidae)
- ❏ Purple Martin*
- ❏ Tree Swallow*
- ❏ *Violet-green Swallow*
- ❏ Northern Rough-winged Swallow*
- ❏ Bank Swallow*
- ❏ Cliff Swallow*
- ❏ Barn Swallow*

Chickadees & Titmice (Paridae)
- ❏ Black-capped Chickadee*
- ❏ Boreal Chickadee*
- ❏ *Tufted Titmouse*

Nuthatches (Sittidae)
- ❏ Red-breasted Nuthatch*
- ❏ White-breasted Nuthatch*
- ❏ *Pygmy Nuthatch*

Creepers (Certhiidae)
- ❏ Brown Creeper*

Wrens (Troglodytidae)
- ❏ *Rock Wren*
- ❏ *Carolina Wren*
- ❏ House Wren*
- ❏ Winter Wren*
- ❏ Sedge Wren*
- ❏ Marsh Wren*

Kinglets (Regulidae)
- ❏ Golden-crowned Kinglet*
- ❏ Ruby-crowned Kinglet*

Gnatcatchers (Sylviidae)
- ❏ *Blue-gray Gnatcatcher*

Thrushes (Turdidae)
- ❏ *Northern Wheatear*
- ❏ Eastern Bluebird*
- ❏ Mountain Bluebird*
- ❏ *Townsend's Solitaire*
- ❏ Veery*
- ❏ Gray-cheeked Thrush*
- ❏ Swainson's Thrush*
- ❏ Hermit Thrush*
- ❏ *Wood Thrush*
- ❏ American Robin*
- ❏ *Varied Thrush*

Mockingbirds & Thrashers (Mimidae)
- ❏ Gray Catbird*
- ❏ *Northern Mockingbird*
- ❏ *Sage Thrasher*
- ❏ Brown Thrasher*
- ❏ *Bendire's Thrasher*

Starlings (Sturnidae)
- ❏ European Starling*

Pipits (Motacillidae)
- ❏ *Yellow Wagtail*
- ❏ American Pipit*
- ❏ Sprague's Pipit*

Waxwings (Bombycillidae)
- ❏ Bohemian Waxwing*
- ❏ Cedar Waxwing*

Silky-flycatchers (Ptilogonatidae)
- ❏ *Phainopepla*

Wood-Warblers (Parulidae)
- ❏ *Blue-winged Warbler*
- ❏ Golden-winged Warbler*
- ❏ Tennessee Warbler*
- ❏ Orange-crowned Warbler*
- ❏ Nashville Warbler*
- ❏ Northern Parula*
- ❏ Yellow Warbler*
- ❏ Chestnut-sided Warbler*
- ❏ Magnolia Warbler*
- ❏ Cape May Warbler*
- ❏ Black-throated Blue Warbler
- ❏ Yellow-rumped Warbler*
- ❏ Black-throated Green Warbler*
- ❏ Blackburnian Warbler*
- ❏ *Yellow-throated Warbler*
- ❏ Pine Warbler*
- ❏ *Prairie Warbler*
- ❏ Palm Warbler*
- ❏ Bay-breasted Warbler*
- ❏ Blackpoll Warbler*
- ❏ *Cerulean Warbler*
- ❏ Black-and-white Warbler*
- ❏ American Redstart*
- ❏ *Prothonotary Warbler*
- ❏ *Worm-eating Warbler*
- ❏ Ovenbird*
- ❏ Northern Waterthrush*
- ❏ *Kentucky Warbler*
- ❏ Connecticut Warbler*
- ❏ Mourning Warbler*
- ❏ *MacGillivray's Warbler*
- ❏ Common Yellowthroat*
- ❏ *Hooded Warbler*
- ❏ Wilson's Warbler*
- ❏ Canada Warbler*
- ❏ *Yellow-breasted Chat*

Tanagers (Thraupidae)
- ❏ *Summer Tanager*
- ❏ Scarlet Tanager*
- ❏ *Western Tanager*

Sparrows & Allies (Emberizidae)
- ❏ *Green-tailed Towhee*
- ❏ Spotted Towhee*
- ❏ Eastern Towhee*
- ❏ American Tree Sparrow*
- ❏ Chipping Sparrow*
- ❏ Clay-colored Sparrow*
- ❏ *Brewer's Sparrow*
- ❏ *Field Sparrow*
- ❏ Vesper Sparrow*
- ❏ Lark Sparrow*
- ❏ Lark Bunting*
- ❏ Savannah Sparrow*
- ❏ Grasshopper Sparrow*
- ❏ Baird's Sparrow*
- ❏ *Henslow's Sparrow*
- ❏ Le Conte's Sparrow*
- ❏ Nelson's Sharp-tailed Sparrow*
- ❏ Fox Sparrow*
- ❏ Song Sparrow*
- ❏ Lincoln's Sparrow*
- ❏ Swamp Sparrow*
- ❏ White-throated Sparrow*
- ❏ Harris' Sparrow*
- ❏ White-crowned Sparrow*
- ❏ *Golden-crowned Sparrow*
- ❏ Dark-eyed Junco*
- ❏ *McCown's Longspur*
- ❏ Lapland Longspur*
- ❏ Smith's Longspur*
- ❏ Chestnut-collared Longspur*
- ❏ Snow Bunting*

Grosbeaks & Buntings (Cardinalidae)
- ❏ *Northern Cardinal*
- ❏ Rose-breasted Grosbeak*
- ❏ *Black-headed Grosbeak*
- ❏ *Blue Grosbeak*
- ❏ *Lazuli Bunting*
- ❏ Indigo Bunting*
- ❏ *Dickcissel*

Blackbirds & Allies (Icteridae)
- ❏ Bobolink*
- ❏ Red-winged Blackbird*

- ❏ *Eastern Meadowlark*
- ❏ Western Meadowlark*
- ❏ Yellow-headed Blackbird*
- ❏ Rusty Blackbird*
- ❏ Brewer's Blackbird*
- ❏ Common Grackle*
- ❏ Brown-headed Cowbird*
- ❏ Orchard Oriole*
- ❏ Baltimore Oriole*
- ❏ *Bullock's Oriole*

Finches (Fringillidae)
- ❏ *Brambling*
- ❏ *Gray-crowned Rosy-Finch*
- ❏ Pine Grosbeak*
- ❏ Purple Finch*
- ❏ *Cassin's Finch*
- ❏ House Finch*
- ❏ Red Crossbill*
- ❏ White-winged Crossbill*
- ❏ Common Redpoll*
- ❏ Hoary Redpoll*
- ❏ Pine Siskin*
- ❏ American Goldfinch*
- ❏ Evening Grosbeak*

Old World Sparrows (Passeridae)
- ❏ House Sparrow*
- ❏ *Eurasian Tree Sparrow*

INDEX OF SCIENTIFIC NAMES

This index references only the primary species accounts.

INDEX OF COMMON NAMES

Page numbers in boldface type refer to the primary, illustrated species accounts.

ABOUT THE AUTHORS

Inspired by wild creatures and wild places, Andy Bezener has developed a keen interest in the study and conservation of birds. Fieldwork with the Canadian Wildlife Service and a degree in conservation biology have given Andy joyful insight into the lives of many North American birds. His admiration and concern for wilderness and wildlife has led him across much of North America and southern Africa. Andy is coauthor of Lone Pine's *Rocky Mountain Nature Guide, Birds of Ontario, Birds of Northern California, Birds of Boston* and *Birds of New York City, Western Long Island and Northeastern New Jersey.*

Ken De Smet is an endangered species biologist with the Manitoba Wildlife Branch. He has conducted extensive research on rare or declining grassland birds in southern Manitoba and currently works with local conservation groups and national recovery teams to help endangered species. For his master's thesis, he studied the nesting ecology of the Red-necked Grebe in Manitoba's Turtle Mountain Provincial Park. He has spent time working on and managing projects for Ducks Unlimited and the Canadian Wildlife Service, and he has written numerous articles and reports on birds and wildlife conservation, including Canadian status reports for several bird species. Much of his spare time is spent organizing and participating in bird watching, ecotourism and bird surveys. Ken lives in Stonewall with his wife Bev and their two daughters, Shannon and Melissa.